COSMO HANDBOOKS OF EDUCATION

A CONTINUING SERIES

HOW TO DO RESEARCH IN EDUCATION

COSMO HANDBOOKS OF EDUCATION

A CONTINUING SERIES

OTHER TITLES IN THE SERIES RELEASED SO FAR

1. NEW SCHOOL MUSIC HANDBOOK
   P. W. DYKEMA & H. M. CUNDIFF

2. A HANDBOOK FOR TEACHERS
   J. S. BUTTERWECK & G. A. MUZZEY

3. HOW TO DO RESEARCH IN EDUCATION
   CARTER V. GOOD

4. STUDENT GUIDANCE TECHNIQUES
   PATERSON, SCHNEIDLER & WILLIAMSON

5. THE MODERN LANGUAGE TEACHER'S HANDBOOK
   T. E. OLIVER

OTHER EXCITING NEW SERIES LAUNCHED BY COSMO PUBLICATIONS

- TEACHING METHODOLOGY SERIES
- EDUCATIONAL THEORY, CLASSICAL RESOURCES
- INTERNATIONAL LIBRARY OF EDUCATION
- COSMO TEACHER'S TRAINING SERIES

WRITE TO US FOR THE DETAILS OF THESE SEREIS

HOW TO DO RESEARCH IN EDUCATION

A HANDBOOK FOR THE GRADUATE STUDENT, RESEARCH WORKER, AND PUBLIC-SCHOOL INVESTIGATOR

By
Carter V. Good, PH.D.
PROFESSOR OF EDUCATION IN MIAMI UNIVERSITY,
OXFORD. OHIO

INDIGO BOOKS

AN
INDIGO BOOK
PUBLISHED BY INDIGO BOOKS
Paperback division of
COSMO PUBLICATIONS,
24-B, Ansari Road, Darya Ganj,
New Delhi 110 002, India.

INDIGO BOOKS and
COSMO PUBLICATIONS
are publishing subsidiaries of
GENESIS PUBLISHING PVT. LTD.,
New Delhi, India

HOW TO DO RESEARCH IN EDUCATION
Fisrt Published by Cosmo in 2006

First INDIGO Edition 2006

ISBN 81-292-0163-1

PRINTED AND BOUND IN INDIA

PREFACE

When the average student begins his graduate work he is almost wholly innocent of any knowledge of the techniques of research. A discouragingly large number of these students manage to remain in the graduate school a year or two without having become particularly adept in methods of research. Possibly the institution or department itself is partly to blame. Too frequently the student must discover information concerning research procedures by the wasteful trial and error method, although there is always the opportunity for profiting by conferences with professors, class instruction, contacts with more mature students, and individual reading. However, it should be necessary neither for the student to waste time in discovering by chance basic information concerning research principles nor for the professor to consume his time in repeating to different students information which could be presented systematically in an organized class group. It is true that until quite recently one of the difficulties involved in giving systematic instruction concerning the principles of research has been the lack of concrete organized materials which could be placed in the hands of the student. Within the last three or four years the efforts of educational workers have partly eliminated this shortage of working materials. In fact, it now seems that enough scattered material on educational research has been published in widely separated monographs, bulletins, articles, and editorials to make it worth while to bring together and organize such contributions.

Such an organization and interpretation should prove of service not only to the large number of graduate students, but also to senior-college students, investigators, workers in research bureaus, superintendents, principals, teachers, and others interested in conducting educational studies. An examination of the selected bibliography of references in the appendix and of the large number of citations in footnotes indicates how recent and extensive, yet how scattered, this interest and activity in educational research have been.

A survey of the practice of graduate departments and schools of education with regard to guidance of graduate students in the techniques of research reveals essentially the conditions set forth in the preceding paragraph. Considerable interest is expressed in the guidance problem at the graduate level, but a frequently recurring comment concerns the relatively small amount of comprehensive and organized material which is available for placing in the hands of the student. The inquiry was made in the form of the following questions: Do you compile lists of problems suitable for investigation as thesis projects? Do you have graduate theses on file in the library which are recommended for examination to graduate students? Do you make suggestions concerning the mechanics and form of thesis construction? Do you have seminar or research courses which are conducted almost exclusively for the benefit of students who are preparing theses? Are there other materials or suggestions for the benefit of graduate students? The following institutions were good enough to answer the writer's inquiry and in many instances forwarded mimeographed or printed materials and detailed personal letters: California, Chicago, Columbia, Illinois, Indiana, Iowa, Michigan, Minnesota, New

York, Northwestern, Ohio State, Pennsylvania, Pittsburgh, Stanford, Texas, Wisconsin, and Yale.

The present writer is indebted to the large number of educational workers and investigators whose writings are cited frequently in this volume. Obviously, without their efforts, this summarization and organization of the literature of educational research would not have been possible. Especially heavy is the obligation to the work of the Bureaus of Research of the University of Illinois and Ohio State University, the *Journal of Educational Research*, the educational publications of the University of Chicago Press and Teachers College of Columbia University, and the United States Bureau of Education. Recognition of the contributions of other writers too numerous to mention by name is made in footnotes at the appropriate times.

It is hoped that this handbook of the literature of educational research may prove of service to the individual graduate or senior-college student, the research worker and investigator, the seminar group in education or cognate subjects, the public-school worker interested in experimentation or investigation, and others in any way concerned with the conducting and reporting of research or the publication of educational writings.

C. V. G.

OXFORD, OHIO,

TABLE OF CONTENTS

HOW TO DO RESEARCH IN EDUCATION

CHAPTER I

THE VALUE OF EDUCATIONAL RESEARCH

What is Educational Research?—The following quotations selected from the writings of four workers prominent in education will assist the reader to a better understanding of the fundamental meaning of real educational research. Two of these writers are directors of research bureaus at the university level, the third is a university president, and the fourth is editor of a journal famous in the field of secondary education.

An apt brief statement of the nature of educational research is as follows:

> The ultimate purpose of all educational research is the discovery of procedures, rules and principles relating to the various aspects of education. Critical reflective thinking is required in which discovered facts and principles may be utilized, as well as original data. Thus the answering of any question about education by means of critical reflective thinking, based upon the "best" data obtainable, may properly be called educational research.[1]

A fuller statement by the same writer[2] concerning the nature of educational research may be found elsewhere.

[1] Walter S. Monroe and Nell Bomar Johnston, *Reporting Educational Research*, p. 8. University of Illinois Bulletin, Vol. XXII, No. 38. Urbana, Illinois: University of Illinois, 1925.

[2] Walter S. Monroe, "Service of Educational Research to School Administrators," *American School Board Journal*, LXX (April, 1925), 37–39, 122, 125.

The following explanation[3] of the meaning of educational research is worth careful study.

Research is a "careful or critical inquiry or examination in seeking facts or principles; a diligent investigation to ascertain something," according to *Webster's New International Dictionary*. This definition makes clear the fact that research is not merely a search for truth, but a prolonged, intensive, purposeful search. In the last analysis, research per se constitutes a method for the discovery of truth which is really a method of critical thinking. It comprises defining and redefining problems; formulating hypotheses or suggested solutions; collecting, organizing, and evaluating data; making deductions and reaching conclusions; and, at last, carefully testing the conclusions to determine whether they fit the formulated hypotheses.

The emphasis of research work upon data, controls, and experimentation has conveyed the impression that research must be undertaken in the laboratory and must involve statistical analyses, but such is far from the whole truth, for any careful examination of facts or principles constitutes research. This may be undertaken in the library or the schoolroom, instead of the laboratory, and criticism may be substituted for statistics in evaluating the data obtained. Any individual who attempts to substitute deductions based on carefully collected facts for those based upon opinions without supporting evidence, and who strives to advance the frontiers of knowledge, is a research worker.

A quotation[4] from an address by a university president may add something to what has been said concerning the nature of research.

There exists in the public mind much uncertainty as to the nature and purpose of research. The problem of research is the problem of searching for the truth—of searching for what is "so," as the man in the street would probably express it. It is not a search for those fragments of the truth which have already been found and are now described in books, more or less scarce, or

[3] Clifford Woody, "The Values of Educational Research to the Classroom Teacher," *Journal of Educational Research*, XVI (October, 1927), 172–78.

[4] W. W. Campbell, "Universities and the Truth," *School and Society*, XX (September 6, 1924), 289–96.

obscure, but a search for existing truth which has not yet been found by anybody. A professor engaging in research work is looking for something that already exists. He does not invent the truth, he does not develop the truth, he does not do anything whatever to the truth except to uncover it or discover it, and expose it to the comprehension of his fellowmen . . .

. . . .

We must guard against a too narrow use of the words "research" and "science." When a scientist is spoken of, most people have the chemist or biologist or astronomer or the modern farmer in mind. The chances are that they will leave out the student of Greek or of the history of religions; and that is frequently a mistake. A classical scholar who devotes himself seriously to the study of the evolution of the Latin language, or who searches for the forces which produced the wonderful Greek civilization, and for the other forces which later operated to destroy it, is as truly a scientist as he who studies X-rays or the decomposition of radium. If a professor of history endeavors to trace the effects of the continuous working of ethnic, economic, climatic, religious, and other forces upon the development of nations and civilizations, he is a real scientist. A scientist is one who studies any subject with due and impartial regard to the facts, and always with reference to cause and effect.

A Caution Concerning the Use of the Term "Research." There is, as certain research workers recognize, danger that the term, research, may come to be applied indiscriminately to writings which are useful to the profession, but in no real sense fundamental educational research. An editorial writer[5] calls attention to a bulletin, *Bibliography of Secondary Education Research, 1920–1925*, published by the United States Bureau of Education, and raises a question concerning the use of the word, research, to cover many of the titles included in the bulletin.

As one reads the titles and comments in this bulletin, one wonders whether the demand for fundamental research has yet secured adequate recognition in the minds of the members of the

[5] "What is Research?" *School Review*, XXXIV (September, 1926), 488–89.

committee or of secondary-school teachers and principals. At least nine-tenths of the titles cited in the bulletin refer to purely descriptive accounts of what is going on in some department of some high school. It cannot be denied that the distribution of information about practical experiments in classrooms is very desirable and worthy of all possible encouragement. There is danger, however, that a certain commonplace and consequent neglect of real research will result from the use of the word "research" to cover descriptive and trivial writings on educational matters.

. . . .

Would it not be well for those who have undertaken to foster research to begin drawing a distinction between different types of contributions to educational literature? There are good articles on the content of courses; there are good articles on administrative devices. Should these not be listed as articles worth reading but containing no research? Would it not promote true scientific work to reserve the title "research" for publications which contribute to the understanding of fundamental principles?

The same editorial includes a quotation taken from an editorial in the *School of Education Record of the University of North Dakota.* This interesting editorial comment is as follows:

We have heard much during the last few years of what is called "research." True and genuine research is one of the finest performances of human intelligence and ingenuity, but 99 per cent of the so-called research in both undergraduate and graduate work is far from "research." Indeed, much of it is a veritable "idol of the theatre." The work of some men is genuine research; but, where you find one such piece of work, you will find thousands and thousands of mediocre students who are kept busy collecting and collating, in small puttering ways and sometimes with the scissors, work that is passed off and palmed off in ponderous theses as "research." It would remind one of Carlyle's saying that "some people are noted for fussy littleness and an infinite deal of nothing." Professors set students to collecting data that might be gathered by an eighth-grade pupil and call it "research." The result is only what is of common knowledge, and in most cases leads nowhere. As someone has aptly said of such "research," "it is trying to find out for the hundredth time what everybody knows and then expressing it in language that nobody understands." Much of the so-called "research" work is absolute inflation, and the theses embodying it very soon find their place on musty and dusty shelves to be heard of no more.

One often wonders whether there is not so much pretension and inflation in the whole modern educational world that there is very likely to be a "blowout" in the near future; it would suggest the truth of Aesop's fable of the frog. Nearly every institution and every department seems to be "playing" research in order to exploit itself in a public and advertising way; they must know that much of it is only a "game."

I know that, when one strikes at one extreme, one is likely to be accused of the other extreme by those who are unable to think straight, to infer sanely, and to interpret justly. It is only the sham work that I am hitting—there is nothing finer than genuine research and artistic expression and formulation.

The Need for Research in Education.—Woody[6] has called attention in a vigorous manner to the urgent need for research in educational institutions. He advances a number of reasons for this stand: the effect of research in stimulating good teaching, the desirability of extending research to the secondary and elementary institutions, the fact that research in higher institutions of learning and in business and industry is not keeping pace with advancing civilization, the responsibility of the United States for carrying forward research work due to the impoverished condition of Europe since the World War, and the desirability of securing more reliable data concerning economical and appropriate teaching and learning procedures. The point of view set forth is very well stated in the following paragraph:

> In no field is the need for research more apparent than in that of teaching, which now is done largely by rule of thumb. The superiority of one teaching method over another has never been definitely determined. No scientifically established curriculum exists,

[6] Clifford Woody, "The Values of Educational Research to the Classroom Teacher," *Journal of Educational Research*, XVI (October, 1927), 172–78.

although some promising efforts have been made to effect one. As yet little has been revealed to indicate that one classroom organization is superior to another. The best method of marking pupils or evaluating instruction has never been scientifically determined. Little evidence is available on the most satisfactory size of class or length of recitation. Virtually no data have been gathered upon how the child learns, although, within recent years, considerable emphasis has been given to investigations in this field. This list could be extended indefinitely and the enumerated activities analyzed in much greater detail. Further analysis would only present more proof that in the science of teaching there has been but little research.

Another writer[7] shows the necessity for research in education by pointing to the increasing complexity of society and the resulting intricacy of the educational problem, the excellent results secured in private and industrial research, and the large range of administrative, supervisory, instructional, and curricular problems to be solved.

Desirability of Making Practical Applications of the Results of Research Investigations.—Charters[8] makes an interesting and clear distinction between pure research and practical research. His apt characterization of the two types of research follows:

Pure research, therefore, consists of two steps: it attacks any problem anywhere that appeals to the fancy of the investigator. If he desires to investigate the composition of the stones in the gall-bladder of a South Sea Island turtle, he has an inalienable right to do so. Then when he has selected his problem all that is demanded of him is that he apply scholarly methods to its solution. When he has done this and published his findings for the use of other investigators who may be interested in them his task is completed. He need feel no concern about whether or not his findings have any practical social use for the layman.

[7] A. N. Jorgensen, "The Necessity for Research in Education," *American School Board Journal*, LXXIII (August, 1926), 41–42.

[8] W. W. Charters, "Pure Research and Practical Research," *Journal of Educational Research*, XII (September, 1925), 95–101.

When, however, we enter the field of practical research, the situation becomes much more complicated. The practical research investigator cannot pick his problems from the air. They are localized within practice and in the end they must again be applied to the improvement of practice. His selection is narrowed by the practical situations in which he works.

The practical research worker must also be protected and nourished by society. His contribution, study by study, is socially more valuable than is that of the pure research worker. His batting average is higher. He also works for the love of the game, but he cannot indulge in those wide gestures of selection which accompany untrammeled freedom.

Practical research workers are growing in numbers and power as their contributions are realized to be valuable beyond computation. They cannot with justice be derided by the pure research worker. They use the same careful technique and often discover startlingly important new methods and facts which, indeed, are quite as often as not used by the pure research worker.

. . . .

. . . In practical research there are five steps. (1) *A going concern is studied*, measurements made, and points of weakness discovered. (2) Some one of these weaknesses is *selected* for investigation. (3) Then follows *solution in the laboratory*. (4) This is succeeded by the step of *installation* in which modifications must be made so that the solution will work in practice. (5) Finally, the solution must be *maintained* by placing it into the organization so that it will become a permanent part of the system. The pure research worker must, upon entering the practical research field, never lay the blame for the lack of use of his solution upon the organization. It is absolutely essential that he consider the failure to use it to be a failure in his solution, and he must seek to make the necessary changes and set up the proper routine to secure its permanent use.

An editorial writer[9] presents a convincing plea for the application of the results of educational research to educational practice. He says in part:

[9] "Educational Research and Educational Practice," *Educational Research Bulletin*, VI (September 28, 1927), 274–75. Columbus, Ohio: Bureau of Educational Research, Ohio State University.

A great many of the readers of this Bulletin attended summer school this past summer. In courses in school administration, principles of teaching, and psychology, new evidences on old problems were presented. New ways of presenting material, new theories regarding selection and organization of subject-matter, suggestions on administrative and supervisory practice were expounded by those who had either conducted research themselves or had carefully studied the record of research done by others. The question may well be raised whether the new ideas received in these summer-school courses are going to modify our practice during the current school year. If we do not use any of the new things we have learned, how can they affect our students or our school organization? Furthermore, if teachers, principals, and superintendents in regular positions do not attempt to apply the findings of research, research workers are deprived of the best means of knowing the validity of their findings. The regular workers in the public school can make as great a contribution to the progress of education by careful efforts at applying the results of educational research as by doing what is ordinarily called by that name.

The Service of Research to Society.—A very able representative of the field of practical research pictures pure research as an insurance premium paid by society against stagnation and as requiring no more justification than play. He points out that both pure and practical research workers must be protected and nourished by society. A previous quotation has indicated the great social value of practical research, while the following statement[10] shows the value of pure research to society.

Pure research may be considered from the point of view either of the research worker or of society. From the individual research worker's point of view its only standard of evaluation is the satisfaction that it gives him. From the point of view of society its practical and social value is to be considered. If pure research is protected and encouraged, society is often repaid for the outlay. Here and there some principle, fact, or solution is discovered in the course of the research game which may prove of significant importance to society. And these results might possibly never have been

[10] W. W. Charters, *op. cit.*, 95–96.

discovered if some child of research had not happened upon them in his play. It frequently happens that what originally was of use only to give satisfaction to the research worker becomes a powerful method for controlling the needs, desires, and satisfactions of society. When Benjamin Franklin, for instance, played with his kite and his key the neighbors might well have smiled at his childish and impractical curiosity, yet these objects of derision have become a cornerstone of recent civilization and have given us electric lights, street railways, the automobile, the radio, and thousands of articles of commerce now listed as social necessities. Franklin and his colleagues, the pure research workers, will always be protected as long as the leaders of society possess ordinary wisdom.

The Value of Research in Harmonizing Opinion.—One of the fathers of the testing and measuring movement has expressed himself as finding the true value of research not only in the discovery of truth but also in the supreme power of truth to harmonize conflict of human opinion and to make cooperation possible. He points out that the seven major types of conflict may be harmonized by the master tool of cooperative, impersonal, objective, scientific research. These seven types of conflict are: (1) the pseudo-conflict of misunderstanding, (2) the intentional conflict of dishonesty, (3) the irrational conflict of emotional bias, (4) conflict based upon conclusion drawn from different facts, (5) disagreement as to what the facts are, (6) disagreement caused by defects in the generalizing process, and (7) conflicts caused by differences in interpretation.[11]

Value of Research in Teacher-training and Higher Institutions.—The president and research director of a large teacher-training institution have presented an interesting statement of the service performed by a

[11] S. A. Courtis, "The Contributions of Research to the Harmonization of Opinion," *School and Society*, XXIII (June 5, 1926), 707–710.

department of educational research.[12] The work of their research department has included: (1) investigations for the administration, (2) studies for committees, (3) aid to departments in solving problems of a research nature, (4) assistance to graduate students in the field of research, (5) cooperation with outside agencies, and (6) cooperation with public-school systems.

Reference may be made to a discussion of the service rendered to both students and faculty by personnel research in a university.[13]

Graduate Student Benefits by Doing a Minor Piece of Research.—Reeder has indicated an aspect of graduate work which differs fundamentally from the undergraduate program.[14]

> The thesis requirement is perhaps the most characteristic respect in which a graduate curriculum of a university differs from an undergraduate one. In the work of the undergraduate curriculum the student is guided at practically every step in his work, but in the work of the graduate curriculum he is placed more and more on his own resources and responsibility; moreover, he is expected to show a high and constantly increasing degree of intellectual independence. Preparing the thesis aids in developing this intellectual independence; furthermore, the quality of the thesis produced is one of the best measures of the degree of intellectual independence which the student has attained.
>
> The preparation of the thesis is calculated to give the student definitely intensive and scholarly training in the collection, organization, and presentation of facts. Since it does these things, it should not be looked upon as only another chore to be perfunctorily performed or as only another requirement designed to

[12] George Willard Frasier and Frederick Lamson Whitney, "Experiments in Teachers College Administration: I, Educational Research," *Educational Administration and Supervision*, XIV (January, 1928), 1–8.

[13] Howard R. Taylor, "The Need for Personnel Research in a University," *School and Society*, XXVI (November 19, 1927), 653–55.

[14] Ward G. Reeder, *How to Write a Thesis*, pp. 5–6. Bloomington, Illinois: Public School Publishing Co., 1925.

make a graduate degree a little more difficult to secure, but rather should be regarded as one of the most worth while types of training which the graduate curriculum gives.

Research in the Public-school Program.—Judd[15] has shown in a convincing manner the value of research in the American school program. After tracing briefly the historical development of the movement, he urges a union of forces in the careful study of school problems and a formulation of principles of organization and methods of work through cooperative inquiry such as would be made possible by the establishment of a federal department equipped to make scientific studies and to supply that coordination and reinforcement which are the greatest needs of our present-day science of education.

The last decade has witnessed an interesting development in the form of organized research bureaus or departments in the public-school field as well as in the university and teacher-training institutions. In 1923 Baldwin[16] published a list of bureaus of educational research together with extended comment on the contributions of educational research of various types during the preceding biennium, 1920–22. A significant monograph[17] published in 1927 reports the status of organized research in the field of education. This publication not only provides a detailed statement of the agencies for educational research in America but

[15] Charles H. Judd, "Educational Research and the American School Program," *Educational Record*, IV (October, 1923), 165–77.

[16] Bird T. Baldwin, *Educational Research.* Bureau of Education Bulletin No. 42, 1923. Washington: Bureau of Education. Pp. 76.

[17] Harold B. Chapman, *Organized Research in Education with Special Reference to the Bureau of Educational Research.* Bureau of Educational Research Monographs, Number 7. Columbus, Ohio: Ohio State University Press, 1927. Pp. x + 222.

also describes similar agencies in Europe and traces the historical development of the research movement in America.

However, attention has been called to the fact that on many occasions research bureaus are prevented from attacking fundamental problems in education due to the immediate pressure of practical service problems which the supporting institution or community wishes solved.[18] Frequently fundamental problems relating to teaching or curriculum construction which can be solved only through the development of critical scientific techniques and laborious experimentation are pushed into the background in order to conduct urgent service investigations which affect immediate administrative procedures.

The Service of Research to School Administrators.—Newlon[19] points out certain fields such as finance, testing and measurement, and the curriculum in which the research worker can be of great service to the school superintendent, although he states that adequate evidence is not yet available to solve the major problems of these fields. He emphasizes, as the two most important needs in educational research, the desirability of devising better methods of presenting results and the necessity for basing research on a sound educational philosophy.

Monroe[20] discusses the service of research to school administrators in terms of reduction of school

[18] "Research versus Service," *Elementary School Journal*, XXVIII (December, 1927), 248–49.

[19] Jesse H. Newlon, "What Research Can Do for the Superintendent," *Journal of Educational Research*, VIII (September, 1923), 106–112.

[20] Walter S. Monroe, "Service of Educational Research to School Administrators," *American School Board Journal*, LXX (April, 1925), 37–39, 122, 125.

costs, increased educational efficiency, measurement of achievement, and other positive values of educational research. However, he points out certain dogmatisms of research and shows that collection and statistical treatment of facts will not serve as a substitute for real thinking. The study of some problems must be based partially or wholly upon principles and theories derived from psychology, sociology, philosophy, and ethics. While the greatest service of educational research will probably be through promoting clearer and more critical thinking about educational problems, this service applies not only to the study of those problems based upon objective facts but also to problems for which it is necessary to introduce other types of data.

Value of Research to the Individual.—Crawford[21] lists six ways in which the individual research worker profits by reason of his investigations: (1) it is the only sure avenue to outstanding achievement as a scholar; (2) it is the only road to intellectual independence; (3) it enables one to understand and appreciate the research of others; (4) ability in research enables one to qualify for responsible positions of leadership; (5) results of research often yield attractive financial rewards; and (6) it is an attractive and pleasant pursuit.

Possibilities of Research by Teachers.—An editorial writer[22] comments on a suggested plan for the organization and stimulation of research among classroom teachers which involves the use of teacher-training institutions as centers for conducting such investigation. The library facilities and staffs of such institutions would provide the necessary guidance for the teachers

[21] Claude C. Crawford, *Methods of Study*, pp. 156–57. Published by the author, University of Idaho, Moscow, Idaho, 1926.

[22] "Educational Research by Teachers," *Elementary School Journal*, XXVI (April, 1926), 564–66.

who are turning their classrooms into research laboratories. The editorial writer sounds a wholesome note of caution concerning the premature innovation of research on a wholesale basis among classroom teachers.

Such a plan is certainly worthy of serious consideration. However, it involves certain elements which cannot be overlooked. Vigorous scientific attack on educational problems means the expenditure of energy. If energy is to be available for this purpose, it must be provided by the public, which is to profit through research. At the present time boards of education and the public do not recognize the importance of continuous research in order to keep the educational system at a high level of efficiency. Research and certain very essential phases of central supervision are limited by the fact that the public is willing to have the schools move along traditional lines and makes little or no demand for innovation. Under such conditions teachers will be very slow to follow the plan suggested by the writer quoted, but public complacence is certainly no adequate justification for inaction on the part of teachers. Perhaps the most promising suggestion is that concrete examples of school improvement supplied to the public by voluntary work on the part of teachers will do more than anything else to bring the kind of support necessary for a change in the whole situation.

The director of a research bureau lists seven values[23] which accrue to teachers and educational workers who participate in a program of research: (1) gives expert training in research; (2) results in superior teaching; (3) provides a great stimulus to professional growth; (4) provides a mass of information with which to interpret current articles in educational periodicals; (5) aids in establishing teaching as a profession; (6) often involves directly or indirectly monetary rewards; and (7) results in certain spiritual satisfactions.

Another director of a research bureau, who is also editor of a number of research publications, has prepared

[23] Clifford Woody, "The Values of Educational Research to the Classroom Teacher," *Journal of Educational Research*, XVI (October, 1927), 172–78.

a book[24] which provides the teacher interested in classroom investigations with information concerning the learning processes, statistical methods, new-type examinations, etc. The same worker[25] has expressed a point of view which shows clearly the value of experimental investigation to the research worker, especially to the individual who works with human beings; this statement seems very appropriate as the concluding paragraph of this chapter.

> Finally, their [experiments'] reaction upon the teacher spiritually must not be left out of account. The fresh point of view which research always engenders should not be denied to the teacher. The spirit of inquiry, of open-minded alertness to the problems which arise in teaching, will make the teacher free. It will lead him to seek problems and do something, even though it may be but a little, in their solution. Moreover, it will make him expert as a teacher and will make his calling more attractive. Indeed, when looked at from this point of view the teacher's occupation becomes fascinating. He has children to study—not stones, bugs, fossils or old manuscripts, but the most interesting of all possible materials—namely, human beings. Moreover, he has at hand human beings at their most engaging period—childhood and youth. And his children never grow old. In constant procession they present to him, always at the level of childhood, their innumerable interesting aspects. Yet each is different from the other—different in strength, talent, and character; different in origin, growth, and need. If teaching these children is to include studying them, the job of teaching takes on new meaning. Its scope is broadened. Its meaning is enriched. No other calling may then be compared with it. It is the great adventure.

[24] B. R. Buckingham, *Research for Teachers.* New York: Silver, Burdett and Co., 1926. Pp. viii + 386.

[25] B. R. Buckingham, "The Public-School Teacher as a Research Worker," *Journal of Educational Research,* XI (April, 1925), 235–43.

Chapter II

SOURCES OF INFORMATION IN EDUCATION

Are Graduate Students and Educational Workers in the Field Familiar with Educational Literature?—It seems reasonable to expect graduate students in education and school administrators to be fairly well acquainted with leaders in the field and with the contributions of these men to educational literature. Graduate students, administrators, supervisors, and high-school department heads ordinarily have completed an undergraduate program which included a certain amount of work in education and in many cases have pursued some graduate courses in education. The assumption is that the groups mentioned have read more or less regularly one or more of the educational periodicals. The fond hope, then, of the professor of education is that his graduate students, many of whom have been, are, or will be public-school executives, know something about prominent workers in education, their contributions, their institutional connections, and something about the educational periodicals, monograph series, bulletins, book-review departments, school survey reports, yearbooks, and volumes in which educational contributions appear.

Ashbaugh's Investigation of Student-familiarity with Educators.—However, there is evidence of several kinds to indicate that the college professor's dream, as expressed in the preceding sentence, falls far short of realization. Two interesting studies[1] present some specific information to this effect. Worcester, in the monograph edited by Pressey, shows the rather distressing lack of information on the part of students in education relative to educational and scientific organizations, honorary professional organizations, educational journals, universities prominent in education, educational leaders, and requirements for graduate degrees.

Professor Ashbaugh listed the names of thirty well-known educators, each name preceded by a number. A list of twenty statements was also prepared and the student was expected to match each statement with the appropriate name. The list of thirty names and the twenty statements which follow render the procedure employed self-explanatory.

1. Cornelia S. Adair
2. David A. Anderson
3. F. W. Ballou
4. Franklin Bobbitt
5. B. R. Buckingham
6. W. W. Charters
7. J. L. Clifton
8. Frank Cody
9. J. G. Collicott
10. R. J. Condon
11. E. P. Cubberley
12. W. M. Davidson
13. John Dewey
14. Susan Dorsey
15. J. M. Gwinn
16. C. H. Judd
17. W. H. Kilpatrick
18. Max Mason
19. William McAndrew
20. Mary McSkimmon
21. C. S. Meek
22. W. J. O'Shea
23. W. F. Russell
24. Payson Smith
25. C. L. Spain
26. Geo. D. Strayer
27. E. L. Thorndike
28. J. J. Tigert
29. A. E. Winship
30. Will Wood

[1] E. J. Ashbaugh, "Should School Administrators Know Something about People Prominent in Education?" *Educational Research Bulletin,* VI (October 12, 1927), 291–93. Columbus, Ohio: Bureau of Educational Research, Ohio State University.

S. L. Pressey, L. C. Pressey, and Others, *Research Adventures in University Teaching,* pp. 63–65. Bloomington, Illinois: Public School Publishing Co., 1927.

Place in the parentheses before each of the following statements the number which precedes the name of the proper person.

( ) 1. United States Commissioner of Education
( ) 2. President of the National Education Association
( ) 3. Superintendent of Schools, Los Angeles
( ) 4. Author, *The Principal and His School*
( ) 5. President, State Teachers College, Kent, Ohio
( ) 6. Superintendent of Schools, New York City
( ) 7. Editor, *Journal of Educational Research*
( ) 8. President, Ohio State Teacher Association
( ) 9. State Superintendent of Public Instruction, Massachusetts
( )10. Superintendent of Schools, Columbus
( )11. Dean, Teachers College, Columbia University
( )12. Author, *Democracy and Education*
( )13. President, University of Chicago
( )14. Superintendent of Schools, Washington, D. C.
( )15. President, Department of Superintendence, National Education Association
( )16. State Superintendent of Public Instruction, Ohio
( )17. Author, *How to Make the Curriculum*
( )18. Superintendent of Schools, Detroit
( )19. Editor, *Educational Review*
( )20. Superintendent of Schools, Pittsburgh

While it must be admitted that certain of the names listed have local or statewide significance rather than national prominence, the results secured from forty-eight graduate students who took the test are rather illuminating. Correct responses were given on 38 per cent of the items, and only 63 per cent of the total number were tried. Seven different people were designated as the president of the N.E.A., as the dean of Teachers College, Columbia University, and as the president of the University of Chicago; six different persons were named as the editor of the *Educational Review.*

Professor Ashbaugh also investigated the information sixty-six graduate students possessed concerning the positions held by fifty writers who had contributed three or more articles to educational journals of national scope during a few years immediately preceding the date of the investigation. The results show that of the total 3,300 possible responses (50 names and 66 students) only 615 were attempted and but 420 were correct. In terms of per cents, only 18.6 per cent of the items were tried, and only 68 per cent of those tried were answered correctly.

The Graduate Student in Search of a Thesis Problem.—An editorial writer[2] comments on the graduate student who wishes to begin work on a thesis, but has no problem in mind and evidently has done nothing toward examining the literature. The problem finally suggested by the floundering student, whose haziness is pictured in the quotation given below, indicates his lack of familiarity with current educational literature. The graduate student enters the professorial sanctum and after a preliminary remark or two gets down to business as follows:

> "I've got to write a Master's thesis," says he, "and I'd like to talk to you about a topic." The statement ends with a slight upward inflection as if, in spite of its grammatical form, a sort of question were implied. After an awkward pause Mr. Blank [the student] repeats that he would like to talk about a thesis topic. Whereupon the editor [and professor] suggests that he go ahead and do so.
>
> It transpires, however, that the editor-professor has misconceived Mr. Blank's meaning. He has no topic to talk about. In fact, instead of coming with a topic, he has come to get one. He looks so expectant, too; purely, as one might say, in a receptive mood.
>
> No, he has no problems to suggest. He gives one the impression of having just learned about this thesis business, and of being entirely open-minded on the subject. At least, one gathers that

[2] "The Editor Turns Professor," *Educational Research Bulletin*, VI (September 14, 1927), 252–53. Columbus, Ohio: Bureau of Educational Research, Ohio State University.

he has no bias toward any particular topic and certainly no preconceived notions.

A conversation ensues. The editor—playing for the nonce his professorial role—asks in what department Mr. Blank is majoring, what courses he has taken, what positions he has held, and for what type of educational service he is fitting himself. At one stage of the resulting exchange of ideas Mr. Blank brightens. With some modesty, yet with the undeniable air of a discoverer, he suggests that he might correlate intelligence and achievement in the high school. He could give some tests in the school with which he is connected; and his friend, the principal of the X school, would probably let him give some tests there; and maybe he could get one or two more schools if he stopped to think about the matter. And, O yes! how many schools does the professor think would be needed to get results that you could depend on? On being told that intelligence and achievement—so far as either are now measurable—have already been correlated by hundreds of people, Mr. Blank helplessly withdraws within himself, a discouraged seeker after truth in a world where all the problems have been solved.

The Candidate for a Graduate Degree and the Oral or Written Examination.—Probably at no other time is one's familiarity with educational workers and literature subjected to a more severe test than at the time of the examination preliminary to the granting of a graduate degree. In fact, the candidate may have prepared a quite acceptable thesis and may have finished his individual courses in education with credit, yet is denied his graduate degree for a time because of ignorance of current educational literature. The writer has in mind two such men who found it necessary to spend a considerable part of an extra year in familiarizing themselves with present-day developments in education before being granted the Doctor's degree in education. In one instance the candidate had done a good part of his graduate work in six or seven summer quarters and in the other case the candidate had been engaged for a year or two in work other than teaching after finishing his graduate courses.

An illustration of a different type may be used to show how certain candidates for a graduate degree profit by reason of familiarity with current educational literature. One of two men who received the Doctor's degree in education with highest honors from a famous graduate school was granted this recognition in a large measure because of his ability to indicate the body of literature containing the answer to a given question. Even though this candidate was unable in some cases to quote the specific facts in answer to the question asked, his reply was, "I do not know the answer to that question, but I can tell you where to find the information."

If it is not giving away a secret of the graduate school, the writer suggests that it will be to the advantage of every graduate student in education to familiarize himself with the prominent leaders in the field, their contributions, the subdivisions of the field in which they are working, the current projects being carried forward by these men, their institutional connections, educational periodicals and their editorial staffs, monograph series, bulletins, book-review departments, school-survey reports and staffs, professional organizations and yearbooks, and educational publishers and their current offerings. It is trite to suggest that a similar procedure would be of value to the individual who is no longer engaged in graduate study and to workers in the public-school field of endeavor.

Many Educational Writings Reveal Unfamiliarity with Current Literature.—Too frequently authors fail to keep in touch with current educational literature. In some cases writers have a book virtually finished and allow it to remain in their files over a period of two or three years, while attempting to locate a publisher or trying to find the necessary time to complete the work. Too many such authors, when the book is finally completed, send the manuscript to the publisher without bringing the references and citations up to date. It seems not unreasonable to expect significant contributions appearing a year or more before the date of publication of a given book to be represented in some way in the volume in question.

Several examples will serve to illustrate the point made in the preceding paragraph. A 1927 book dealing with the problems of special method in high school makes no mention of the following significant contributions: Gray's summary of reading investigations, Curtis' summary of science investigations, Buswell and Judd's studies of reading and foreign languages, Washburne and Vogel's canvass of children's reading interests, Huber, Bruner, and Curry's study of preferences in poetry, Marshall and Judd's work in social science, Rugg's method of unification of the social studies, and the important contributions of Breslich and Schorling in mathematics. The author of the same book has an exceedingly vague style of referring to the work of the writers who are cited and is taken to task by a reviewer[3] for this lapse:

> The glaring disregard of the accepted principles of citation is utterly inexcusable in a writer in a technical field. Such statements as "Judd's study reveals," "as set forth by Dewey," "Dewey has shown," "Parker gives the following," "according to Dewey," "as Thorndike suggests," "Davis has discovered," "Lancaster found," "as Nutt reminds us," "Kline believes," and "according to Cubberley" show an indefensible writing technique in dealing with technical materials.

A 1927 book, dealing with the development of character and personality, which ran through a mimeo-

[3] *School Review*, XXXV (November, 1927), 708.

graphed edition at least two years before being printed makes no mention of a number of pertinent contributions: Betts and Hawthorne's *Method in Teaching Religion*, 1925; Burnham's *Great Teachers and Mental Health*, 1926; Downey's *The Will Temperament and Its Testing*, 1923; Freeman's *Mental Tests*, 1926; and Hartshorne and May's investigations covering two or three years at Teachers College, Columbia University. A 1927 monograph which deals with the problem of feeblemindedness in the public schools includes only one reference each to Goddard and Wallin, two of the outstanding figures in the field under consideration. No mention whatever is made of such workers as Bronner, Doll, Healy, Mateer, and the Presseys who are interested in the problems of feeblemindedness or its related issues of abnormality and delinquency. Only four of the references listed reveal dates of publication later than 1924; undoubtedly this is a monograph which must have lain fallow two or three years before going to press. It is of interest to note that the volume was reported as a plagiarism shortly after publication and was withdrawn from circulation.

Graduate Theses are Valuable Sources of Information.—It is a matter of interest to note the relatively large number of significant problems attacked in Masters' and Doctors' dissertations in education. In most fields the graduate thesis is of insufficient general interest to attract a sale large enough to defray the cost of publication. However, in the field of education, a considerable number of these investigations made during the past few years have been published by commercial houses which of course expect to be reimbursed through sales for the expenditure involved. Yet, it must be admitted that except for the individual who visits in person the library of the department of education, the large number of graduate theses are comparatively inaccessible. It is true that under certain conditions the graduate thesis is forwarded from the library to the distant applicant, but the number of copies available and the "red tape" involved limit materially dissemination of the information included in these studies The Bureau of Educational Research of the University of Illinois, covering the period since January, 1917 has issued annual or biennial mimeographed lists of graduate theses in education. These lists are adequately classified.

Graduate schools and departments of education call the attention of students to theses which have been accepted in the past and urge that they be examined carefully. A number of large graduate schools suggest an appropriate list of accepted theses which represent a variety of types of interest and a variety of methods of procedure. The University of Chicago at intervals publishes a volume of abstracts of the Doctors' theses accepted in the various fields of graduate work.

The Student Needs to See the Field of Education as a Whole.—Too frequently, even the graduate student fails to picture the various subdivisions of education as component parts of a unified whole. It is hardly to be expected that the typical undergraduate possesses any adequate overview of the field of education and the various relationships involved between the several subdivisions. It is true that the comparatively recent development of a course of an introductory nature does something toward giving the undergraduate this initial survey or overview of the field of education. Certainly it seems that the graduate student and the experienced worker in the field should be able, without serious difficulty, to recognize the various divisions of the field and to group information acquired accordingly.

However, since even graduate students and public-school workers have failed to see interrelationships between courses in education and often have covered bodies of subject matter in education as separate and isolated bits of information without apparent connections with preceding or subsequent courses, some comment on this matter seems desirable at this point. The writer suggests below a rough outline of the field of education which may be of some assistance to the student. This scheme of organization may be suggestive as a means of grouping leaders in the field of education, educational periodicals current educational developments, and new publications. It will be recognized that this tentative outline is suggestive rather than final and makes no attempt to list fully the numerous smaller subdivisions of interest which may be grouped under certain of the major divisions.

I. General Problems of Education

A. School administration and supervision
1. Educational administration, organization and management
2. Business administration, finance, buildings and grounds
3. School legislation
4. School surveys
5. Extra-curricular activities
6. Educational and vocational guidance

B. Educational psychology and measurement
1. Psychological tests
2. Educational tests and measurements
3. Statistical methods
4. Psychology of learning
5. Child study
6. Individual differences
7. Education of exceptional children
8. Mental hygiene
9. Psychology of the school subjects
10. Experimental education

- C. General theory and method
  1. Educational philosophy
  2. Educational sociology
  3. General methods of instruction
- D. History of education
  1. Educational biography
  2. Current educational conditions
  3. International aspects of education, comparative education
- E. Rural education
- F. Pre-school and elementary education
  1. Pre-school and kindergarten education
  2. Elementary education
  3. Elementary curriculum
- G. Secondary education
  1. Junior high school
  2. Senior high school
  3. Junior college
  4. Secondary curriculum
- H. Higher education
  1. Teacher-training
  2. Professional education

II. Teaching and Curriculum of the Special Subjects

- A. Commercial and business education
- B. English (reading, spelling, etc.)
- C. Fine arts
- D. Foreign languages
- E. Home economics
- F. Manual and industrial arts
- G. Mathematics
- H. Moral, religious, and character education
- I. Music
- J. Physical and health education
- K. Science
- L. Social studies

Information Concerning Leaders in the Field of Education.—The writer debated for a time the advisability of including a list of prominent educators, research workers, and educational periodicals grouped according to the outline presented above, but decided limitations of space did not permit. Likewise, it seemed impracticable to present a list of contributions made by individual workers in the various fields or a statement of current research projects. By the time this chapter reaches the reader such a list of contributions would not be complete and the research projects would no longer be contemporary. The intellectual activity and growth of the student will be stimulated more vigorously and his individual interests met more adequately if he performs these services for himself. The following sources of information, some rather homely to be sure but enlightening nevertheless, concerning educational workers and their interests may be mentioned: direct contact in teacher-training institutions, educational publications, educational periodicals (articles, book reviews, editorial staff, editorial comment, news items, advertisements of publishing houses, and lists of publications), school survey reports, monograph series, series of educational textbooks, yearbooks of professional organizations, membership lists of professional organizations usually found in yearbooks where such are published (National Society for the Study of Education, National Society of College Teachers of Education, Sections Q and I of the American Association for the Advancement of Science, Educational Research Association, Department of Superintendence, and the American Psychological Association), addresses and papers at professional and educational gatherings, educational directories (national and state), catalogues of teacher-training institutions, *Who's Who in America*, *American Men of Science*, bibliographies, and the *Phi Delta Kappan* (publication of a national professional fraternity in education).

The authors of an introductory book[4] in education had the happy thought of including the pictures of ten prominent living educators, even though such a practice is contrary to ordinary practice. These photographs together with the accompanying captions help to make real great personalities who have been in many cases only names.

Probably many of the younger, and older, workers in education receive more benefit at educational gatherings from contact with great personalities in education than from the actual speeches heard. No doubt the fact that addresses at educational gatherings are frequently reiterations or restatements of previously published articles, books, or chapters in yearbooks diminishes the benefits to be secured from attendance on the various sessions. At a recent meeting of a national educational society the chairman of the yearbook committee read almost verbatim his published introduction to the yearbook which most of the large audience had had an opportunity to read for themselves. Most of the papers presented before this educational organization, as well as those read before two other similar groups, consisted in the main of material which had been published in the yearbooks of the educational organizations in question; the addresses of two men in particular were reiterations of their views which had been previously expressed and published a number of times. Two speakers on the

[4] George Willard Frasier and Winfield D. Armentrout, *An Introduction to Education.* Chicago: Scott, Foresman and Co., 1927.

Also see Ching-Ju Ho, *Personnel Studies of Scientists in the United States.* Teachers College Contributions to Education, No. 298. New York: Teachers College, Columbia University, 1928. Pp 60. Includes an analysis of the vocational histories of prominent psychologists.

program of a research organization occupied a considerable part of the time allotted them by quoting or paraphrasing material from the same monograph. An able editor and research worker on the same program read a lengthy editorial of his own composition which had appeared in print a few months before. A luncheon speaker who appeared before a prominent educational organization read a paper which had been delivered two months before at another national educational gathering and which had appeared in print less than a month before the second delivery. Possibly many, or most, of the hearers at the various meetings were not conscious of the reiterations and restatements enumerated. Although this amount of repetition is generally undesirable, it is no doubt true that something was gained by coming into contact with great personalities, even by the listener who was familiar with the material presented.

The Student of Education Should Read Systematically and Keep an Organized Record of Such Reading.—The outline of the field of education, as given in a preceding section of this chapter, may be of some service in indicating phases of education concerning which knowledge is necessary for well-rounded development. Of course it is to be expected that each worker has a special line of interest which consumes a major part of the available time and attention. Succeeding portions of this chapter will suggest research journals, monograph series, bulletins and pamphlets, school survey agencies, professional organizations and yearbooks, educational foundations, and educational publishers with which the student of education should be familiar. The advantage of keeping a systematic record of one's reading will be recognized. Many workers have found cards preferable for use in filing away references and annotations. It may be emphasized that one should copy the complete reference with an adequate annotation at the time the material is read. Otherwise many valuable references escape one's memory and can with difficulty be relocated. No doubt many of the incomplete references found in educational publications are due to failure on the part of the author to use a little more time and care in copying the complete information at the time of the original reading.

Educational Bibliographies and Abstracts.—The student of education may save himself much searching in the library and some mental anguish by becoming familiar with available bibliographies. The United States Bureau of Education publishes bibliographies covering a wide range of interest and at frequent intervals publishes classified lists of current educational literature. Specific information concerning publications of the Bureau of Education may be obtained by examining the Bureau's list of publications. There is available a partial list of important educational bibliographies in the *Teachers Journal and Abstract.*[5] Another bibliography of bibliographies[6] presents a valuable list of 231 items.

The *Teachers Journal and Abstract* published by Colorado State Teachers College, Greeley, Colorado, is a valuable aid in that each month it summarizes the important educational contributions, especially the magazine articles, of the preceding month. The *Loyola Educational Digest* (Chicago) is a similar publica-

[5] Frederick L. Whitney and Earle U. Rugg, "Sources of Current Literature in Education," *Teachers Journal and Abstract*, I (January, 1926), 47–53.

[6] Walter S. Monroe and Ollie Asher, *A Bibliography of Bibliographies.* University of Illinois Bulletin, Vol. XXIV, No. 36. Urbana, Illinois: University of Illinois, 1927. Pp. 60.

tion. At least one large institution, the University of Chicago, publishes in bound volumes abstracts of the Doctors' theses accepted. A number of the educational periodicals include book reviews, which are reasonably adequate abstracts and evaluations of current literature in book form, and a monthly list of educational publications received. The *Educational Review* prints annually a list of publications received, grouped according to publishers.

Educational Directories.—The United States Bureau of Education publishes an annual educational directory which is of great interest to students of education and public-school workers. A partial list of the items of information included is: principal state school officers, county superintendents, superintendents of public schools, presidents of universities and colleges, presidents or deans of professional schools, educational boards and foundations, educational and learned associations, and educational periodicals. An annual directory published by the Brewer Teachers Agency of Chicago contains certain information with regard to number of teachers in school systems and higher institutions of learning, salaries of school officials, number of pupils or students enrolled, and heads of school systems and educational institutions. Certain states publish educational directories containing information similar to that included in the directories mentioned above. It is likely that a number of the larger city systems print annual educational directories. It will be recognized that there are numerous occasions on which workers in education find the information included in such educational directories of real value. Patterson's *American Educational Directory* (American Educational Co., Chicago) is a valuable and complete handbook.

Educational Periodicals Which Report Quantitative Investigations.—A complete list of educational periodicals currently received by the library of the Bureau of Education will be found in the annual educational directory of the United States Bureau of Education. In this directory the reader will find the various educational interests more or less adequately represented; hardly any subdivision of the field fails to be represented by one or more of the publications listed, although many of the periodicals rarely print original or experimental investigations containing quantitative data. It seems sufficient at this point to list only those educational periodicals of rather general interest to the student of education which place considerable emphasis on quantitative evidence. The journals preceded by an asterisk place especial emphasis on research studies.

American Educational Digest. 1126–28 Q Street, Lincoln, Nebraska. Monthly.

**American School Board Journal.* Bruce Publishing Co., 354 Milwaukee Street, Milwaukee, Wisconsin. Monthly.

Chicago Schools Journal. Board of Education, Chicago Normal College, Sixty-eighth Street and Stewart Avenue, Chicago, Illinois. 10 numbers.

Education. Palmer Co., 120 Boylston Street, Boston, Massachusetts. 10 numbers.

**Educational Administration and Supervision.* Warwick and York, Inc., Baltimore, Maryland. 9 numbers.

**Elementary School Journal.* School of Education, University of Chicago, Chicago, Illinois. 10 numbers.

**Journal of Applied Psychology.* Williams and Wilkins Co., Mount Royal and Guilford Avenues, Baltimore, Maryland. Quarterly.

Journal of Educational Method. 525 West One hundred and twentieth Street, New York City. 10 numbers.

**Journal of Educational Psychology.* Warwick and York, Inc., Baltimore, Maryland. 9 numbers.

**Journal of Educational Research.* Public School Publishing Co., Bloomington, Illinois. 10 numbers.

**Journal of Experimental Psychology.* Psychological Review Co., Princeton, New Jersey. Bimonthly.

**Peabody Journal of Education.* George Peabody College for Teachers, Nashville, Tennessee. Bimonthly.

**Pedagogical Seminary and Journal of Genetic Psychology.* Clark University, Worcester, Massachusetts. Quarterly.

School and Society. Science Press, Garrison, New York. Weekly.

School Life. United States Bureau of Education, Washington, D. C. 10 numbers.

**School Review.* School of Education, University of Chicago, Chicago, Illinois. 10 numbers.

**Teachers College Record.* Teachers College, Columbia University, New York City. 10 numbers.

Teachers Journal and Abstract. Colorado State Teachers College, Greeley, Colorado. 9 numbers.

An Investigation of the Helpfulness of Educational Journals.—A questionnaire study[7] was made to find which of ten designated professional journals were read most by senior high school principals. Replies were received from 381 senior high school principals located in 375 cities which include all the states and the District of Columbia. An effort was also made to find which of the ten periodicals were considered most helpful in the work of the principals. A percentage index of helpfulness was secured by dividing the number of times a journal was mentioned as most helpful by the total number of times it was mentioned as being read. The first column of Table I gives this index of helpfulness, the second column lists the rank in helpfulness, and the third and fourth columns indicate the number of research articles appearing in the journals within a stipulated period of time.

[7] James L. La Poe, "The Senior High School Principals' Professional Magazines." *Educational Research Bulletin,* VI (September 14, 1927), 259–61. Columbus, Ohio: Bureau of Educational Research, Ohio State University.

TABLE I.*—THE HELPFULNESS OF CERTAIN PROFESSIONAL JOURNALS

Journals	Index of helpfulness	Rank in helpfulness	Number of research articles	
			1925	1924
School Review	45.5	1	24	28
Educational Administration and Supervision	32.1	2	23	12
American School Board Journal	21.2	3	7	4
Teachers College Record	19.8	4.5	14	7
Journal of Educational Research	19.8	4.5	47	51
Journal of Education	18.8	6	†	†
Educational Review	14.5	7	†	2
School and Society	13.3	8	26	18
State Journals of Education	12.2	9	†	†
Education	10.3	10	1	2

* Rearranged from author's data.
† Not analyzed or not mentioned.

Bulletins, Monographs, and Studies Published by Teacher-training Institutions.—Some of the most valuable information in education appears in the publications of the larger schools of education. The following list[8] of college and university publications dealing with education should be of some service to the worker in locating original studies and contributions.

Colorado State Teachers College, Greeley, Colorado—*Bulletins.*
George Peabody College for Teachers—*Contributions to Education.*
Harvard University, School of Education, Cambridge, Massachusetts—*Bulletins, Monographs,* and *Studies.*
Indiana University, Bureau of Cooperative Research, Bloomington, Indiana—*Bulletins.*
Johns Hopkins University, Baltimore, Maryland—*Studies in Education.*

[8] Adapted from the article by Whitney and Rugg, *op. cit.*

Kansas State Teachers College, Extension Division, Emporia, Kansas—*Bulletins.*

Ohio State University, Bureau of Educational Research, Columbus, Ohio—*Bulletins* and *Monographs.*

State University of Iowa, Iowa City, Iowa—*Bulletins, Monographs,* and *Studies*—(a) Iowa Child Welfare Research Station, and (b) College of Education Series.

Teachers College, Columbia University, New York City—*Contributions to Education* and Lincoln School *Monographs.*

University of California, Bureau of Research in Education, Berkeley, California—*Studies.*

University of Chicago, School of Education, Chicago, Illinois—*Supplementary Educational Monographs.*

University of Illinois, Bureau of Educational Research, Urbana, Illinois—*Research Bulletins* and *Research Circulars.*

University of Michigan, Bureau of Educational Reference and Research, Ann Arbor, Michigan—*Bulletins.*

University of Minnesota, College of Education, Minneapolis, Minnesota—*Monographs, Studies,* and *Bulletins.*

University of Wisconsin, Bureau of Educational Research, Madison, Wisconsin—*Bulletins.*

Upon request lists of the publications issued by the various institutions mentioned above will be provided by the schools in question. Probably at the present time the publications of Teachers College of Columbia University, the University of Chicago, Ohio State University, and the University of Illinois are best known to students of education. The number of volumes in the monograph series, *Teachers College Contributions to Education.* which consists of Doctors' dissertations, at this writing numbers approximately 300; the monograph series, *Supplementary Educational Monographs,* which includes studies of a somewhat higher grade than the ordinary Doctor's dissertation, at this writing numbers 35 investigations.

Bulletins and Reports of State and City School Systems.—As a rule libraries do not have an adequate supply of state and city manuals, programs of study, school-board reports, superintendents' reports, etc. However, this is a valuable source of information for the student of education and the worker in the public-school field. In most cases such materials can be secured from the school system in question free of charge or for a nominal fee which covers cost of printing. Space does not permit a listing of the city bureaus of educational research, boards, and state departments which publish useful monographs, bulletins, and pamphlets; for such information the reader is referred to the previously mentioned article[9] in the *Teachers Journal and Abstract*. Of course most of the larger cities publish manuals, courses of study, and superintendents' and school-board reports.

School Survey Reports and Survey Staffs.—Valuable data concerning public-school systems and even higher institutions of learning are available in school-survey reports. Among the agencies making school surveys during the past twelve or fifteen years are the United States Bureau of Education; the General Education Board; the Russell Sage Foundation; the educational staffs of such institutions as Teachers College of Columbia University and the University of Chicago; and city school boards and state departments of education working together with outside educational experts. Lists of school surveys made by the agencies in question and price lists of the reports may be secured from the agencies themselves; in many cases, especially when surveys have been made by state departments, the United States Bureau of Education, and the General Education Board, copies may be secured free of charge or at a nominal cost. Usually such survey agencies are especially generous in providing libraries with copies of the reports. Sears[10] has provided a selected list of surveys.

[9] Whitney and Rugg, *op. cit.*

[10] Jesse B. Sears, *The School Survey*, pp. 429–33. Boston: Houghton Mifflin Co., 1925.

Professional Educational Organizations and Their Journals, Bulletins, Yearbooks, Proceedings, and Reports. There is a growing tendency among educational organizations, both national and state, to issue a publication which represents the interests of the group in question. Many state teachers' associations sponsor a state journal for teachers. Various national organizations with specialized interests issue a publication, usually at intervals of a month, which serves as the official organ of the group in question. Some of the national or sectional organizations and their official organs are as follows:

Association of American Colleges Bulletin. Association of American Colleges, Lime and Green Street, Lancaster, Pennsylvania. 4 times a year.

Bulletin of Elementary School Principals. National Education Association, 1201 Sixteenth Street, N. W., Washington, D. C. 5 times a year.

Bulletin of the American Association of University Professors. American Association of University Professors, Nineteenth and Northhampton Streets, Easton, Pennsylvania. 8 numbers.

Educational Record. American Council on Education, 24–26 Jackson Place, Washington, D. C. Quarterly.

English Journal. National Council of Teachers of English, University of Chicago Press, Chicago, Illinois. 10 numbers.

Journal of Educational Method. National Conference on Educational Method, 525 West One hundred and twentieth Street, New York City. 10 numbers.

Journal of Educational Research. Educational Research Association, Public School Publishing Co., Bloomington, Illinois. 10 numbers.

Journal of Home Economics. American Home Economics Association, 1211 Cathedral Street, Baltimore, Maryland. Monthly.

Journal of the National Education Association. National Education Association, 1201 Sixteenth Street, N. W., Washington, D. C. 9 numbers.

Mathematics Teacher. National Council of Teachers of Mathematics, 425 West One hundred and twenty-third Street, New York City. 8 numbers.

Modern Language Journal. National Federation of Modern Language Teachers, University of Pennsylvania, Philadelphia, Pennsylvania. 8 numbers.

North Central Association Quarterly. North Central Association of Colleges and Secondary Schools, University High School Building, room 407, University of Michigan, Ann Arbor, Michigan. Quarterly.

Research Bulletin. National Education Association, Research Division, 1201 Sixteenth Street, N. W., Washington, D. C. 5 times a year.

It is a matter of interest to workers in education to note the number of educational associations which issue yearbooks or volumes of annual proceedings of a more pretentious nature than the bulletins and journals listed above. These annual publications are concerned with the problems discussed at the yearly conventions of the organizations in question. Below is a list of some of the important educational associations of national or regional scope which were not mentioned in the preceding list of organizations and their organs. Attention will be called to the associations which publish yearbooks or volumes of proceedings. Since officers, addresses of officers, and places and dates of meeting are subject to change, this information will not be included. The reader may secure such information from the annual educational directory of the United States Bureau of Education.

American Association for the Advancement of Science, Section Q (Education).

*American Association of Teachers Colleges, *Yearbooks.*

American Classical League.

American Psychological Association.

Association of American Universities.

Association of Colleges and Secondary Schools of the Middle States and Maryland.

Association of Colleges and Secondary Schools of the Southern States.

*National Association of Secondary School Principals, *Yearbooks.*
National Committee on Research in Secondary Education.
*National Education Association, Department of Elementary School Principals, *Yearbooks.*
*National Education Association, Department of Superintendence, *Yearbooks.*
*National Education Association, *Proceedings.*
National Education Association, National Council of Education.
National Research Council, Division of Educational Relations.
*National Society for the Study of Education, *Yearbooks.*
*National Society of College Teachers of Education, *Yearbooks.*
New England Association of Colleges and Secondary Schools.
Northwest Association of Secondary and Higher Schools.
Progressive Education Association.

The organizations preceded by an asterisk are of especial interest to students of education because of their annual volumes of proceedings or yearbooks. The last yearbook of an organization usually gives the titles of preceding publications. Attention may be called to some of the topics which have been discussed within the past few years in two of the series of yearbooks. The National Society for the Study of Education, since 1920, has been concerned with the problems of new materials of instruction, the education of gifted children, silent reading, intelligence testing, English composition, social studies, vocational education, adapting the schools to individual differences, safety education, extra-curricular activities, and curriculum-making. The 1928 yearbook of this body is a report of the society's "Committee on the Possibilities and Limitations of Training." Part I is entitled *Nature and Nurture: Their Influence upon Intelligence* and Part II is entitled *Nature and Nurture: Their Influence upon Achievement.* This professional group expects to publish, in 1929, yearbooks dealing with the problems of "Preschool and Nursery Education" and "The Textbook."

Valuable contributions in the curriculum field have been made by the yearbooks of the Department of Superintendence. This association, beginning the series in 1924, has published yearbooks under the following titles: *The Elementary School Curriculum*, *Research in Constructing the Elementary School Curriculum*, *The Nation at Work on the Public School Curriculum*, and *The Junior High School Curriculum*. The 1928 yearbook is a treatment of the senior high school curriculum and the yearbook for 1929 is concerned with the problem of the articulation of the units of the American school system.

Special attention may be directed to the yearbooks of the International Institute of Teachers College, Columbia University, which describe current educational conditions in foreign countries. The first of these yearbooks appeared in 1925 and covered the year, 1924.

National Foundations or Boards for the Promotion of Education and the United States Bureau of Education and Their Publications.—The best known national foundations and boards for the advancement of education are:

Carnegie Foundation for the Advancement of Teaching, 522 Fifth Avenue, New York City.

Commonwealth Fund, 1 East Fifty-seventh Street, New York City.

General Education Board, 61 Broadway, New York City.

Russell Sage Foundation, secretary, 130 East Twenty-second Street, New York City.

These organizations have advanced the cause of education materially through encouragement of research, subsidies granted to investigators in the field, and through their own investigations and publications. Lists of the publications and studies sponsored by these foundations may be secured from the organizations in question. For purposes of illustration, one type of activity sponsored by these foundations may be mentioned. The Commonwealth Fund has subsidized much of the investigation of reading carried forward at the University of Chicago; this work has been particularly concerned with photographing the eye-movements in reading.

Space is available only for calling attention to the valuable work done by the Bureau of Education. The numerous publications of this agency should be known to every student of education. They cover a wide range of interest and include probably the best available source of information on current educational conditions, contemporary educational literature, educational statistics, and current movements in education. A list of the publications referred to may be secured from the United States Bureau of Education at Washington, D.C. Most libraries have these bulletins on file.

Educational Publishers and Their Offerings of Books and Reference Volumes.—Educational publishers are glad to supply the applicant with catalogues of their publications. Certain houses publish books in series grouped around some appropriate educational title such as, *Riverside Textbooks in Education, Lippincott Educational Guides,* etc. A list of these series in education may be found in an article [11] to which reference has previously been made. Upon application workers in education may be placed on the mailing lists of educational publishers and thereby receive notices of new publications. Certain publishers send notices on cards suitable for filing. Book reviews and lists of current publications received, as found in professional journals, as well as advertisements in periodicals, are of assistance to the reader in keeping in touch with new books. *School and Society* prints an annual

[11] Whitney and Rugg, *Teachers Journal and Abstract, op. cit.*

list of pedagogical literature. The *Educational Review* publishes an annual list of professional books received during the preceding twelve months, grouped by publishers. The *Journal of the National Education Association* publishes an annual selected bibliography, with annotations, of new books chosen by experts in the field. The list for 1926 includes some sixty selected titles plus a number of additional titles which receive mention only. More than 250 publications on teaching and school administration were issued in 1926. A report[12] in *School and Society* includes a classified list of more than 400 volumes dealing with teaching, school administration, and educational research which appeared in 1927. The complete list of educational books published in 1927 includes approximately 450 titles; the selected list[13] of 60 books for 1927 appeared in print in March, 1928.

Books may be traced by author, title, and subject in the card indexes of the library, the *United States Catalogue*, *Supplements to the United States Catalogue*, and the *Cumulative Book Index*. The *Book Review Digest* indexes important books and gives abstracts of reviews found in many of the leading periodicals. In addition, the student may find it helpful to familiarize himself with the "Dewey Decimal" system of classification and to examine the books on the shelves of the library; sometimes valuable material is located in this way which was not discovered by convassing the card index. The number for education is 370, while the appropriate subdivisions of education may be located under numbers ranging from 370–379 inclusive. Sometimes it is worth while to canvass the related fields such as sociology and

[12] Joseph L. Wheeler, "Educational Books of 1927," *School and Society*, XXVI (December 31, 1927), 823–35.

[13] "Sixty Educational Books of 1927," *Journal of the National Education Association*, XVII (March, 1928), 95–98.

psychology when investigating special problems in education.

Certain educational reference books are of value, although they are soon out of date. Expense of revision prevents them from being brought up to date at frequent intervals and therefore such sources present only a partial treatment of educational problems. In this connection may be mentioned Paul Monroe's *An Encyclopedia of Education*, F. Watson's *The Encyclopedia and Dictionary of Education*, J. M. Baldwin's *A Dictionary of Philosophy and Psychology*, and the general reference works and encyclopedias such as the *Britannica* and *International.*

Some of the publishers of educational books are given below; the houses which appear rather frequently in the role of educational publishers are indicated by an asterisk.

American Book Co., New York City.
*D. Appleton and Co., New York City.
A. S. Barnes and Co., New York City.
Bruce Publishing Co., Milwaukee, Wisconsin.
*The Century Co., New York City.
Thomas Y. Crowell, New York City.
Doubleday, Page and Co., Garden City, New York.
E. P. Dutton and Co., New York City.
*Ginn and Co., Boston.
*D. C. Heath and Co., Boston.
Henry Holt and Co., New York City.
*Houghton Mifflin Co., Boston.
*J. B. Lippincott Co., Philadelphia.
Little, Brown and Co., Boston.
*Macmillan Co., New York City.
*Public School Publishing Co., Bloomington, Illinois.
Rand, McNally and Co., Chicago.
Row, Peterson and Co., Chicago.
Chas. Scribner and Sons, New York City.
*Scott, Foresman and Co., Chicago.
*Silver, Burdett and Co., New York City.

*Teachers College, Columbia University, Bureau of Publications, New York City.
*University of Chicago Press, Chicago.
*Warwick and York, Inc., Baltimore, Maryland.
*World Book Co., Yonkers, New York.

Keeping Pace with Current Periodical Literature.—While it is hardly within the powers of a single individual to read all the periodicals of interest to workers in education, several useful means of keeping in touch with articles are available. The *Readers' Guide to Periodical Literature* and the *International Index to Periodicals* contain references to the contents of a number of important educational journals. The *Psychological Index* is a valuable list of references in a somewhat specialized field, but of interest to students of psychology, research workers, and investigators. Two recently established periodicals of a rather distinctive character issue monthly digests of important magazine articles appearing during the preceding month. Both the *Loyola Educational Digest* (3441 North Ashland Avenue, Chicago, Illinois) and the *Teachers Journal and Abstract* (Greeley, Colorado) have met with favorable receptions at the hands of the teaching profession. The annual or semi-annual indexes of educational periodicals are of assistance in locating material readily. Attention has previously been called to the useful bibliographies of the United States Bureau of Education and its frequently published lists of current educational literature.

Other Sources of Information.—Professor Alexander[14] has published a very useful bulletin of information, with special reference to administration, concerning educational books; public documents, national and state; publications of universities, educational institutions, and

[14] Carter Alexander and Others, *Educational Research.* New York: Bureau of Publications, Teachers College, Columbia University, 1927. Pp. vi + 42.

private foundations; periodical references; statistics, published and unpublished; bibliographies, etc. An especially helpful feature of the bulletin is the list of notes and bibliographies on individual items in administration, alphabetically arranged. Sources of information concerning many of the major problems of education are listed. Reference should be made to several other useful sources of information.[15]

Conclusion.—The writer is neither facetious nor unreasonable when he suggests that the graduate student in education, the research worker and investigator, and the scientific and forward-looking public-school worker should become familiar with the sources of educational information listed in this chapter. Such a statement does not mean that any single individual will read conscientiously or even skim rapidly all the sources of information mentioned. However, to recall the case of the candidate for the Doctor's degree who profited much by his familiarity with current educational literature, even though one may not have at tongue's end specific information on all educational problems that arise, he will be a much-respected and sought-after worker in education who knows *how* and *where* to locate desired information readily.

[15] Claude C. Crawford, *The Technique of Study*, Chapter X. Boston: Houghton Mifflin Co., 1928.

Harold O. Rugg, *Statistical Methods Applied to Education*, Chapter II. Boston: Houghton Mifflin Co., 1917.

Harold O. Rugg, "How to Keep in Touch with the Quantitative Literature of Education," *Elementary School Journal*, XVIII (December, 1917), 301–10.

L. Belle Voegelein, *List of Educational Subject Headings.* Columbus, Ohio: Ohio State University, 1928. Pp. xiv + 338.

CHAPTER III

TECHNICAL VOCABULARY AND TERMINOLOGY IN EDUCATION

Each Profession Has Its Own Vocabulary and Terminology.—Before a profession can exist there must be present a sufficient body of subject matter and practice to provide information, training, and guidance for those individuals following the calling in question. Of course such a body of subject matter and practice involves a considerable range of technical vocabulary and terminology appropriate to, and in part peculiar to, the profession in question. The professions of law and medicine have such highly specialized vocabularies as to leave the layman in a state of confusion when lawyers and doctors for one reason or another choose to be learned and mystifying. New terms are added daily to the science of medicine in order to label the numerous new discoveries that are made. In recent years aeronautics and radio have added probably hundreds of new terms to the languages of today.

The ancient professions of medicine and law have developed uniform and exact technical vocabularies which make for common understanding among practitioners and make possible accurate interchange of information and practice between workers in different parts of the world. Whether these facts caused medical and legal dictionaries to be prepared or whether the publication of dictionaries has brought about standardization of terminology may not be determined definitely by a layman such as the writer; probably influences toward standardization have emanated from both sources. It is said that the science of botany did not develop rapidly until manuals had been prepared which aided in common identification of a plant which had been known under different names and colloquialisms in separate communities and regions. It may not be out of place at this point to raise a question as to whether the technical vocabulary employed in education is not sufficiently large and the terminology sufficiently diversified to make desirable a dictionary of educational terms. In fact small beginnings in this direction have been made in the cases of educational books which include rather highly specialized material and on this account provide a glossary of the more unusual terms.

Size of Technical Vocabulary in Education.—A question may be raised relative to the size of the technical vocabulary to which the young student is introduced. Fortunately some evidence which throws light on this problem is available. An investigation,[1] including 98 students who were asked to prepare a statement of what they considered the characteristics of good and poor textbooks, shows that "too much technical vocabulary" heads the list of specific sources of difficulty in the textbooks mentioned. Analysis of ten textbooks in educational psychology revealed 559 selected technical terms considered important by four psychology instructors. Since a class in educational psychology ordinarily meets approximately 50 regular class days, equal distribution of these terms means that about ten new terms must be taken up each class period. Analyses of the technical vocabularies found in textbooks in

[1] S. L. Pressey, L. C. Pressey, and Others, *Research Adventures in University Teaching*, pp. 61–63. Bloomington, Illinois: Public School Publishing Co., 1927.

history of education, school administration, and principles of education were made. It was found that 36 per cent of the 559 selected psychological terms appeared in the "principles" list, 19 per cent in the "history" list, and 15 per cent in the "school administration" list. A comparison of the three technical vocabularies with Thorndike's ten thousand most common words of the English language showed that in the list in history of education there were 1,831 words not found in Thorndike's list; there were 1,076 such words in the list in school administration and 1,833 such words in the list in principles of education. Such figures indicate that vocabulary problems are a matter of real concern in the courses mentioned.

Pressey made a similar investigation[2] of English literature, American history, and zoology. A text in English literature contained references to 2,461 different items such as authors, historical and literary characters, literary compositions, places and dates. Of these items 57 per cent appeared only once, while 77 per cent were mentioned in only one chapter. Thirty-six per cent of the dates did not appear at all in a second text in English literature. A college text in American history mentioned 983 different persons of whom 83 per cent appeared only once. A college text in zoology commonly used in beginning courses was found to contain 4,226 technical terms not included in the 10,000 words of the Thorndike list of most commonly used words. Since teachers of foreign languages consider the acquisition of 1,000 new words a fair achievement for the first year's work in a foreign language, the technical vocabulary in the zoology text appears to be about four times as great as the vocabulary students are expected to master in a foreign language. Such facts indicate that the problem

[2] S. L. Pressey, L. C. Pressey, and Others, *op. cit.*, pp. 127–33.

of technical vocabulary is one worthy of consideration in the textbooks of fields other than education.

Nomenclature in Professional Educational Journals.—The highly technical character of the articles appearing in certain of the educational journals has inspired an editorial comment[3] which describes the situation so well that it is quoted in full:

Sometime ago a layman interested in the progress of education said to a university president, "What are the best educational magazines you read?" The reply was, "I don't read any of them. It is not because I haven't time, but because they have such technical vocabularies I can't read them without constant reference to a dictionary and I haven't time for that."

This bit of conversation raises several important questions with reference to educational magazines in general and our own in particular. Are the articles too technical for university presidents to read? Are they too technical for the members of the Educational Research Association of which the journal is the official organ? Are they too technical for college teachers of education whom we expect to be interested in the field of educational research? Are they too technical for school administrators, supervisors, and teachers upon whom lies the responsibility for putting into practice the findings of research? Where should material be published which reports new technical procedure, new formulas, new applications of the old?

The question is raised frankly because a question of policy is involved. For whom should educational magazines be published? What is their mission? Is their primary object simply to report or is it to report in order to modify practice? Are they publicity agencies for their contributors or are they service instruments for the benefit of the school children of the country? How much technical education have we a right to assume on the part of readers or to what extent may these magazines be expected to be the source of this technical education?

As we examine educational magazines we find evidence of various policies. Some are so free from technical terms that it is safe to assume that anyone can read them—even university presidents, and that without a dictionary. Most of these relate

[3] "Are We Too Highbrow?" *Journal of Educational Research,* XIV (December, 1926), 384–85.

personal experiences and opinions and savor little of contact with research and the scientific movement in education. They are apparently written for teachers who are neither trained nor critical. Others show evidence of an awareness of present educational tendencies. Their articles report the results of a variation of procedure which was to some extent at least checked by control methods. The language is relatively simple though the statements at times are dogmatic. Some discrimination is evidently expected of the reader though all the data are practically never presented. A third type of magazine is also available. This type fairly bristles with technical terms—quartiles, percentiles, and ogives, P.E.'s and sigmas, correlations multiple and partial, and regressions. Statistics by which to validate procedure and test the results have become an important instrument in scientific educational work, and therefore the authors, having made use of statistical procedure, feel the necessity of reporting all of it in the reports of their experiments.

Whenever anyone develops a new formula or a new use for an old formula, technical workers will certainly be pleased to know about it. Every worker should safeguard himself by every means at his disposal in the conduct of an educational experiment and the interpretation of his findings. On the other hand, when reporting investigations which are of value to public-school people, it is certainly a mistake to burden the report with a technical vocabulary which few understand. Research findings are valuable only as they modify educational practice.

This editorial inspired two letters of very different character with regard to technical terminology in educational journals. These letters[4] are interesting enough to quote; the first writer waxes somewhat ironical in his criticism of articles containing a large amount of technical nomenclature.

In reply to your editorial questions in the December number of the *Journal of Educational Research*, I venture to suggest that the cause of apathy, not only of the "laity" (a detestable usage) but of the profession, toward much of the so-called, "educational research" is perennial disappointment through failure to glean anything of real merit from the long and tedious articles which,

[4] *Journal of Educational Research*, XV (March, 1927), 214–15.

even under intriguing titles, prove to be but academic pedantry, camouflaged behind pseudo-technical lingo, in a strained effort, not to give real information, but to get into print or to satisfy the undiscriminating demands of institutionalized scholarship.

The practice of a few of the best scientific journals, of requiring their contributors to submit a brief, intelligible summary in well-established language, representing the final "conclusion of the whole matter," is certainly a boon to the busy, serious reader.

There is a very characteristic tendency in the field of education, particularly, to undue prolixity and often "sciosophistic" palavering.

An imposing repertoire of technical conventionalisms and Greek or other lettered symbols and formulas is in no sense a guarantee of erudition or profound insight; rather, like the noisy and spectacular whitecap, it is an index of shallowness or rockbound limitations. Most authors take too many presumptive liberties with their readers. When symbols or abbreviations are used they should, if intended for the general reader, be parenthetically explained. There is, in fact, little need for many "technical" expressions, and only rarely does an honest-to-goodness idea call for new terminology. That periodical is fortunate which succeeds in capturing one or a few fundamentally new ideas or expressions during a year. The mad scramble to produce something "new," if nothing more than a name, has developed almost to a mania, a *nomophobia*, that is more appropriately described as counterfeiting than as coinage.

Some question may be raised as to whether this vigorous writer has practiced what he preached in selecting the vocabulary used in the preceding quotation. The second letter as quoted below expresses a different point of view and the reader may draw his own conclusions as to the merits of the arguments presented in the editorial comment and in the subsequent comments on the same problem.

While I have my typewriter at hand, I am tempted to free my mind of some things which have been circulating around there for some time and which have been precipitated by your editorial in the Journal, "Are We Too Highbrow?" While I have as little use as anybody for the notion that a thing is valuable only in proportion to its difficulty or that the "pure" scientist has no responsibility to make his researches intelligible, I am wondering whether it be not possible to swing to the other extreme and overemphasize the value of the simplified. Take, for example, this question of the technical vocabulary of educational journals—to be specific, take the *Journal of Educational Research.* This journal is the official organ of an association all of whose members can be assumed to have had quite a bit of technical training. And, is it not true that a very large proportion of its readers, other than the members of the E.R.A., have had some professional training, and that this proportion is getting larger? If technical terms are to be eliminated largely from the Journal, then would not the same logic favor eliminating them from professional courses in education? Where shall the process stop? Shall we insist that all university courses be taught in terms of the high-school pupils' vocabulary? If rather, laying the customary cynicism aside, the function of language is to convey thought; and if a technical term will, when learned, make for greater clearness and brevity—and, of course, that is the only condition for which I am arguing—is it not desirable to employ that term, and to teach the use of it? Furthermore, is it not reasonable to suppose that any person who is fit to direct public education, even a college president, should have the ability and the willingness to understand those terms which refer to those particular phases of work with which he is concerned? My point is, instead of considering the elimination of technical terms from our journals, why should we not see to it that each person who leaves a college of education can understand such terms?

Desirability of an Exact and Uniform Terminology in Educational Writings.—A well-known author has taken to task contributors to periodical literature for failure to employ an exact and uniform educational nomenclature.[5]

One who reads carefully the articles that appear in the successive issues of the *School Review* cannot fail to be struck by the loose use of terms which constantly occurs in the educational writings of the present day. For example, one author in the March number uses the term "grades" in the title of his article, while another

[5] Franklin W. Johnson, "Educational Terminology," *School Review*, XXXII (June, 1924), 407–408.

employs the terms "mark" and "grade" interchangeably. "Grade" is the term in general use to distinguish the successive groups of pupils in their progress through the school and should be used exclusively for this purpose. The term "mark" is accurately descriptive and has but one use which is clearly understood. There is a similar, but less confusing, use of the terms "pupil" and "student" in articles in the secondary field. The more careful writers use "pupil" when speaking of the high school and "student" when referring to the college. There is also the confused use of "schedule" and "program of recitations." The former is distinctive; the latter is properly used only in the expression "program of studies" which is applied to all of the curriculum offerings of a school. School men in other countries avoid the confusion into which we have fallen by using the terms "schedule" and "time-table." "Extra-curricular" is another descriptive word which is now inaccurate. When the activities thus designated first appeared, they were quite outside the formal studies comprising the curriculum. With the broader aims now accepted, the curriculum has expanded to include all educative experiences, among which the great variety of social activities now organized and directed by the modern school are recognized as having an important place. The term "extra-classroom" should be used as more accurately descriptive in designating these.

The claim that teaching is a profession would be strengthened by a more exact use of language in our professional journals.

Desirability of Some Uniformity in Education Courses.—Evidence is available which indicates a decided lack of common agreement and uniformity with regard to the problems and content of a given course in education, authorship of textbooks used, and course titles. As long as this state of affairs exists it will be difficult to develop an exact technical vocabulary and a uniform educational nomenclature.

Watson,[6] on the basis of topics included in texts, courses, and examinations in educational psychology,

[6] Goodwin B. Watson, "What Shall be Taught in Educational Psychology?" *Journal of Educational Psychology*, XVII (December, 1926), 577–99.

formulated a series of problems deemed important in this field. The list of problems was submitted to 400 subjects with the request that they add topics not included in the series. Various groups of individuals were asked to rate the importance of the different psychological problems included in the list. The author's conclusion was that psychological textbooks do not agree with one another in their emphases or with the criterion based upon judgment of value. Representative educational psychologists, in their ratings of the problems suggested, differed widely from the distribution of emphasis suggested by other educators and from the lines of emphasis in textbooks.

Worcester[7] analyzed eleven outlines of the first course in educational psychology as received from ten colleges and universities. He calls attention to the lack of agreement as to the material included in this first course. The same writer found on investigating twelve texts in educational psychology that the topic of instinct was the only item discussed under the same name in all the books analyzed. The space devoted to this topic varied from one-half of 1 per cent to 14 per cent of the whole text.

An article[8] published as early as 1920, based on material collected some years previous to publication of the data, indicates a fairly large number of course titles covering in a large measure the same general body of subject matter. For instance, the 57 courses in methods of instruction found in 32 college catalogues were distributed under 16 course titles. The author calls attention to the confusion which results when

[7] Dean A. Worcester, "The Wide Diversities of Practice in First Courses in Educational Psychology," *Journal of Educational Psychology*, XVIII (January, 1927), 11–17.

[8] G. M. Wilson, "Uniform Nomenclature for College Courses in Education," *Educational Review*, LX (September, 1920), 150–55.

students examine descriptions of such courses in college catalogues, especially when transferring from one institution to another. Certainly the officers charged with evaluating the work of students who transfer from other institutions find their task greatly complicated by the wide range of educational terminology in current use.

A more recent study[9] of course titles in educational psychology, based on catalogues for the year 1926 secured from state normal schools and teachers' colleges, shows, if anything, that the range of terminology in assigning course titles has increased during recent years. The 155 institutions whose catalogues were analyzed were found to offer a total of 897 courses in psychology under 182 different course titles. The distribution of titles was as follows: educational psychology, 21; educational tests and measurements, 36; mental tests and measurements, 19; general psychology, 13; child study, 18; psychology of adolescence, 8; psychology of subject matter, 12; social psychology, 2; abnormal psychology, 11; individual differences, 10; and miscellaneous, 32; total, 182. It will be recognized that the person making the analysis may have grouped the course titles more or less arbitrarily under the general divisions of subject matter listed in the preceding sentence, since the decision was based only on the title of the course.

Douglas[10] made a questionnaire study of the status of the introductory course in educational psychology in

[9] Marion E. MacDonald, "A Catalog Study of Courses in Psychology in State Normal Schools and Teachers Colleges," *Educational Administration and Supervision*, XIII (April, 1927), 272–82.

[10] O. B. Douglas, "The Present Status of the Introductory Course in Educational Psychology in American Institutions of Learning," *Journal of Educational Psychology*, XVI (September, 1925), 396–408.

American universities and colleges and received 65 usable replies. His conclusions indicate that there is little or no uniformity of opinion as to the subject matter of educational psychology except where the course is offered in a designated college year. Consequently the textbooks in use vary widely in authorship and content.

Lack of a Common Terminology at the Secondary-school Level.—It is of interest to consider whether there is any unanimity of expression in secondary education with respect to general objectives. On first thought one might expect rather general agreement along this line among secondary-school workers due to the work of the committee of the National Education Association which framed the seven cardinal principles of secondary education and due to the work of such writers as Bobbitt and Parker. However, an analysis of the objectives listed or stated indirectly in manuals and programs of studies published by state departments of education and city secondary-school systems reveals a wide range of terminology employed in stating general aims or objectives.

The present writer has previously published data[11] which are concerned with this problem. An effort was made to tabulate each objective in the exact words of the course of study from which it was taken. Such a procedure of course involves considerable duplication, but is of value in revealing the wide scope of the aims emphasized and the diversified terminology in use. In not all cases were the statements of the courses of study listed in numerical array as specific objectives of the schools in question, but in such instances it could be deduced from the context that the items were goals

[11] Carter V. Good, "The Objectives of Secondary Schools in 1926–27," *Education*, XLVII (June, 1927), 585–92.

toward which the schools were working. As a result of the analysis 106 general objectives of the secondary school were discovered, although it is true that in some cases essentially the same objective was listed several times under varying forms of nomenclature. Such data indicate that many secondary-school officers, according to their printed courses of study, are hazy or at least disagree in terminology, with regard to the aims of the high school. The present writer does not venture to suggest that all secondary courses of study should recite in a parrot-like fashion the same ten or twelve or twenty objectives. However, unless there is more general agreement among high-school workers than the foregoing analysis indicates, laymen, high-school pupils, and students of education may be expected to have hazy ideas with regard to the real purposes of secondary education.

The writer has employed virtually the same technique of analysis and the same printed programs of studies in determining the titles of parallel high-school curriculums, secondary course titles, and the specific objectives of the various divisions of subject matter. The results secured indicate a diversity of terminology comparable with that used in stating the general objectives of the secondary school. A study[12] of parallel-curriculum titles revealed 130 different titles in use, although curriculums including much the same type of work often appeared under different nomenclature. For instance, the work frequently offered under the title "home economics" also appears under other titles—"college entrance home economics," "dietetics," "domestic arts," "general home economics," "girls' vocational," "home training,"

[12] Carter V. Good and Raymond E. Good, "Titles of Curriculums Offered or Suggested in Secondary Schools," *School Review*, XXXV (September, 1927), 503–509.

"household arts," "industrial (girls)," and "vocational home economics."

It is hardly in place at this point to suggest the number of titles under which the curriculums of secondary schools should be grouped. Certainly, any definite effort on the part of those interested in high-school curriculum-making to adopt a more uniform terminology should reduce the number of titles used considerably below 130. Probably the number of curriculum titles could be reduced one-half or even three-fourths. Increased uniformity in terminology should lessen the confusion which may arise when a pupil transfers from one school system to another, when a school officer speaks or writes of his secondary-school curriculums for the benefit of a group of workers from other secondary-school systems, or when students of education and investigators canvass the educational offerings of different high schools. Undoubtedly the problem is one worthy of careful study. Probably a movement toward standardization of nomenclature could be most effectively initiated in the secondary field by such professional organizations as the North Central Association of Colleges and Secondary Schools, the Association of Colleges and Secondary Schools of the Southern States, and the National Association of Secondary School Principals.

An analysis[13] of the course of study in social science in 29 senior high school systems disclosed 48 different course titles. It is likely that a number of the courses and titles involved were the result of the whims of an individual school officer or instructor or of the idiosyncrasies of a particular school system rather than

[13] Carter V. Good, "The Variables of the Senior High School Curriculum and the College-Entrance Problem," *School Review*, XXXV (November, 1927), 686–91.

an expression of social need or careful planning. Among the course titles discovered were community-life problems, community civics, citizenship, civic science, modern problems, problems of democracy, problems of government, and social problems. Certainly if such courses have, in any sense, or could be made to include, a common body of subject matter, a blanket title should be adopted to cover such material. This standardization of terminology would eliminate confusion for those who have charge of college admissions, for the pupils who transfer from one secondary school to another, and for the workers in the field of secondary education. This is also a problem which accrediting organizations and professional associations of secondary-school officers could take up with profit to both college and high school.

Data concerning the titles of courses in 78 junior high school centers,[14] and concerning the specific objectives[15] of certain of the great divisions of secondary subject matter and the course titles[15] of the same divisions of subject matter in the senior high school are also available.

[14] R. M. Tyron, H. L. Smith, and Allan F. Rood, "The Program of Studies in Seventy-Eight Junior High School Centers," *School Review*, XXXV (February, 1927), 96–107.

[15] Carter V. Good, "The Mathematics and Science Curricula in Junior and Senior High Schools," *School Science and Mathematics*, XXVII (November, 1927), 863–69.

Carter V. Good, "The High School Curriculum in Home Economics," *Journal of Home Economics*, XIX (December, 1927), 686–90.

Carter V. Good, "The High School Curriculum in Commercial Education," *Journal of Commercial Education*, LVI (November, 1927), 263–65.

Carter V. Good, "The Objectives and Status of Art Education in Secondary Schools," *Journal of Educational Method*, VII (February, 1928), 209–13.

Carter V. Good, "English Objectives and Constants in Secondary Schools," *Peabody Journal of Education*, V (January, 1928), 230–35.

The conclusions reached are much the same as those stated in the preceding discussion of social science and in a previous discussion of the general objectives of the secondary school.

Efforts toward Establishing an Exact and Uniform Educational Nomenclature.—It is not within the province of this chapter or book to present a list of definitions of educational terms. Such a dictionary of educational definitions would probably comprise a fair-sized volume. However, the reader may be referred to four creditable attempts to standardize portions of the vocabulary in the field of education. The late Charles Hughes Johnston has prepared a chapter[16] on high-school terminology which, if read carefully and applied conscientiously in the speaking and writing of school workers, should do much to eliminate the haziness and diversification of nomenclature in the field of secondary education. A recent bulletin[17] has been prepared which is concerned especially with problems of terminology at the college level. Professors Monroe[18] and Odell[19] have sought to define the terms in the field of educational measurements. Certainly it seems that some worker might now carry these attempts at standardization of terminology in education beyond the scope of the four

[16] Charles Hughes Johnston, Jesse H. Newlon, and Frank G. Pickell, *Junior-Senior High School Administration*, pp. 65–88. New York: Charles Scribner's Sons, 1922.

[17] David A. Robertson, *Standard Terminology in Education*. Educational Record Supplement (January, 1927). Washington, D. C.: American Council on Education. Pp. 32.

[18] Walter S. Monroe, *Definitions of the Terminology of Educational Measurements*. University of Illinois Bulletin, Vol. XX, No. 6. Urbana, Illinois: University of Illinois, 1922. Pp. 18.

[19] Charles W. Odell, *A Glossary of Three Hundred Terms Used in Educational Measurement and Research*. University of Illinois Bulletin, Vol. XXV, No. 28. Urbana, Illinois: University of Illinois, 1928. Pp. 68.

contributions mentioned and perform for education the service Noah Webster did for the English language and spelling a century or more ago in his famous speller and dictionary.

Conclusion.—While education is a relatively new science when compared with the old professions of law and medicine, a sufficient body of educational literature has developed to make highly desirable a uniform and exact educational vocabulary. The problem of mastering the technical vocabularies used in educational textbooks is found no easy task for young students in teacher-training work. If workers are somewhat divided with respect to the use of highly technical terms in educational periodicals, they are entirely agreed as to the desirability of an exact and uniform terminology in educational writings, notwithstanding present practice to the contrary. There is a wide diversity of practice in the titles and nomenclature used to label teacher-training courses, educational objectives, and even secondary-school courses and objectives. While a few isolated and scattered efforts have been made toward the standardization of vocabularies involved in selected portions of the field of education, there is a large field of service open to the worker or workers who will complete, and secure general adoption of, this standardized nomenclature.

At one time it was the practice of medicine man, priest, and orator to be mystifying, voluble, and to indulge in high-sounding phraseology; probably the maintenance of the offices in question depended on such procedures. It is possible that some writers in education have used these methods. However, the real scientist uses the simplest terminology compatible with correct expression of his ideas and with clear understanding on the part of the reader or hearer; certainly he is consistent in the use of the nomenclature appropriate to the science represented.

Chapter IV

CHARACTERISTICS OF SCIENTIFIC INVESTIGATIONS

The Nature of Educational Research.—In Chapter I an attempt was made to define research; several statements from competent research workers were quoted in order to establish a clear conception of the fundamental meaning of real educational research. The value of research to society, the educational system, the various levels of the school system, and to the individual worker or teacher was discussed at some length. It seems appropriate at this time to present two somewhat fuller statements[1] of the first brief characterization of educational research as given in Chapter I.

"Reflective thinking" is the name given to the mental process of discovering rules and principles. Since men began to be concerned about the preparation of children for the activities of adult life, "thinkers" have been discovering from their experience and observation rules and principles relating to the learning process, the teaching process, the curriculum, the organization of a school, the preparation of teachers, and so forth. Many of these "discoveries" we now know have been faulty due to incorrect or incomplete data or to failure to think with sufficient accuracy. Recently under the name of "educational research," specific attention has been given to improving the technique of discovering knowledge about education. Particular emphasis has been placed

[1] Walter S. Monroe and Nell Bomar Johnston, *Reporting Educational Research*, p. 7. University of Illinois Bulletin, Vol. XXII, No. 38. Urbana, Illinois: University of Illinois, 1925.

Walter S. Monroe and Max D. Engelhart, *The Techniques of Educational Research*, p. 7. University of Illinois Bulletin, Vol. XXV, No. 19. Urbana, Illinois: University of Illinois, 1928.

upon collecting objective data and summarizing them by employing statistical procedures with the result that some persons appear to consider these two phases of educational research as constituting the whole of it. This is an unfortunate conception. Reflective thinking is required in the discovery of new procedures, rules and principles.

Although the authors . . . are not attempting to define educational research, there is one other point which should be noted here. The process of producing knowledge is one of growth. Discovered principles become data which may be used in making other discoveries. In the course of our racial experience, particularly during modern times, a considerable store of knowledge relative to education has been accumulated. Most of this knowledge is recorded in treatises on educational theory, educational psychology, philosophy of education, and school administration. Unfortunately, not all that one finds in books relating to education is true but much valid knowledge is contained which a "discoverer" of educational procedures, rules and principles will find helpful to use.

The statement which follows probably expresses the point of view of the senior author better than the first quotation, since it was made some three years later. However, essentially the same conception of educational research is found expressed in the two statements.

Educational research is the name for a type of procedure employed in answering thought questions about education; that is, questions for which answers must be manufactured by reflective thinking. This procedure is one in which the best data obtainable are used and the thinking is critical. At times a research worker may be concerned with fact questions answerable by routine clerical activities. If the answers to such questions are needed as a means of dealing with thought questions, such activities are a phase of educational research.

The ultimate purpose of all educational research is the discovery of procedures, rules, and principles relating to the various aspects of education. Or to express it in a somewhat different way, the function of educational research is to determine what we should do or attempt to do in educating children and adults. However, many of the activities of research workers have as their immediate purpose the determination of what is, or what has been, rather than what should be. This is not inappropriate provided the securing of this information is looked upon as a means for determining what should be.

Nature of Research in Educational Administration.—The meaning of educational research is made more concrete when the definition of research is narrowed down specifically to a given subdivision of the field of education. Alexander[2] has prepared an able statement of the nature of research in educational administration and in addition has indicated the various phases of educational administration into which the investigator may inquire. These problems in educational administration will be discussed in a later chapter which will consider the selection of an appropriate problem for investigation.

> Research in educational administration seeks to discover, in the light of the purposes of education commonly acknowledged, the most efficient procedures in the organization, supervision, financing, and evaluation of the program of educational service. It results in the statement of principles or the description of procedures essential to the development of an efficient administration of schools.
>
> The research worker in this field employs the methods common to all fields of scientific inquiry. He arrives at the solution of his problems through reflective thinking. In some of the steps in his thinking he is assisted by more or less elaborate techniques. In others he relies solely upon the methods employed in everyday experience. In any case he inquires concerning the validity of any procedure which he proposes to use, accepting nothing solely upon the sanction of tradition or current practice. He tests the results obtained to determine whether they are consistent with all the facts pertinent to the administrative procedure or principle under investigation. He favors objective measures and is satisfied with nothing less than competent evidence.

[2] Carter Alexander and Others, *Educational Research*, p. 1. New York: Bureau of Publications, Teachers College, Columbia University, 1927.

Research Essentially a Method of Procedure.—The foregoing treatment of the nature of research and the discussion of educational research found in Chapter I make quite plain the fact that the essential difference between scientific research and ordinary investigation is found in the care with which the method is worked out and in the precision with which each step of the process is planned. Attention has been called to this distinguishing characteristic of true research in the educational literature available.[3] The last-named reference, by Trow, is of especial interest, since it is devoted entirely to a treatment of scientific method in education. A brief summary of his discussion of scientific method seems appropriate at this point. The summary is adapted from the writer's review of Trow's work in *Educational Administration and Supervision* for April, 1926.

Trow's Discussion of Scientific Method in Education.—Education has reached a stage in its development when it may truly be considered a science, since it possesses both a systematic and orderly arrangement of knowledge and a scientific method of procedure. The empirical and speculative thinking of educators has given way in large part to the scientific investigation of concrete school situations from which data may be drawn for the guidance of the teacher and the modification of school procedure. However, there are two ways in which the term "scientific," if thoughtlessly used, may work positive harm. A school administrator may take over bodily what purports to be scientific in the form of the

[3] W. C. Schluter, *How to Do Research Work*, Chapter I. New York: Prentice-Hall, 1926.

An Outline of Methods of Research with Suggestions for High School Principals and Teachers, p. 5. Bureau of Education Bulletin, No. 24, 1926. Washington: Bureau of Education.

Wm. Clark Trow, *Scientific Method in Education*. Boston: Houghton Mifflin Co., 1925. Pp. xii + 160.

tentative hypothesis of a scientific worker with the result that the smooth running of the school is interfered with and no advantage gained. On the other hand, there is the reactionary who distrusts all innovations to which the descriptive term "scientific" is applied. The *method* of science is far more important than the subject matter involved. Scientific method means literally the "pursuit of knowledge."

In his pursuit of knowledge man has sought simpler ways than the scientific method which involves orderly procedure or a series of steps. Because of the universal need for guidance man has appealed to authority, both religious and civil. At one time authority furnished both the aim and content of education. The sources of such professional knowledge were custom, empirical findings, and speculation; when these sources proved inadequate, there emerged the scientific method. The scientific method involves problem-solving (seeing problems and discovering the solution), degrees of certainty (the hypothesis, theory, and law), and induction and deduction. Scientific procedure makes use of instruments of precision, mechanical inventions, quantitative measurements, the experiment, and definite rules of scientific thinking. The application of scientific method to educational problems has included the methods of psychology in the study of children (the questionnaire, anthropometry, measuring human reactions, the rating scale, and experimentation), the methods of medicine in the study of children and homes (the clinic and case history), a method of sociology in the study of curriculum content (the social survey), and methods of economics in the study of schools (the industrial survey and statistical method).

Trow points out that one of the valuable contributions of educational science is to methods of teaching; too frequently the value of scholarship is lost because method is lacking. Education does more than to borrow the methods of collecting and accurately measuring data as used by the natural and social sciences; it puts such methods to work in its own field and investigates individuals, class groups, and entire schools. The scientific method in education has limitations common to certain other sciences; like all sciences, the science of education does not determine truth unmistakably and for all time; like the biological sciences, education deals with the phenomena of human life which involves an unpredictability that is often baffling. Education may possess certain other limitations peculiar to itself—the hangover of the influence of authority and speculation, the tendency to fall back upon authority and opinion because of too meager scientifically-determined information, too few data, too few accurate measures, and the deficient scholarship and training of too many educators.

Steps in Research. In general, authorities[4] are fairly well agreed with respect to the steps to be observed in research. While the five steps listed below are not necessarily sequential, they must be observed at some time in the course of a given investigation of a scientific nature. It may be said that these five steps in research are the same as those in any process of reasoning: (1) the formulation and definition of the problem, (2) the collection and assembly of necessary and relevant information or data, (3) critical analysis of the data, (4) the development and formulation of hypotheses or possible solutions, (5) testing the validity of the proposed hypotheses until a satisfactory solution is found.

[4] Monroe and Johnston, *op. cit.*, p. 9.
Bureau of Education Bulletin, No. 24, 1926, *op. cit.*, p. 5.

Schluter has listed a sequence of fifteen steps[5] which he uses as an outline in discussing the essential characteristics of research procedure. He devotes a chapter of his book to each of the fifteen items. The reader no doubt will be able to group several of these steps under one of the steps listed in the preceding paragraph. For instance, the first five items proposed by Schluter are concerned with the formulation of the problem. The fifteen steps in research procedure, as listed by Schluter, are:

1. Selecting the field, topic, or subject for research.
2. Surveying the field to apprehend the research problem.
3. Developing a bibliography.
4. Formulating or defining the problem.
5. Differentiating and outlining the elements in the problem.
6. Classifying the elements in the problem according to their relation (direct or indirect) to the data or evidence.
7. Determining the data or evidence required on the basis of the elements in the problem.
8. Ascertaining the availability of the data or evidence required.
9. Testing the solvability of the problem.
10. Collecting the data and information.
11. Systematizing and arranging the data preparatory to their analysis.
12. Analyzing and interpreting the data and evidence.
13. Arranging the data for presentation.
14. Selecting and using citations, references, and footnotes.
15. Developing the form and style of the research exposition.

A Negative Definition of Research and Scientific Procedure.—Crawford has stated an interesting negative definition of research.[6]

It is not the mere collection of a mass of interesting material. The term research is sometimes erroneously used in connection with reading in the library to assemble material for a long term paper or

[5] Schluter, *op. cit.*, p. 5.

[6] Claude C. Crawford, *Methods of Study*, pp. 154–55. Published by the author, University of Idaho, Moscow, Idaho, 1926.

essay. Research is not merely dredging for suggestions or opinions from a great number of people, and picking out a pearl here and there. It is not necessarily the invention of a new machine, instrument or process of manufacture. It is not necessarily the solution of a practical problem. It may be in the realm of pure science, or theory, and have no practical bearings whatever. It is not a form of magic or black art by which a few geniuses perform supernatural feats or discover things which are not revealed to ordinary mortals; nor is it a type of work which an ordinary student who has been doing well in college courses can enter into and pursue successfully without special training.

Reeder has named and illustrated ten common violations of the principles of scientific procedure.[7]

1. Stating one's opinion as a fact without any evidence or without sufficient evidence to support it.
2. Stating the opinion of a reputed authority as a fact.
3. Stating the opinion of a committee as a truth.
4. Stating the opinion of the majority as a fact.
5. Reasoning from analogy.
6. Reasoning from silence.
7. Omission of evidence contrary to a certain theory which the author supports.
8. Failure to indicate how and where data were secured.
9. Inaccurate or vague citations, quotations, dates, etc.
10. Wrong interpretation of data.

Positive Aspects of Research and Scientific Method.—After considering certain negative characteristics of research and scientific procedure, it seems desirable to summarize the positive aspects of research and scientific method. Crawford mentions the following characteristics of research:[8]

1. It centers around a problem.
2. It involves original work.
3. It rests upon a mental attitude of curiosity.

[7] Ward G. Reeder *How to Write a Thesis*, pp. 14–18. Bloomington, Illinois: Public School Publishing Co., 1925.

[8] Crawford, *op. cit.*, p. 155.

4. It requires an open mind.
5. It rests on the assumption that everything is subject to law and order.
6. Its object is to discover laws and generalizations.
7. It is a study of cause and effect.
8. It is based on measurement.
9. It involves a conscious technique.

Characteristics of the Scientist.—An interesting editorial[9] describes two characteristics which distinguish the true scientist, an insatiable desire to know the truth and an absolute honesty in reporting what is found.

. . . But what is a scientist? Not simply one who works the microscope, the telescope, or the retort; not simply one who works in the field of chemistry or physics or biology or astronomy. A scientist is one who is distinguished by two characteristics. First an insatiable desire to know the truth and, second, an absolute honesty in reporting what he finds. These will characterize Galileo and Newton, Faraday, Pasteur, and Michaelson. They will also characterize Plato, Savonarola, Luther, Pestalozzi, and Thorndike. If we are to have a science of education, research must play a big part in the things we do. This means we must be scientists. We must have the characteristics of the scientist.

Probably the vast majority of people fail to qualify on one or both of these characteristics. They have no insatiable desire to know the truth. Gossip is quite as satisfactory as fact. They prefer to take their opinions, ready made, from others, for it requires less effort than thinking. Prejudices are more easily acquired than knowledge. It is easier to express an opinion than to pass judgment upon it; easier to repeat than to revise one's position on the basis of more information. Also, it seems more consistent.

The second characteristic—absolute honesty in reporting what we find—is equally important. Recently a professor of geography in a university was heard to say, "I don't care what the evidence shows, I don't believe it." On another occasion the dean of a graduate school remarked concerning some data reported in a

[9] "Research," *Educational Research Bulletin*, VI (April 13, 1927), 164–65. Columbus, Ohio: Bureau of Educational Research, Ohio State University.

Master's investigation, "I don't believe it, and if it is true, it should never be published." An editorial, which appeared in an educational magazine a number of years ago, said this, regarding a certain investigation: "The study ought never to have been made. Having been made, it ought not to have been accepted as a Doctor's dissertation. Having been accepted, it ought never to have been published." These statements are illustrative of the non-scientific attitude of mind which sometimes appears even among those whom we ordinarily suppose to be scientific. All of us have our prejudices. All of us have our limitations, especially outside of our own field. The true scientist, however, reports with absolute honesty his findings whether or not they agree with tradition, with the findings of his colleagues, or with the theories and philosophy which he holds. Truth is acknowledged and reported regardless of how it cuts across personal inclinations.

Scientific Nature of the Graduate Thesis.—Reeder makes the following statement concerning the thesis as a scientific document:[10]

> A thesis is a report of a research on a given problem or topic; it should be a scientific document. It is presumed that its author stands ready to defend it with the facts that have been collected and organized; it is presumed also that it shall be a contribution to existing knowledge. This contribution to existing knowledge may be made in either one or both of two ways: (1) by the derivation of a new method or technique or by the improvement of an old method or technique; (2) by the use of an old method or technique in making a scholarly collection and organization of facts on a given problem or topic. If it be insisted that a thesis, particularly one for the baccalaureate or master's degree, cannot always be expected to be a *contribution to existing knowledge,* certainly in all cases it should be expected to be a *scholarly* document worthy of the degree for which it is submitted.

Alexander presents a statement of the standards desirable in a thesis in educational administration.[11] Standards for the handling of the problem, data, method, presentation, conclusions and mechanics are listed.

[10] Reeder, *op. cit.*, p. 9.
[11] Alexander and Others, *op. cit.*, pp. 2–4.

Many of the items are applicable to other fields of education.

Some General Principles Concerning the Conducting of Original Investigations.—Crawford mentions a number of general items which he considers important in research work.[12] This list of eleven items may serve as a partial summary of the points made in the preceding discussions of this chapter.

1. Select a suitable subject.
2. Master the general field in which you are to work.
3. Be on guard for hidden factors.
4. Try to relate everything possible to your problem.
5. Adopt a good system of notes.
6. Reduce everything to written form.
7. Use objective devices to eliminate personal factors.
8. Plan your investigation before reading what others have done.
9. Get as much criticism as possible.
10. Rehearse the procedure of your investigation by trying it out upon a friend or a small group before you apply it in final form.
11. Remember that you are seeking after truth instead of confirmation of your personal opinions.

Care in Reporting Educational Research is Essential.—Although a later chapter will discuss at length the problems involved in reporting educational research, attention at this time very appropriately may be called to this important phase of educational research. It is a matter of regret that the reader's attention is so frequently distracted from quite valuable and worth-while information by lapses in the mechanics, form, English usage, and style employed by the author. The writer should never become so wrapped up in his subject or so careless as to neglect such matters.

The following statements which refer to educational publications in general, for the most part will be found especially applicable in the case of reports of educational

[12] Crawford, *op. cit.*, pp. 161–62.

research. Today it is tacitly assumed that the author of a new book, monograph, or study in education has a message to convey which reports the results of original investigation or experimentation, presents a reorganization of subject matter in the field discussed, makes available a summary and interpretation of investigations in a given field, or, much less frequently than formerly, consists of unsubstantiated statements of an individual's theories about educational problems or of an "inspirational" pedagogical address. Most publications of this type require a good working knowledge of the handling of graphical, statistical, and tabular materials; ability to digest and organize effectively large masses of subject matter; development of mechanical devices to expedite the reading of the busy individual who has a little time in which to do much reading; and satisfactory and complete bibliographical forms and methods of referring to the work of other authors in the field treated.

The book, monograph, article, or thesis of limited or questionable value which is lacking in the respects enumerated in the preceding paragraph has nothing to recommend it. The strong publication or report of research with a real message, by virtue of its content value, may transcend lapses in mechanics and form. However, it is interesting to observe that, almost without exception, educational writings most suggestive on the content side are almost perfect in the mechanics of construction. This fact may be due to the editorial watchfulness of a good publishing house, the competent staff of an educational journal, the critical eye of a faculty adviser, the ability of the individual worker, or a combination of such factors. The educational report of inferior content and form, in most cases, probably has two explanations for its lapses, a poorly trained or careless author and an over-worked and harassed editorial staff of limited educational background in a small publishing house. As has been suggested above, the problems involved in reporting educational research will be discussed in detail and at some length in a later chapter.

The Methods of Science as Contrasted with the Methods of Opinion.—Parker presents an excellent statement of five characteristics of scientific procedure.[13] He states that the following five characteristics or terms descriptive of science were derived from Thorndike's discussion[14] of science versus opinion: (1) mathematical precision, (2) objectivity, (3) verifiability, (4) impartiality, and (5) expertness. The reader will note that by using a simple mnemonic scheme the five principles can be kept in mind quite easily; the first letters of the five terms spell the word "movie." A brief statement of the meaning of each characteristic and a few concrete illustrations will provide an appropriate summary of certain points previously discussed in this chapter.

Mathematical Precision and Accuracy.—Science takes the stand that anything which exists can be measured and seeks to discover precise quantitative measures for determining amounts, changes, and differences. Science is not content to guess at differences or similarities or to deal solely with such vague and general terms as "more," "less," "much," "little," "approximately," etc. The worker interested in making the spelling curriculum of the elementary grades determines exactly frequency of usage of words on the part of children and adults in his selection of words, considers on the basis of careful investigation difficulty and social need in the gradation of words, and also investigates the problems of

[13] Samuel Chester Parker, *General Methods of Teaching in Elementary Schools*, pp. 107–111. Boston: Ginn and Co., 1922.

[14] E. L. Thorndike, *Principles of Teaching*, pp. 265–68. New York: A. G. Seiler, 1906.

presentation of words.[15] The old method of formulating the spelling curriculum was on the basis of a single man's opinion or to "spell" through a dictionary. In directing intelligently the reading of children, adult opinion as a basis for selection of books is not sufficient; accurate information concerning preferences of children, sex differences, and both chronological and reading ages of the children involved is necessary.[16] Exact information concerning the play behavior of children has been secured and analyzed from the following angles: general age growth, preferences of children below the third grade, sex differences, differences between town and country children, differences between negro and white children, the influence of certain variables (year-to-year changes, prevailing local fashions in play, home training, and playground space and equipment), individual differences, seasonal variations, school progress, and intelligence.[17]

In three interesting editorials[18] attention is called to the desirability of mathematical precision and accuracy in educational writings and research. The first editorial writer takes to task the author of a study in which American and European secondary systems of education are compared. This study characterizes American high

[15] Frederick S. Breed and William C. French, *The Breed-French Speller*, pp. iv-xiv. Chicago: Lyons and Carnahan, 1927.

[16] Carleton Washburne and Mabel Vogel, *Winnetka Graded Book List.* Chicago: American Library Association, 1926. Pp. 286.

[17] Harvey C. Lehman and Paul A. Witty, *The Psychology of Play Activities.* New York: A. S. Barnes and Co., 1927. Pp. xviii + 242.

[18] "Secondary Education in the United States and in Europe," *School Review*, XXXV (September, 1927), 481–83.

"Accuracy," *Journal of Educational Research*, VIII (June, 1923), 63–67.

"Scientific Accuracy Versus Propaganda," *Elementary School Journal*, XXVI (January, 1926), 323–25.

schools as "enormous" in size, when in reality, in 1923–24, of the total 19,442 high schools only 614 enrolled more than 1,000 pupils and only 13 enrolled more than 5,000 pupils. There were 9,150 high schools with 100 or less pupils and the average enrollment was 199 pupils.[19] The author is also taken to task for other similar inaccuracies in his statements. The third editorial is concerned with a criticism of a study which neglects a scientific and accurate treatment of school costs due to the interest of the investigator in disseminating certain school propaganda, propaganda of a desirable character though resting on an insecure factual basis. The second editorial writer emphasizes mathematical precision and accuracy, but finds it possible to carry precision to the point of absurdity, so far as practical working conditions are concerned.

> Fortunately, however, accuracy in the absolute sense is not for most purposes worth pursuing. It would not, for example, be worth while to obtain the valuation of a school district to the last cent nor to know the floor area of a schoolroom correct to the nearest square inch nor to compute the average writing ability of a class to the third decimal place. A difference of a few cents on the tax duplicate is unimportant. A dozen square inches more or less in a surface containing approximately 100,000 such units is of no consequence. A writing ability of 65.378 on the Ayres scale has little meaning beyond the integer. Evidently, then, there are instances where meticulous accuracy is not worth the labor of attaining it because small differences are immaterial.[20]

Objectivity.—The method of science emphasizes concrete tangible materials and data which are open to the observation and manipulation of workers other than the original discoverer or investigator. For instance, purely

[19] *Statistics of Public High Schools*, 1923–1924, pp. 1–2. Bureau of Education Bulletin, No. 40, 1925. Washington: Bureau of Education.

[20] "Accuracy," *Journal of Educational Research*, VIII (June, 1923), p. 63.

mental materials which consist of the impressions, feelings, ideas, beliefs, or opinions of an individual worker or thinker are not open to such general observation and are considered as *subjective.* Certain of the illustrations used in the preceding discussion of mathematical precision and accuracy are also good examples of the objective type of investigation. The curriculum-maker in spelling analyzes children's themes, children's letters, and adult correspondence which are available for the inspection of other investigators. The worker interested in the reading interests of children ascertains from children themselves their preferences as an aid in formulating a book list instead of depending solely on the opinions of librarians, teachers, and other adults. The investigator of play behavior determines by a canvass of children the games in which they actually engage over a given period of time. The data secured from such investigations are available for the inspection of other workers and have an existence outside the thinking and opinions of one or more theorists or philosophers.

For too many years writing upon the subject of formal discipline was of a bitter and partisan nature. Opinion, belief, and prejudiced arguments so beclouded the real issues that a scientific and experimental solution of the problem was delayed. The following statements[21] from prominent individuals illustrate the rule of opinion that held sway a few years ago and which is still present in many instances. "My opinion of the supreme educational value of the great disciplinary studies has not changed and will never change." "I believe that the slow processes of translation of the classics make good training for the boy who has chosen a business career." "I, for one, regret very keenly that I took a great deal

[21] Carter V. Good, *The Supplementary Reading Assignment*, pp. 95–96. Baltimore: Warwick and York, 1927.

of Latin and Greek and did not spend far more time on advanced mathematics and physics."

It is not to be assumed from the foregoing discussions that authoritative opinion is of no value. Education, in the present stage of development in some of its fields, must depend for a time on the best and most authoritative opinion available as a guide. However, wherever such a state of affairs exists, experimental and objective investigation must be encouraged to support or disprove the theories or opinions which have served as guides. A later chapter will suggest some of the fields of investigation in which experimentation and research are urgently needed. Reference will be made to sources which contain lists of concrete problems in need of solution in education.

At this time attention may be directed to publications which have based conclusions on theory and opinion rather than on concrete and objective data and evidence. It should be kept in mind that certain of the publications mentioned may make worth while contributions to education in spite of lack of objectivity. A clinical psychologist bases his discussion of the differences between bright and dull pupils on the opinions and experiences of 500 teachers.[22] A keen and caustic critic of activity analysis as a technique of curriculum-making offers no substitute other than the reiteration that the philosopher should set up objectives and ideals, which of course is a subjective procedure.[23] A well-known student of method presents a theoretical and philosophical discussion of general principles of teaching rather than an organized treatment of concrete fac-

[22] Harry J. Baker, *Characteristic Differences in Bright and Dull Pupils.* Bloomington, Illinois: Public School Publishing Co., 1927. Pp. viii + 118.

[23] Boyd H. Bode, *Modern Educational Theories.* New York: Macmillan Co., 1927. Pp. xiv + 352.

tual material relating to specific school subjects and problems.[24] The authors of a book list for children use the factors of judgment and opinion in compiling their list.[25] An investigator seeks to determine the effect of tobacco on mental efficiency by basing his conclusions in part on the opinions of prominent men and women.[26]

Reference may be made to two editorials which urge wider use of the objective method in education. The first calls attention to the desirability of objective methods rather than opinion in the rating and recommending of teachers.[27] The second editorial points out that the instructors of teachers in training need to draw freely upon the experimental evidence available rather than on their own pet theories.[28]

Verifiability.—Educational research, to be scientific, must be reported in such a way that other competent workers can repeat and verify the investigation in question, if desired. This makes it necessary that each step, method of procedure, source of data, and every other essential aspect of the experiment or investigation be described fully. If certain data are of minor importance or render the body of the report unnecessarily complicated, they may in many cases be placed in an appendix. The investigations of spelling

[24] William Heard Kilpatrick, *Foundations of Method: Informal Talks on Teaching*. New York: Macmillan Co., 1925. Pp. xii + 384.

[25] Lewis M. Terman and Margaret Lima, *Children's Reading*. New York: D. Appleton and Co., 1926. Pp. 364.

[26] M. V. O'Shea, *Tobacco and Mental Efficiency*. New York: Macmillan Co., 1923. Pp. xx + 258.

[27] Grover H. Alderman, "Subjective Versus Objective Judgments," *University of Pittsburgh School of Education Journal*, II (September-October, 1926), 20–21.

[28] "Research Versus Propaganda in Education," *Peabody Journal of Education*, V (July, 1927), 46–47.

vocabularies, play behavior, and children's reading preferences which were mentioned in the previous discussion of mathematical precision and accuracy describe the procedures involved in such a way that competent workers may verify such investigations, if desired.

An all too common lapse in educational writings is failure on the part of the author to give the exact source of an expressed opinion, statement, quotation, or data. Two reviewers[29] of Pringle's *Methods with Adolescents* have criticized the author vigorously for his failure to give such information. The author draws freely upon the writings of Judd, Thorndike, Dewey, Bagley, and others, but never gives page references and frequently neglects to cite volume or article. To quote the first reviewer indirectly, this glaring disregard of the accepted principles of citation is utterly inexcusable in a writer in a technical field and shows an indefensible writing technique in dealing with technical materials.

Impartiality.—The scientist seeks assiduously for the truth and nothing but the truth with no consideration for his own personal opinions, feelings, or interests. He undertakes an investigation or experiment without preconceived prejudices which might interfere with proper manipulation of scientific procedures. Certainly, if the ordinary citizen is expected to begin jury service without preconceived opinions or prejudices concerning the guilt of the individual on trial, the research worker may well adopt a similar attitude toward the outcome of a problem which he attacks. Probably, in the light of the preceding comments, it is a desirable practice to invite an outside group of workers to make a school

[29] *School Review*, XXXV (November, 1927), 707–709.

Educational Administration and Supervision, XIII (December, 1927), 639–42.

survey of a city or state system. It would be fair to neither the author of a series of elementary school readers nor to the school system in question to ask the former to recommend a series of basal readers.

An example of an investigation conducted by biased workers may be found in the first part of the report of the Advisory Committee of the American Classical League. Quotations from an editorial comment[30] on this study are very appropriate in a discussion of impartiality as a characteristic of the scientist.

> The report has two striking characteristics. It is defensive in tone throughout. The reader feels at every turn that there is an enemy in the immediate neighborhood whom the authors are trying bravely to repel. In the second place, the report is amateurish. The authors lack the sure touch of the experienced workman.
>
> . . . .
>
> . . . The favorite method of the investigators . . . is to prove that something comes out of the study of Latin and to rest the case on this fact. For example, pupils who study Latin are superior to pupils who do not study Latin in interpreting the Latin abbreviations found in ordinary English reading. This superiority is accepted as showing the advantage of studying Latin. Let any sober-minded person look impartially at this case. If the time spent in studying Latin were devoted to a good course in English, would the gain in interpreting English be as small as it is now? This question is not asked in the report. The Latin pupils are compared with pupils who have had no training in abbreviations, and, because the Latin pupils can do something—even though it is pitifully little—there is great rejoicing in the Latin camp. If the non-Latin pupils who are found inferior in such a one-sided comparison were measured in knowledge of agriculture or in skill in shopwork or in the facts of botany instead of in Latin abbreviations, and the pupils who had been devoting their time to Latin had to show how much they knew in these fields, as well as in the field of Latin abbreviations, what would the Latinists say? As it is, the investigators ignore the whole field of scientific training and count only the achievements resulting from the study of Latin.

30 "The Classical Investigation," *School Review*, XXXIII (February, 1925), 86–89.

. . . .

The report is written by Latin specialists with a bias so marked that no one will be convinced who is not now prejudiced in favor of all that the committee believes. It is a painful example of the blind offering leadership to their kind.

Expertness.—Scientific investigations are conducted by individuals whose minds are specially trained to seek out the truth in the fields in question. It follows that such scientific studies must be made by experts who are masters of the techniques needed to determine truth in the fields under investigation. It is recognized that the graduate student, when he first undertakes a thesis investigation, may not be an expert in the field involved, but he must make up his deficiency by careful reading and study along the line of the problem under consideration. In many instances, especially in the case of the Doctor's dissertation, by the time the study has been completed the candidate for a graduate degree is, and should be, better informed than anyone else on the given problem. It has been deplored that so many graduate students, after having become expert in a given field, do not carry forward their investigations after leaving the graduate school.[31]

A few instances may be cited to illustrate the demand for expertness in educational investigations. The committee in charge of the Modern Foreign Language Investigation invited the cooperation of an outstanding expert in the photography of eye movements in reading.[32] The largest state in this country invited a group of outstanding leaders to make a survey of the status of the public school system; a nationally known leader in

[31] B. R. Buckingham, "The Greatest Waste in Education," *School and Society*, XXIV (November 27, 1926), 653–58.

[32] G. T. Buswell, *A Laboratory Study of the Reading of Modern Foreign Languages*. New York: Macmillan Co., 1927. Pp. xii + 100.

education inquired into the secondary schools of the state;[33] dozens of similar instances could be mentioned. Those interested in a revision of the pharmaceutical curriculum secured the cooperation of the best known advocate of the technique of activity analysis in curriculum-construction.[34] When the city of Los Angeles wished to undertake a revision of its curriculum, a pioneer student of the curriculum was called to direct the work.[35]

Conclusion.—The chief characteristics and requirements of educational research may be summed up under the five points discussed in the preceding paragraphs: (1) mathematical precision, (2) objectivity, (3) verifiability, (4) impartiality, and (5) expertness. Many of the points made in this chapter will be found summarized in Downing's excellent article.[36]

[33] C. H. Judd, *Secondary Education.* Texas Educational Survey Report, Volume III. Austin, Texas: Texas Educational Survey Commission, 1924. Pp. 104.

[34] W. W. Charters, A. B. Lemon, and Leon M. Monell, *Basic Material for a Pharmaceutical Curriculum.* New York: McGraw-Hill Book Co., 1927. Pp. 366.

[35] Franklin Bobbitt, *Curriculum-making in Los Angeles.* Supplementary Educational Monographs, No. 20. Chicago: Department of Education, University of Chicago, 1922. Pp. vi + 106.

[36] Elliot R. Downing, "The Elements and Safeguards of Scientific Thinking," *Scientific Monthly*, XXVI (March, 1928), 231–43.

Chapter V

SELECTING AND DEFINING A PROBLEM FOR INVESTIGATION: NEEDED RESEARCH IN EDUCATION

Have Most of the Problems of Education Been Solved?—A rather common attitude on the part of the graduate student who is just beginning his work is that most of the problems of education have been solved. He is prone to point to the relatively large number of Masters' and Doctors' theses completed each year, monographs, contributions of research organizations and bureaus, studies published in research periodicals, and other scientific contributions to education as evidence that the supply of problems in education requiring solution is virtually exhausted. Of course such a conception of the state of affairs in education is far from the real truth, as subsequent portions of this chapter will make quite clear.

Education may well take its cue from such fields as industry, commerce, and other applied sciences as well as the pure sciences. The automobile and airship industries are notable examples of fields in which an enormous amount of industry is expended in bringing about improvement through the solution not only of presented problems but of discovered or sought out problems. Radio workers are not satisfied merely with broadcasting sound, but at this writing have broadcast successfully visual images. The movie industry was not content merely to represent the behavior of actors by pictures thrown on a screen, but synchronized the reproduction of the human voice with the appropriate actions of the players on the screen. Parker calls attention to the large number of mechanical, diplomatic, moral, expressional, aesthetic, scientific, and mathematical problems present in the everyday life of the world.[1]

Unquestionably in many of the subdivisions of the field of education the final word has not been said; new problems continually present themselves or are discovered, tentative solutions must be verified, and partial solutions must be completed. Even the much worked over field of reading still presents a large number of problems in urgent need of solution; just as one of the so-called "whole" methods of teaching reading seems superior to the old A B C method, there may be a method much superior to any in current use. While a spelling vocabulary selected and graded on the basis of frequency of use, need, and difficulty is much superior to the old speller the content of which was selected according to an individual author's opinion or was the dictionary itself, there are yet other problems in spelling in need of solution. The subdivisions of the field of measurement are yet in their infancy so far as accurate measures of human traits and characteristics—psychological, educational, emotional, character, etc.—are concerned.

Seeing and Finding Problems.—The preceding paragraphs and a subsequent portion of this chapter indicate that the difficulty of many graduate students and educational workers is in sensing or finding the multitudinous problems which confront on every hand the trained investigator who has eyes to see such issues. Trow calls attention to this rather characteristic inability to

[1] Samuel Chester Parker, *Types of Elementary Teaching and Learning*, Chapter X. Boston: Ginn and Co., 1923.

see problems on the part of students, graduate and undergraduate.[2] "Oftentimes students finish college and go on to graduate school before they discover that they need to do some original research before they will be awarded a graduate degree. So they confer with some member of the graduate faculty and ask him for a problem to work on; they can't seem to think of any. Can't think of any, and the world fairly bursting with them!" An editorial writer quoted in Chapter II gives an interesting and rather humorous account of the graduate student who went to a professor with the fond expectation of having a thesis problem "assigned" to him.[3]

McCall mentions five ways in which experimental problems may be discovered: (1) by becoming a scholar in one or more specialties as early as possible; (2) by reading, listening, and working critically and reflectively; (3) by considering every obstacle an opportunity for the exercise of ingenuity instead of an insuperable barrier; (4) by starting a research problem and watching problems bud out of it; and (5) by not losing those problems already found, that is, by keeping a systematic record of original ideas and problems.[4]

Selecting a Problem for Investigation.—Obviously, after problems in a given field have been located, the research worker must make a choice with regard to the particular problem which he wishes to attack. It should be emphasized that in the case of a graduate student responsibility for choosing a problem rests on the student and not on a member of the faculty, although

[2] Wm. Clark Trow, *Scientific Method in Education*, p. 40. Boston: Houghton Mifflin Co., 1925.

[3] "The Editor Turns Professor," *Educational Research Bulletin*, VI (September 14, 1927), 252–53. Columbus, Ohio: Bureau of Educational Research, Ohio State University.

[4] William A. McCall, *How to Experiment in Education*, pp. 7–8. New York: Macmillan Co., 1923.

the latter is almost without exception generous in the matter of consultations concerning thesis problems. In the field of education, at least, ability on the part of the student to select and plan a study is considered as essential to the completion of work leading to a graduate degree. In the preceding paragraph attention was called to the desirability of keeping a systematic record of original ideas and problems that arise; a card index seems quite appropriate for such a purpose.

It should be emphasized in the case of the graduate student that early selection of a problem is highly desirable; otherwise a hurried and careless piece of work, often accompanied by delay in the granting of the degree, is likely to result. Usually the Doctor's problem is under way a year before the granting of the degree and in many cases the candidate has been working on his problem two or three years. A few candidates for the Master's degree may concentrate their thesis work so as to finish the project within three or four months, but as a rule a considerably longer period of time is required for the completion of a creditable thesis.

Reeder[5] suggests the following criteria which the student should keep in mind when selecting a problem for investigation: (1) the novelty of the problem, (2) the student's interest in the problem, (3) the practical value of research on the problem to the student and others, (4) the student's special qualifications to attack the problem, (5) the availability of data on the problem, (6) the cost of investigating the problem, and (7) the time probably required for the investigation of the problem.

Schluter lists six criteria which he considers especially important in choosing a problem in the social sciences.[6]

[5] Ward G. Reeder, *How to Write a Thesis*, pp. 21–23. Bloomington, Illinois: Public School Publishing Co., 1925.

[6] W. C. Schluter, *How to Do Research Work*, pp. 11–12. New York: Prentice-Hall, 1926.

1. Does the field appeal to my interest?
   a. Is the interest purely intellectual?
   b. Is the interest present because of reward—pecuniary returns, possibility of advancement in position, increased authority, and so forth?
2. Are the results that may be obtained of practical or utilitarian significance?
   a. May they be of use in business?
   b. May they be of use to society, to government, or to others?
3. Does the field present gaps in verified knowledge which need to be filled?
4. Does the field require reworking?
5. Does the field permit extension of inquiry beyond the present limits of verified knowledge?
6. Is the field pivotal or strategical from the standpoint of the immediate purposes which the possible results of investigation are to serve?

Naturally, in selecting a problem and in the later formulation and definition of the problem, a bibliographical survey is essential. Otherwise, the investigator may be pursuing a problem which has already been solved. McCall tells of a student who submitted a manuscript to Thorndike with the hope that it would be accepted as a Doctor's thesis; the student said he knew it was original because he had read nothing on the subject.[7] It will be recognized that a survey of the literature pertinent to a given problem will prevent repetition of an investigation previously conducted by another experimenter or worker, may suggest additional problems for solution, aids in perfecting techniques and procedures, and provides a summary of related investigations and previous experiments. An editorial writer to whom reference has previously been made tells of a graduate student who wished to correlate intelligence and achievement in high school as a thesis problem and seemed chagrined when informed that this had been done by

[7] William A. McCall, *op. cit.*, p. 8.

hundreds of people.[8] The information in Chapter II of this book should suggest a wide range of sources for the preparation of a bibliography.

Alexander[9] suggests that the student interested in choosing a problem in educational administration should: (1) acquire the attitude of questioning every administrative procedure in education and inquire what evidence there is to support one procedure in preference to another; (2) really *know* the most important fifty studies in educational administration; and (3) chart the issues which superintendents of schools must meet, list the kinds and amounts of knowledge, and estimate the reliability of the knowledge available.

Formulating and Stating the Problem.—After the general problem to be investigated has been selected it must be definitely formulated and stated. McCall says there are three types of workers in educational research who are clearly indicated by the way in which they formulate their problems.[10] The first type of experimenter formulates problems which are so broad in their scope as to offer little practical aid in planning the details of an investigation. This first type is illustrated by the worker who came with the problem: "What is the effect of various factors upon learning?" McCall reports that later the experimenter came with the formulation: "What are the effects of distribution of time upon learning?" At a later stage the problem became: "Will a typical fourth-grade class in silent reading, spending three thirty-minute periods per week, accomplish more or less than an equivalent class spending five periods of

[8] "The Editor Turns Professor," *Educational Research Bulletin*, *op. cit.*, pp. 252–53.

[9] Carter Alexander and Others, *Educational Research*, pp. 4–6. New York: Bureau of Publications, Teachers College, Columbia University, 1927.

[10] William A. McCall, *op. cit.*, pp. 9–11.

eighteen minutes each per week?" The second type of experimenter is described as the "pot-hole" type who works on such narrow problems as to be considered an experimental drudge and as failing to see any relation between his isolated researches and the general scheme of education. The third type is the scholarly worker who formulates the general problem, then breaks it up into smaller issues or specific working units. The solutions of these specific problems are brought together in a unified whole as contributions to the solution of the large problem which alone may have real practical significance.

Monroe and Engelhart[11] point out that the problem should be expressed either in the form of a question or so that the question to be answered is clearly apparent. They take the point of view that a statement of the topic, such as the title of a thesis, merely names the particular field in which the problem is to be formulated and is not satisfactory as a statement of the problem itself. The authors have selected from the literature excellent references which illustrate the various possible methods of stating a problem. The various forms used in the general statement of the problem are as follows:

1. A question or questions.
   a. A single question.
   b. Several questions.
   c. A single question followed by several sub-questions.
2. Declarative statement.
   a. A single statement.
   b. A single statement containing several phases.
   c. A series of complete statements.
   d. A general statement followed by subordinate statements.
3. Statement followed by restatement in the form of a question.
4. A statement followed by a series of theses.

[11] Walter S. Monroe and Max D. Engelhart, *The Techniques of Educational Research*, p. 14. University of Illinois Bulletin, Vol. XXV, No. 19. Urbana, Illinois: University of Illinois, 1928.

Defining and Delimiting the Problem.—A quotation from Monroe and Engelhart[12] seems appropriate in a discussion of defining and delimiting the problem under investigation.

> To define a problem means to specify it in detail and with precision. Each question and subordinate question to be answered is to be specified. The limits of the investigation must be determined. Frequently, it is necessary to review previous studies in order to determine just what is to be done. Sometimes it is necessary to formulate the point of view or educational theory on which the investigation is to be based. If certain assumptions are made, they must be explicitly noted.
>
> The definition of the problem affords a basis for the subsequent phases of educational research. It is the guide for the collecting of data. The data are to be analyzed, organized, and summarized so as to be most useful for answering the questions specified in the definition of the problem and the conclusion is merely a statement of the answers resulting from the investigation.
>
> The basic importance of the problem and its definition indicates that they should appear early in a report of educational research. However, it is not unusual to find reports in which a large amount of introductory material precedes the statement of the problem. Occasionally this may be desirable but frequently a critical reader wonders if the formulation of this introductory material did not precede the formulation of the problem.

The same authors include a valuable list of references to studies which illustrate several ways of defining the problem. The types of definition represented are:

1. Analysis of the major problem or problems in terms of subordinate problems.
2. Statement of the limits or scope of study.
3. Orientation of the problem.
   a. A historical account, remote or recent.
   b. A survey of previous studies or related studies.
   c. An analysis of previous studies or related subjects.
   d. Preliminary survey.

[12] Walter S. Monroe and Max D. Engelhart, *op. cit.*, Chapter II.

4. Description of the general nature of the problem.
   a. Type.
   b. Source.
   c. Procedure.
5. Statement of limitations of technique employed.
6. Recognition of assumptions and implications.
7. Importance, value, or significance of study of education.
8. Definition of terms.

Alexander[13] presents a list of steps to be followed in defining and outlining the problem for a dissertation in educational administration; the suggestions are quite applicable to other fields. The case of the student who wished to study the effect of various factors on learning, as cited in a preceding paragraph of this chapter, illustrates the way in which this very general and vague problem had to be narrowed and delimited. A specific study may be used to make more concrete the statement and definition of the problem.[14]

The purpose of the study here reported was to determine the comparative success of extensive reading and intensive reading in the social-science field.

The investigation requires little justification because of the wide variation in the amount of supplementary reading assigned by college and high-school instructors . . .

. . . .

The Advisory Committee on the Social Studies of the Commonwealth Fund suggested the need for the investigation of the problem of extensive and intensive reading . . .

The terms "extensive reading" and "intensive reading" as used in this study may be defined in two ways . . .

The terms "comparative success" and "merits" as used in this study mean the ability of the student (1) to answer questions which test range and accuracy of information, (2) to apply material which has been read to the solution of problem situations, (3) to reproduce

[13] Carter Alexander and Others, *op. cit.*, pp. 6–7.

[14] Carter V. Good, "An Experimental Study of the Merits of Extensive and Intensive Reading in the Social Sciences," *School Review*, XXXIII (December, 1925), 755–70.

ideas or thought units gained from assigned reading material, (4) to retain material once acquired, as shown by a retest, and (5) to sense relationships, as evidenced by proficiency in outlining the main points and subpoints of a short article . . .

Two types of experiments were made: (1) experiments involving reading done outside the regular class period to determine the merits of extensive and intensive reading of the subject matter of a given course and (2) experiments involving reading done under controlled conditions within the regular class period to determine the merits of extensive and intensive reading of material extraneous to the subject matter of a given course . . .

The general technique of the investigation involved (1) the selection of classes for experimentation, (2) the division of the classes into parallel groups, (3) the selection of reading assignments, and (4) the construction of tests with which to measure the five elements selected for purposes of experimentation.

A number of the points made in preceding paragraphs are summed up in Alexander's list of standards which the thesis problem in educational administration at Teachers College, Columbia University, must reach.[15]

1. Must be within the field of educational administration.
2. Must be unsolved, so that its solution will be a "contribution to education."
3. Must be real in the senses that its solution is a felt need and that it is capable of fairly definite solution based on adequate actual data.
4. Must make a worthwhile or significant contribution to education.
   a. Discover additional facts or new practices.
   b. Substantiate questioned facts, theories, or practices.
   c. Perfect a previously discovered technique.
5. Must be definite in that its conclusions may have real value.
6. Must be sufficiently limited to permit of exhaustive treatment.
7. Must be of sufficient value to justify the effort and time employed in the research.

Completed Research in Education.—Obviously, the educational worker does not wish to attack a problem which has been satisfactorily solved. On more than

[15] Carter Alexander and Others, *op. cit.*, p. 2.

one occasion a research worker has spent much time in the investigation of some problem only to find that some other person has previously arrived at the same conclusion. In some cases the results were even available in print, but the investigator in question had failed to make a thorough bibliographical survey. Probably graduate students are more likely to duplicate the work of some student in another institution due to the difficulty involved in ascertaining the problems being investigated by students in graduate schools. The reader will recall the classic examples of James and Lange who worked out a similar theory of the emotions concurrently and of Lancaster and Bell who discovered independently the monitorial system of instruction.

It may be repeated that the sources of educational information listed in Chapter II furnish a reasonably complete guide in making a bibliographical survey to ascertain previously investigated problems in education. Special attention may be called to the fact that the United States Library of Congress has a list of American doctoral dissertations, printed each year, beginning with the year, 1912. The Bureau of Educational Research of the University of Illinois has issued mimeographed bulletins containing the titles of Masters' and Doctors' theses in education, beginning with January, 1917; these bulletins have been issued at intervals of approximately two years. Mention may be made of the bulletins and bibliographies of the United States Bureau of Education which provide valuable information concerning completed research in education.[16] To enumerate specifically other sources of information

[16] For example, E. E. Windes and W. J. Greenleaf, *Bibliography of Secondary Education Research*, 1920–1925. Bureau of Education Bulletin, No. 2, 1926. Washington: Bureau of Education. Pp. viii + 96.

concerning completed research in education would be to recapitulate the material of Chapter II, although the following general types of material may be brought to the attention of the reader: educational bibliographics and abstracts, guides to current literature, research periodicals, publications of teacher-training institutions, bulletins and reports of state and city school systems and bureaus, school survey reports, publications of professional educational organizations and societies, publications of national foundations and boards, and the books and monographs of a selected group of publishers who make available a considerable number of research contributions.

For a number of years (beginning in 1923) the *Phi Delta Kappan*, publication of a national educational fraternity which numbered in 1926–27 more than 8,000 members most of whom have done graduate work in education and who have adopted the guiding principles of research, service, and leadership in education, has issued a list of the completed studies of the members of Phi Delta Kappa. At this writing there are thirty-six chapters of the organization, including the larger graduate schools and departments of education of this country. The list of studies is usually published in the August number of the journal, although it is often necessary to devote parts of succeeding issues to this list.

A number of the larger graduate schools and departments of education have available lists of Masters' and Doctors' theses which are furnished on request; special mention may be made of Teachers College, Columbia University, which publishes annually a register of its doctors of philosophy from 1899 to date and a bulletin of Masters' theses accepted for the year.

Research under Way.—It is possible in some instances to secure through the administrative offices of graduate schools and departments of education a list of current investigations on which students and staff are engaged. News items in periodicals provide valuable information concerning yearbook topics, school surveys, and other important investigations under way. Advance notices of teacher-training institutions, research bureaus, and educational publishers are well worth careful reading in order to keep in touch with studies well under way or nearing completion. Certain news-letters of local chapters of Phi Delta Kappa have been accustomed to print lists of the projects on which members are engaged; *Zeta News* of the University of Chicago chapter is a case in point. Frequently in the yearbooks of professional organizations and learned societies may be found a list of the topics for projected yearbooks on which work is going forward. In February, 1926, and in March, 1927, the National Committee on Research in Secondary Education published through the United States Bureau of Education a *Bibliography of Current Research Undertakings in Secondary Education.* It is planned to continue this series of reports.

NEEDED INVESTIGATION IN EDUCATION

General Problems.—The literature of the past few years indicates that educational workers have been active in suggesting problems which should be solved. The *Phi Delta Kappan* for October and December, 1926, includes a list of research problems proposed by the members of the fraternity in response to the request that they indicate the educational problems which seemed most important in terms of real need for solution. The problems are classified under three headings, administrative, pedagogical, and professional. Occasionally the news-letters of local chapters of Phi Delta Kappa contain valuable suggestions concerning needed investigations in education, for example, *Zeta News* for November 15, 1924, of the University of Chicago; this list was prepared by certain members of the staff of the School of Education. A number of graduate schools and departments of education have available a suggested list of problems which may offer valuable assistance to students who wish to select a thesis project for investigation. However, it must be kept in mind that such lists of needed investigations are in no sense to be interpreted as "assignments" of problems. The student who selects his problem independently of any such proposed list and comes to a faculty adviser with his technique at least tentatively worked out is considered as possessing one of the most essential characteristics of the successful graduate student and research worker. Naturally many useful and stimulating suggestions relative to possible research studies in education are made at one time or another in connection with graduate courses; the same thing is true in fields other than education.

In succeeding paragraphs reference will be made to suggested lists of problems needing investigation in a number of the subdivisions of the field of education. Two matters of interest are the recency of publication of the suggested lists of investigations and the wide range of interests represented. On the whole, an open-minded and inquiring attitude, which should be stimulating to the graduate student and other educational workers, is suggested. Before considering the more specialized problems in the various fields of education, attention may be directed to an article which mentions a number of general problems which have not been satisfactorily solved.[17]

[17] U. L. Light, "Muddling Through from Guess to Science," *Educational Review*. LXVIII (June, 1924), 5–9.

Higher Education and Teacher Training.—Koos[18] points to the dearth of scientific inquiry into collegiate education and emphasizes the disagreement found among college workers with regard to the aims of the liberal-arts college. He suggests the desirability of investigating the following problems: the functions appropriate to the last two years of the four-year college course, the occupational destination of college graduates, differentiation of work to meet the needs of students of varying mental capacities, the economic and social composition of the students of our colleges, the extent of overlapping in high-school and college courses, the development and use of achievement tests at the college level, and methods of instruction at the college level. Kelly[19] discusses the need for research along several lines in higher education: cost studies, student registration or enrollment, teaching load, miscellaneous statistical studies, experimental colleges, aims of higher education, learning problems, adaptation to different intelligence levels, and measurement of the results of teaching.

Lee [20] points out certain problems in the training of vocational teachers which provide opportunity for research: the selection of candidates for teaching, the measurement of trade ability and trade testing, curriculum construction, evaluating the performance of students, and analysis of the trade teacher's job.

[18] Leonard V. Koos, "Research Problems in Collegiate Education," *School and Society*, XVII (February 17, 1923), 169–74.

[19] F. J. Kelly, "Needed Research in Higher Education," *Studies in Education*, pp. 74–84. Yearbook Number XV of the National Society of College Teachers of Education. Chicago: University of Chicago Press, 1926.

[20] Edwin A. Lee, "Research Problems in Training Vocational Teachers," *School and Society*, XXIV (July 10, 1926), 31–37.

An interesting list of possible studies and researches in the various types of laboratory work involved in the preparation of teachers, supervisors, and school administrators has been suggested by a research committee. The list for 1925 includes forty-eight problems some of which involve a number of smaller problems.[21] A shorter list of types of research needed in supervised student-teaching was published in 1926; this list is accompanied by a useful discussion of five stages of research activity which should be familiar to educational investigators.[22]

Needed Research in Secondary Education.—Briggs[23] canvassed research workers in secondary education to ascertain the problems which in their opinion needed investigation; replies were received from forty-five men who had published in the field. The problems considered of greatest importance at the secondary level, arranged according to frequency of mention, were: methods, 21; organization, 19; teachers, 19; psychology, 17; tests, 16; finance, 9; prognosis, 7; the principal, 6; and supervision, 6. Briggs considers it strange that the history of secondary education has been so neglected as a research field during late years.

Symonds[24] presents a list of eighty problems in the field of measurement in secondary education grouped

[21] A. R. Mead, "List of Possible Studies and Researches in Supervised Student-Teaching," *Educational Administration and Supervision*, XI (May, 1925), 355–56.

[22] A. R. Mead and Others, "Research in Supervised Student-Teaching and Allied Problems: Report of Research Committee, 1926," *Educational Administration and Supervision*, XII (May, 1926), 346–51.

[23] Thomas H. Briggs, "Problems in Secondary Education That Need Solution," *School Life*, XI (February, 1926), 116–18.

[24] Percival M. Symonds, "Needed Research in the Field of Measurement in Secondary Education," *Journal of Educational Research*, XVI (September, 1927), 119–26.

under seven headings: (1) characteristics of tests; (2) new tests; (3) characteristics of mental growth of children of high-school age; (4) use of tests in teaching; (5) problems relating to marks, pupil placement, and program; (6) problems relating to the measurement of efficiency; and (7) problems relating to prediction.

Elementary Education.—Judd[25] emphasizes the desirability of research in elementary education along the following lines: arithmetic, reconstruction of the first six grades, school administration, typical characteristics of pupils of different ages, social institutions to which pupils are introduced in the schools, taxation, personnel management, management of teachers, management of pupils, preparation of textbooks and other mechanical aids to instruction, and problems of classroom procedure.

Classroom Supervision.—Barr[26] discusses seven types of needs in the field of classroom supervision: (1) exact information about the thing to be improved; (2) more information about the probable effectiveness of different training programs; (3) more information about the validity, objectivity, and reliability of the items of teaching observed by supervisors; (4) experimentally determined principles of teaching; (5) more information about the improvability of teachers; (6) more information about the relative effectiveness of various improvement (supervisory) devices; and (7) more exact measures of teaching ability.

The Psychology of Learning.—Henmon[27] calls attention to the large number of unsolved problems in pre-school learning, the general psychology of learning, and the

[25] Charles H. Judd, "Research in Elementary Education," *Journal of Educational Psychology*, XVII (April, 1926), 217–25.

[26] A. S. Barr, "Needed Research in Classroom Supervision," *Peabody Journal of Education*, V (January, 1928), 209–15.

[27] V. A. C. Henmon, "Needed Research in the Field of Learning," *Journal of Educational Research*, XI (May, 1925), 313–21.

special psychology of learning school subjects under school conditions.

Needed Curriculum Research.—Briggs[28] lists twenty-seven questions which he maintains must be answered before the problems in the field of the curriculum can be satisfactorily solved. Salisbury[29] discusses a number of interesting problems in the curriculum field and places special emphasis on that of moral growth. Phelps[30] emphasizes needed research which will utilize the various methods of investigation available in curriculum construction: philosophical study, job analysis, committee-conference curriculum making, quantitative study, and experimental study. Certain of the chapters of the 1928 yearbook of the Department of Superintendence include suggestions relating to problems which should be investigated in the secondary-school subjects.[31] A book by Professor Harap should prove useful to the investigator who wishes to conduct research in the curriculum field, especially in the reorganization of the program of studies in the public-school field.[32]

Educational Finance.—Mort[33] indicates five problems in the field of state aid: (1) the investigation of the demands on the state fiscal program of the principle that the state shall encourage progress of education in

[28] Thomas H. Briggs, *Curriculum Problems.* New York: Macmillan Co., 1926. Pp. xvi + 138.

[29] Ethel I. Salisbury, "Needed Research in Course of Study Making," *Journal of Educational Method,* IV (June, 1925), 410–16.

[30] Shelton Phelps, "Curriculum Construction," *Peabody Journal of Education,* V (January, 1928), 223–29.

[31] *The Development of the High-School Curriculum,* Part II. Sixth Yearbook of the Department of Superintendence. Washington: Department of Superintendence, 1928.

[32] Henry Harap, *The Technique of Curriculum Making.* New York: Macmillan Co., 1928. Pp. xii + 316.

[33] Paul R. Mort, "Needed Research in the Field of State Aid," *Teachers College Record,* XXVII (April, 1926), 707–12.

the localities; (2) the interpretation of a satisfactory minimum educational offering in terms of the unit cost it involves; (3) the development of an index for measuring the burden involved in transporting pupils; (4) the investigation of the effect which the cost of living should have on a true measure of educational need; and (5) the investigation of the part to be played in an equalization program by capital outlay.

Alexander[34] asks eight important questions pertinent to the field of educational finance:

1. What are the available materials in a given unit as a state or the city school systems of a state and to what important uses may such materials be put?
2. Just what practical and reasonably attainable changes are needed in records, reports, methods of reporting, time of making the budget, and the like, of a given unit as a state or the city systems of a state, to make the fiscal data thoroughly useful and why?
3. What are the needed new techniques for securing valuable results from data already available?
4. What prediction techniques are needed?
5. How do certain educational fiscal policies really work?
6. What can a given fiscal area afford to spend for schools, considering its resources and its other civic needs?
7. What are the possible and practical economies?
8. How can adequate funds for education be raised?

Religious and Character Education.—Even in the relatively new field of religious and character education, which has depended largely on subjective methods of procedure in the past, suggestions concerning research problems are available. Watson[35] calls attention to

[34] Carter Alexander, "Opportunities for Research in Educational Finance," *Educational Administration and Supervision*, IX (April, 1923), 209–22.

[35] Goodwin B. Watson, "Needed Investigations in the Psychology of Character," *Religious Education*, XXIII (January, 1928), 66–72.

certain problems in need of investigation, while a group of four writers[36] discusses four possible areas of experimentation: the curriculum in religious education, the local church, teaching methods in the week-day school of religion, and religious education in the family.

Miscellaneous Suggestions Concerning Problems for Investigation.—Reference may be made to several other sources of information relating to problems in need of investigation: miscellaneous problems[37] with a rough plan of attack suggested, school publicity,[38] sociologica problems,[39] and business management of public schools.[40]

Conclusion.—This chapter has presented certain information relative to the discovery, selection, statement, and definition of research problems in education. Sources of information concerning completed investigations and research under way have been cited. Illustrations of the multitudinous problems requiring solution in education have been drawn from the fields of higher education, teacher training, secondary education, elementary education, learning, the curriculum, finance, character education, etc.

[36] George H. Betts, Norris L. Tibbetts, Blanche Carrier, and Jessie Allen Charters, "Four Areas of Experimentation," *Religious Education*, XXIII (March, 1928), 229–39.

[37] William A. McCall, *How to Experiment in Education*, Chapter X. New York: Macmillan Co., 1923.

[38] Carter Alexander, "Research in Educational Publicity," *Teachers College Record*, XXIX (March, 1928), 479–87.

[39] Hugh Carter, "Research Interests of American Sociologists," *Social Forces*, VI (December, 1927), 209–12.

[40] Harry P. Smith, "Research in the Business Management of Public Schools—Progress and Problems," *American School Board Journal*, LXXVI (March, 1928), 53–54; LXXVI (April, 1928), 45, 129–30.

CHAPTER VI

TECHNIQUES OF EDUCATIONAL RESEARCH AVAILABLE FOR THE COLLECTION OF DATA

What are Data?—Obviously, after the problem for investigation has been selected and defined, a decision must be made concerning the selection of an appropriate technique or method to be used in the collection of data. This raises a question with regard to the meaning of data as employed in educational research. Monroe and Engelhart[1] have recently made a good statement of the types of data available.

Data include all concepts, facts, and principles used in thinking out the answers to thought questions. In other words, data are the things we use in thinking. The meaning of these statements will be more apparent if we note some of the types of data:

1. Ages of school children.
2. Scores made on standardized tests.
3. School marks, and other facts from school records.
4. Answers to questionnaires.
5. Expenditures for educational purposes.
6. Assessed values and tax rates.
7. Measures of school buildings.
8. Statements of beliefs or opinions.
9. School laws.
10. Counts of things such as school children, number of pages, etc.
11. Principles.
12. Descriptions of schools, events, etc.

[1] Walter S. Monroe and Max D. Engelhart, *The Techniques of Educational Research*, p. 27. University of Illinois Bulletin, Vol. XXV, No. 19. Urbana, Illinois: University of Illinois, 1928.

13. Observations.
14. Historical information.
15. Errors in children's compositions.
16. Stenographic reports of lessons.

Collection of Data.—The same authors[2] continue with a discussion of collecting data which is well worth quoting.

> When a problem has been adequately defined, the data needed for its solution are clearly indicated. Hence "collecting data" does not mean bringing together whatever data may be easily accessible. Instead, it means collecting the data specified by the problem.
>
> When data are such that there has been very little or no opportunity for them to be affected by the person collecting them, they are described as "objective." The term "subjective data" has the opposite meaning; that is, they are data of such a character that they might be affected by the prejudices, opinions, and judgment of the person collecting them.
>
> It is apparent from the above list of types of data that many different procedures are employed in collecting data. In general, each type requires unique techniques, and within each type the required techniques may vary according to the problem.

Alexander[3] gives a good description of the procedures necessary in collecting school statistics and other data of a similar nature. He discusses such sources as the superintendent's own school records, questionnaires, printed reports, school surveys, magazine articles, etc. He also includes a helpful treatment of good and bad sampling in the collection of data.

Techniques Available for the Collection of Data.—Monroe and Engelhart[4] have prepared a valuable list of references which illustrate the various techniques or methods of educational research available for the

[2] *Ibid.*, p. 27.

[3] Carter Alexander, *School Statistics and Publicity*, pp. 58–71. New York: Silver, Burdett and Co., 1919.

[4] Walter S. Monroe and Max D. Engelhart, *op. cit.*, pp. 28–38.

collection of subjective and objective data. The outline of techniques minus the references is as follows:

A. Subjective data.
  1. Formulation of criteria to be used as a basis for estimates.
  2. Use of criteria.
B. Objective data.
  1. Techniques employed in collecting.
    a. Analysis.
      (1) Analysis of textbooks.
      (2) Analysis of pupil performances.
      (3) Analysis of records.
    b. Experimental procedures.
      (1) One group method.
      (2) Equivalent group method.
      (3) Rotation method.
    c. Historical.
    d. Interview.
    e. Legal.
      (1) Statutes.
      (2) Decisions.
    f. Questionnaire.
      (1) Opinion.
      (2) Facts.
    g. Survey.
    h. Test construction.
      (1) Scale.
      (2) Tests.
    i. Observation.
  2. Forms in which used.
    a. Raw.
    b. Transmuted.

The discussion of techniques of research, as treated in this chapter, will not follow the preceding outline, although most of the procedures listed will be in some way represented. It is possible in some instances to combine to advantage under one major heading or type of research two or more of the items enumerated above. It must not be concluded that any investigation cited in subsequent discussion as an illustration of a particular technique of research represents only one method of procedure, since frequently a given study must employ several modes of attack in the collection of adequate data. Symonds[5] has very appropriately expressed this point of view.

> . . . . The analysis of the problem leads one to believe that research cannot be broken up into types, such as the experimental type, the questionnaire type, the survey type, the case study type. Research offers a united front. There is always the necessity for a review of previous work, always the necessity for determining matters of sampling, always the problem of statistical treatment of results. Yet each separate problem has its own peculiarities. There are differences in the method of collecting the data, and different emphases are needed in the question of the treatment of data. But whatever the difference in emphases and in techniques, there is in all research an underlying similarity which overshadows the differences. Probably historical research is as distinct a type of investigation as any, and yet it does not cut loose entirely. Every piece of research should involve a certain amount of documentary study, and only those students are excused from documentary study who tread new fields in the van of the movement of scientific education. Perhaps historical research would disclaim any use of statistical methods, but one should hesitate to generalize on a single case even in history—and where there are two or more cases there are statistical methods.

Although Symonds' point is well taken and while all research does have certain elements in common, there seems to be sufficient justification, in the form of differentiated modes of procedure employed in the collection of data, for discussing techniques of research under the following headings: philosophical, historical, survey, questionnaire, statistical, experimental, case study, and activity analysis. It may be repeated that when studies are cited as illustrations of a particular technique of investigation in the collection of data, they may in

[5] Percival M. Symonds, "A Course in the Technique of Educational Research," *Teachers College Record,* XXIX (October, 1927), 24–30.

addition represent other techniques of research. However, in the selection of illustrative studies mentioned in subsequent paragraphs of this chapter, an effort has been made to choose investigations whose major methods of attack adequately represent the modes of procedure under which they are respectively classified.

The fact that there are available very acceptable treatises on certain of the techniques of research is evidence that educational investigators recognize rather clearly differentiated modes of attack in the collection of data. Specific illustrations may be given for the experimental,[6] case study,[7] and survey[8] methods. Numerous standard treatments of the statistical method of investigation are available, while the other methods of research listed in the preceding paragraph have received extended comment in the educational literature which will be taken up at the appropriate time in subsequent portions of this chapter.

Philosophical and Other Subjective Methods of Investigation.—The use of the philosophical method in the solution of educational problems was much more common in the early days of education than today. This was a rather natural consequence of the close relation between education or "pedagogy" and philosophy; in fact education may be considered an offshoot of philosophy, and in a number of smaller institutions work in psychology, education, and philosophy is offered in and by the same department. Today many students and workers have come to dispute or question the use of

[6] William A. McCall, *How to Experiment in Education.* New York: Macmillan Co., 1923. Pp. xvi + 282.

[7] William Claude Reavis, *Pupil Adjustment in Junior and Senior High Schools.* Boston: D. C. Heath and Co., 1926. Pp. xviii + 348.

[8] Jesse B. Sears, *The School Survey.* Boston: Houghton Mifflin Co., 1925. Pp. xxx + 440.

the philosophical method in the solution of educational problems. Symonds[9] presents an interesting statement which expresses this questioning attitude toward philosophy as a method of research:

> . . . It does not seem possible to me that there should be such a thing as "philosophical research." There may be "philosophizing," or "deductive reasoning," or "organization," but not "philosophical research." Perhaps this goes back to the definitions of both philosophy and research. By philosophy is meant the philosophy of education, and as usually considered in this country it treats of such matters as the aims and end of education, the relation of education to the nature of the individual and the society in which he lives, general characteristics of method and moral education. The philosophy of education employs principally the method of ratiocination and tends to work from generals to particulars. Research, on the other hand, reduced to its simplest terms, is *the arrangement of observations.* Research depends in the first place on *data* of some kind, something that has been *collected* or *observed* and *evaluated* or *counted.* Anything may be observed or counted in research in education from natural objects, movements of people, and the products of activity (as in test results) to people's expressed likes and dislikes or opinions. But all research involves the collection and arrangement of data of some kind. Now philosophy is not interested in the reduction of observations and as soon as it is it becomes a science. To be sure, philosophy accepts the generalizations of science and strikes out from them. But the generalizations of science are only a starting point and not an ending point. The up-to-date philosopher is constantly using the latest results of science, but he uses them in his study and not in the laboratory. His purpose is not to inquire further into science but to synthesize the results of science, to show their relationship to one another and to the unstudied phenomena of the world and above all to show the meaning and significance of science. So I would not call the development of a new system of philosophy an act of research. Wide reading it demands, yes; but all is done in the library or the study and not in the laboratory or testing room. Sometimes philosophy may claim that it is doing research in such fields as character education or child welfare. That is because until very recently these fields

[9] Percival M. Symonds, *op. cit.*, pp. 29–30.

have been outside the domain of science and have been the paramount interest of the philosophers. But character is now a very proper study of the psychologist and child welfare has its own research protagonists. As soon as any field becomes a matter for research it leaves philosophy and enters the domain of some science. Philosophy must of necessity dwell in an area where its methods are not the methods of research.

A somewhat different point of view is expressed by the editorial writer who pleads in the following quotation for a union between philosophy and research.[10]

> . . . It is the task of research to disclose the worthy aims of education, to devise means for attaining them, and to record the success which attends the use of the methods and materials thus selected as appropriate for the purposes of society. Therefore, research from one point of view includes philosophical inquiry; and from another point of view it tests, selects, and renders effective the solutions which philosophy offers. To divorce philosophy and research is impossible—as impossible as it is to divorce experimental from introspective psychology. And for the same reason. Without the descriptive and speculative processes the experimental or scientific activities lack interpretation. Without the scientific methods, philosophical inquiry lacks concreteness. Without science, philosophy is uncertain, conflicting, and unconvincing. Without philosophy, science is blind, unmeaning, and petty. We can imagine no more helpful educational organization than that which should exalt both philosophy and research. For example, a school of education in a great university should, in our judgment, elevate its research activities through the directive and refining influence of the best philosophical thought. This does not appear to be thought of. The craze today is for measurement—for counting and comparing in quantitative terms. It would be as silly as it would be untrue for us to deprecate this type of thinking. But there come times when the merely quantitative seems incomplete and unsatisfactory. We observe, moreover, that those research workers are most influential who appeal most frequently to higher sanctions than central tendencies or curves of error.

[10] "Research and Philosophy," *Educational Research Bulletin*, VI (May 11, 1927), 208–209. Columbus, Ohio: Bureau of Educational Research, Ohio State University.

In spite of the conflicting views now current with regard to the place of philosophical methods in the solution of educational problems, important contributions to educational literature have been made by the use of procedures which are primarily of a subjective nature. No less important a body than the 1926 yearbook committee of the National Society for the Study of Education,[11] composed of Bagley, Bobbitt, Bonser, Charters, Counts, Courtis, Horn, Judd, Kelly, Kilpatrick, Rugg, and Works, agreed on 58 statements which they considered expressive of the best available principles to be observed in taking the next forward steps in curriculum-making. In addition, most of the members of the committee issued supplementary statements which expressed the individual curriculum philosophy of the worker in question. Two other major contributions[12] to the curriculum field have made wide use of a philosophical or subjective procedure. Bobbitt, in his curriculum work in Los Angeles, placed before the 1,200 high-school teachers of the city a list of educational objectives which had been drawn up with the cooperation of several hundred graduate students at the University of Chicago and secured the reactions of the teachers together with such additions to the list as they cared to make. In an interesting discussion of curriculum construction Phelps states briefly the con-

[11] *The Foundations of Curriculum-Making.* Twenty-Sixth Yearbook of the National Society for the Study of Education, Part II. Bloomington, Illinois: Public School Publishing Co., 1926. Pp. xii + 238.

[12] Franklin Bobbitt, *Curriculum-Making in Los Angeles.* Supplementary Educational Monographs, No. 20. Chicago: Department of Education, University of Chicago, 1922. Pp. vi + 106.

Franklin Bobbitt, *The Curriculum.* Boston: Houghton Mifflin Co., 1918. Pp. viii + 296.

tribution of the philosophical method to the solution of this educational problem.[13]

One of the best-known and staunchest supporters of educational philosophy, Charles McMurry, has published a numbered list of principles which he has formulated as a guiding philosophy of education.[14] Of course such a list of guiding principles was compiled by the use of a subjective method, in other words, it expresses the individual theory and experience of the author. The same writer has put into print a statement which expresses very well the conception of the educational philosopher concerning the place of philosophy in the field of education.[15]

A treatment of the philosophical method which is of such a nature as to be especially helpful to the public-school worker ends with a caution concerning its use that should be of significance to any research worker.[16]

> While this method is not often used exclusively in educational research, it occupies an important place in many investigations. Indeed, it might be said that one of the greatest needs of education today is this type of research, in order that there may be developed a real philosophy of education that takes into account the most up-to-date contributions of modern science.
>
> It also has an important place in the evaluation of certain methods and procedures in the classroom. A good example of this is found in the evaluation of the Dalton and Winnetka plans,

[13] Shelton Phelps, "Curriculum Construction," *Peabody Journal of Education*, V (January, 1928), 223–29.

[14] Charles A. McMurry, "My Philosophy of Education," *Peabody Journal of Education*, IV (March, 1927), 261–71; also *Phi Delta Kappan*, IX (April, 1927), 145–46, 152–53.

[15] Charles A. McMurry, "Philosophy as Sponser for Education," *Peabody Journal of Education*, V (January, 1928), 197–208.

[16] *An Outline of Methods of Research with Suggestions for High School Principals and Teachers*, p. 18. Bureau of Education Bulletin, No. 24, 1926. Washington: Bureau of Education.

by W. H. Kilpatrick.[17] This type of research problem possesses less value and has more danger for the ordinary research student than any other type of problem . . . It should seldom be undertaken by the high-school principal or teacher.

Three additional illustrations of the use of the philosophical method and subjective factors in the collection of data will be cited. Cox raises a series of questions which he seeks to answer philosophically and check by convassing current practices.[18] Loomis uses the four criteria of reliability, adequacy, flexibility, and simplicity as a basis for testing methods of estimating school-equipment costs; of course the data collected are of the subjective type.[19] Kennon employed certain criteria in the selection of words to be used in literary vocabulary tests for English teachers.[20] It will be recognized that subjective factors operated in the selection of the words included in the vocabulary tests.

Reference may be made to a school system which has a school code based on a definitely stated philosophy of education and of school organization.[21]

[17] William H. Kilpatrick, "An Effort at Appraisal," *Adapting the Schools to Individual Differences*, pp. 273–86. Twenty-Fourth Yearbook of the National Society for the Study of Education, Part II. Bloomington, Illinois: Public School Publishing Co., 1925.

[18] Philip W. L. Cox, *Curriculum-Adjustment in the Secondary School.* Philadelphia: J. B. Lippincott Co., 1925. Pp. x + 306.

[19] Arthur Kirkwood Loomis, *The Technique of Estimating School Equipment Costs.* Teachers College Contributions to Education, No. 208. New York: Teachers College, Columbia University, 1926. Pp. vi + 112.

[20] Laura Hall Vere Kennon, *Tests of Literary Vocabulary for Teachers of English.* Teachers College Contributions to Education, No. 223. New York: Teachers College, Columbia University, 1926. Pp. viii + 78.

[21] *The Public School Code of the Hamtramck, Michigan, Public Schools.* Research Series No. 2. Hamtramck, Michigan: Board of Education, 1927. Pp. 260.

Historical and Legal Methods of Research.—Probably the historical method of research was employed more frequently in education a decade or two ago than at present. However, if the popularity of the historical method has waned, legal research in education, which resembles historical investigation very closely or may even be considered a phase of historical research, has shown a corresponding increase in popularity over the same period of time. In fact, the attention of some workers who formerly gave their time to research in the history of education in general has been diverted to a study of the specialized problems of educational legislation and court decisions affecting school matters. This state of affairs seems to justify a discussion of historical and legal research in education under the same heading; both procedures involve painstaking documentary study.

Two quotations which follow are clear statements of the historical method. The first is intended particularly to meet the needs of high-school principals and teachers.[22]

> This type of research problem deals, as its name indicates, with historical material. It may seek to discover some historical facts or to present in a connected way the development of a certain type of school . . .
>
> In this type of problem there are certain crucial points of method that are of special importance. The first has to do with the reliability of the source . . . By no means all statements that are found in print or in manuscript are reliable. Just because a statement is recorded in the minutes of a school committee or printed in a superintendent's report, it should not be taken as a fact unless it meets the tests laid down. It must be ascertained, in the first place, whether the document itself is genuine; whether it was written at the time when it is supposed to have been written. If found to be genuine, are the statements of fact records of happenings or of *opinions* of the writer regarding what happened?

[22] *An Outline of Methods of Research with Suggestions for High School Principals and Teachers, op. cit.*, pp. 12–13.

This opinion or observation may be valuable, and often is, as corroborative evidence, but it is by no means as valuable as a statement of a fact. The opinion of an eyewitness or contemporary, especially if he is a trained observer, is much more valuable than that of a person who was not an eyewitness and untrained. After all data are in and checked, there is still the problem of proper and legitimate interpretation and inference. Great care must be taken in treating facts as facts and not reading into them other things that, in the light of recent developments, might be expected to have been in the original statements. Great care and rigid integrity should be exercised in dealing with all facts and all inferences. It is not wise to undertake this type of research unless one has been thoroughly trained in its technique or has the advantage of the guidance of expert advice.

Many opportunities will be found for investigations of an historical nature; original material will often be brought to light in cleaning out old closets, basements, and attics. Principals should never allow old reports and records to be destroyed until they have been very carefully looked over to see whether they contain material that may prove of value.

While the statements made in the following quotation are intended to apply particularly to the field of pure history, they are also applicable in large part to the use of the historical method in the solution of educational problems.[23]

The purpose of historical research is to determine what events actually took place in the past and to discover their causes and effects. Some of the outstanding steps in the procedure involved in historical research may be summarized briefly as follows, (From Fling, *The Writing of History*, Yale University Press):

(1) Finding historical remains to use as partial sources of information from which to make out a complete picture of what happened. The historian uses whatever remains of the past he can find, such as portraits, weapons, legends, traditions, documents, memoirs, etc. Usually the greater number of his sources are in written form.

[23] Claude C. Crawford, *Methods of Study*, p. 158. Published by the author, University of Idaho, Moscow, Idaho, 1926.

(2) Criticism of the source in order to determine such things as the following: (a) whether it is genuine or forged; (b) who wrote it—whether he was an idiot or a knave; when he wrote it and where; whether he was biased or fair-minded; whether he had good opportunity to observe the events; whether he wrote his report at the time or years afterward, etc.; (c) whether the different reports about the event are completely separate and independent or whether they were borrowed one from the other, or both borrowed from a third source.

(3) Establishment of facts. After having criticized and evaluated different sources of information, the historian next determines as best he can the facts as they happened. His standard for a fact is that two or more independent sources must agree upon the same thing; but he has to exercise great caution even then, because two sources may agree, and yet both be in error. Much is left to reason and to the weighing of possibilities in the process of establishing fact.

(4) Grouping facts according to some logical plan and writing a historical narrative. This step is not so much research as reporting the results of research.

Schluter[24] presents a treatment of primary and secondary sources that is of special interest to the worker engaged in a study of business and social economy. However, most of the discussion is applicable to research in general.

Grizzell and Stout have used the historical method in the study of problems at the secondary-school level.[25] The reader interested in employing the historical method will find it worth while to make a careful examination of these two contributions to the history of education.

[24] W. C. Schluter, *How to Do Research Work,* Chapters IX, XI. New York: Prentice-Hall, 1926.

[25] Emit Duncan Grizzell, *Origin and Development of the High School in New England Before* 1865. New York: Macmillan Co., 1923. Pp. xxii + 428.

John Elbert Stout, *The Development of High-School Curricula in the North Central States from* 1860 *to* 1918. Supplementary Educational Monographs, No. 15. Chicago: Department of Education, University of Chicago, 1921. Pp. xii + 322.

An editorial writer presents a good discussion of the value of the historical method to education in general.[26]

Edwards has prepared an excellent and detailed guide for those who are interested in finding the law relating to public-school administration.[27] This is probably the best description of the technique of legal research, as applied to school matters, now available to educational workers. Both statute and case law are treated. Of course, it is highly desirable for the reader interested in this type of research to examine and study carefully the procedures employed in the rapidly increasing number of investigations dealing with educational legislation. Reference may be made to a few studies selected from the considerable number of publications now available in the field of school law.[28]

The Comparative and Survey Methods.—At this writing the modern survey movement in its present form covers

[26] "The Historical Method in Educational Research," *Journal of Educational Research*, V (April, 1922), 328–31.

[27] I. N. Edwards, "Where and How to Find the Law Relating to Public-School Administration," *Elementary School Journal*, XXVII (September, 1926), 14–24.

[28] J. Orin Powers, "Legal Provisions and Regulations of State Departments of Education Affecting Junior High Schools," *School Review*, XXXIII (April, 1925), 280–91.

Carter V. Good, "The Present Status of the Law Relating to Certain School Matters," *Peabody Journal of Education*, III (May, 1926), 313–20; IV (July and September, 1926), 31–41, 86–93.

J. B. Edmonson, *Constitutional and Legal Bases of Public School Administration in Michigan*. Bloomington, Illinois: Public School Publishing Co., 1926.

Harry Raymond Trusler, *Essentials of School Law*. Milwaukee, Wisconsin: Bruce Publishing Co., 1927. Pp. xlvi + 478.

Private Schools and State Laws. Compiled by Charles N. Lischka. Education Bulletins, No. 4. Washington: National Catholic Welfare Conference, 1924. Pp. 220.

a period of less than twenty years. The foregoing statement is essentially correct even though the investigations carried forward nearly a century ago by such workers as Barnard and Mann resemble the modern survey movement in certain respects. The technique has been borrowed in a large measure from the social sciences of economics and sociology. Sears indicates that economic and scientific influences have been responsible for the rapid development of the survey movement in education within recent years. The author's discussion of this technique of research is the most comprehensive and adequate treatment now available. Sears presents a discussion of the nature and functions of the school survey, a treatment of the functions of research in the public school, a list of typical research problems, and a bibliography of selected survey reports which are especially suggestive and helpful.[29]

It must be recognized that the use of the survey technique in the collection of data may frequently involve the philosophical, historical, questionnaire, and statistical methods; in fact it is virtually impossible to conduct an adequate survey without resorting to statistical procedures in the manipulation of data. The National Committee on Research in Secondary Education has formulated a very good brief statement of the survey method of collecting data.[30]

The purpose of the survey type of investigation is to describe as accurately, objectively, and quantitatively as possible a class, a school, or a school system—city, State, or National. It usually traces relationships, indicates causes, and suggests improvements. It often employs the historical method in determining the validity of data and the philosophical method in analyzing objectives and

[29] Jesse B. Sears, *The School Survey*, Chapters I, XVII. Boston: Houghton Mifflin Co., 1925.

[30] *An Outline of Methods of Research with Suggestions for High School Principals and Teachers*, *op. cit.*, pp. 18–21.

outcomes. By its very nature it makes more frequent use of statistical methods than any other type

. . . .

The chief difficulties in this type are:

1. Securing reliable data, discriminating between opinion and fact.

2. Selecting relevant material, and distinguishing between useless and unnecessary details and facts and factors that are really important.

3. Relating facts observed and results measured to peculiar conditions, in the school or locality; i.e., interpreting conditions and results with reference to local needs and conditions.

4. Selecting standards of comparison that are valid for the particular school.

5. Distinguishing between facts or conditions closely related in time and place and causal relationship.

6. Describing accurately and adequately the facts and conditions investigated.

In this type of investigation very great care must be taken at all stages. Many otherwise admirable studies have been made valueless by lack of care in securing reliable data. Facts must be obtained; mere opinions alone will not suffice, and such opinions as are considered must be evaluated with careful discrimination. It often takes much time and persistence to get at the real facts, but unless this can be done the investigation is worthless. Great care must also be taken in interpreting facts and conditions and especially in forming conclusions about the cause of a certain effect. The best scientists are often led astray in this particular.

. . . .

Possibly the most difficult phase of a survey investigation is obtaining data covering a series of years. It can not be too strongly urged that records be carefully kept on all phases of the work of the school and as carefully preserved. For example, we should like very much to know what effect the junior high school has had upon school enrollment, elimination, and overageness in each grade. It is practically impossible to secure any reliable data on these points because of the lack of definite records before the introduction of the junior high school and after. Principals and superintendents should always be careful to make adequate records and preserve them.

It is possible to make a number of comparisons in an investigation which employs the survey technique in the collection of data. The following outline indicates some of the comparisons which may be made in arriving at conclusions concerning the status of the school system under examination.

I. Historical, comparing present conditions with those of preceding years.
II. Geographical location.
  A. Comparison with systems outside the system under examination.
    1. National.
    2. Regional.
    3. State.
    4. County.
    5. City.
  B. Comparisons within the system under examination.
    1. County.
    2. District.
    3. School.
    4. Grade.
III. Function or service.
  A. Comparisons between departments or subjects.
  B. Comparisons between enterprises, as kindergarten, junior high school, senior high school, etc.

Butterfield has written a rather caustic criticism of school surveys which may be read with profit by the student who is interested in this technique of collecting data.[31] He takes the point of view that school surveys interfere with the regular work of the school and are often conducted by investigators who take pleasure in tinkering with the machinery of the school system. While some readers may consider the criticisms unnecessarily destructive, the pointed indictments of certain procedures deserve careful attention on the part of those who employ the survey technique.

[31] Ernest W. Butterfield, "Educational Surveys," *Educational Review*, LXVIII (June, 1924), 1–5.

Attention should be called to the important work of the Educational Finance Inquiry Commission which made wide use of survey procedures in studying financial conditions of school systems in New York, Illinois, Iowa, and California. This extensive study has been published in thirteen volumes, several of which may be mentioned specifically as examples of the survey technique.[32] Of course, it must be recognized that such investigations are also almost equally good illustrations of statistical techniques.

Reference may be made to four studies of the survey type which are concerned primarily with problems other than those of educational finance.[33] Two outstanding

[32] Nelson B. Henry, *A Study of Public School Costs in Illinois Cities.* Report of the Educational Finance Inquiry Commission, Vol. XII. New York: Macmillan Co., 1924. Pp. xii + 82.

Floyd W. Reeves, *The Political Unit of Public School Finance in Illinois.* Report of the Educational Finance Inquiry Commission, Vol. X. New York: Macmillan Co., 1924. Pp. xvi + 166.

Charles W. Hunt, *The Cost and Support of Secondary Schools in the State of New York.* Report of the Educational Finance Inquiry Commission, Vol. III. New York: Macmillan Co., 1924. Pp. x + 108.

William F. Russell, Thomas C. Holy, Raleigh W. Stone, and Others, *The Financing of Education in Iowa.* Report of the Educational Finance Inquiry Commission, Vol. VIII. New York: Macmillan Co., 1925. Pp. xxii + 280.

[33] Emery N. Ferriss, *Rural School Survey of New York State: The Rural High School.* Ithaca, New York: Joint Committee on Rural Schools, 1922. Pp. 188.

John Harrison Cook, *A Study of the Mill Schools of North Carolina.* Teachers College Contributions to Education, No. 178. New York: Teachers College, Columbia University, 1925. Pp. viii + 56.

Frederick Earle Emmons. *City School Attendance Service.* Teachers College Contributions to Education, No. 200. New York: Teachers College, Columbia University, 1926. Pp. xiv + 147.

contributions to the curriculum field have utilized survey techniques in investigating the junior and senior high school programs of studies.[34] Space does not permit a listing of other survey reports, but the selected studies cited should provide reasonably adequate examples of the procedures discussed in preceding paragraphs. Of course, it is highly desirable that the student examine carefully selected studies in the field in which he wishes to work. Attention may be called to the educational yearbooks of the International Institute of Teachers College, Columbia University, as examples of studies in comparative education.[35] Reference may also be made to a comparative treatment of education in the United States, England, Germany, and France, although some criticism has been offered with regard to the validity of the conclusions set forth.[36]

Harry Pearse Smith, *The Business Administration of a City School System.* Teachers College Contributions to Education, No. 197. New York: Teachers College, Columbia University, 1925. Pp. x + 130.

[34] James M. Glass, *Curriculum Practices in Junior High School and Grades 5 and 6.* Supplementary Educational Monographs, No. 25. Chicago: Department of Education, University of Chicago, 1924. Pp. x + 182.

George S. Counts, *The Senior High School Curriculum.* Supplementary Educational Monographs, No. 29. Chicago: Department of Education, University of Chicago, 1926. Pp. xii + 160.

[35] At present three volumes: *Educational Yearbooks of the International Institute of Teachers College, Columbia University,* 1924, 1925, 1926. Edited by I. L. Kandel. New York: Macmillan Co., 1925, 1926, 1927.

[36] William S. Learned, *The Quality of the Educational Process in the United States and in Europe.* The Carnegie Foundation for the Advancement of Teaching, Bulletin, No. 20, 1927. New York: The Carnegie Foundation for the Advancement of Teachink. Pp. x + 134.

Questionnaire, Correspondence, and Interview Methods of Investigation.—The questionnaire method attained prominence in education in a large measure because of its extensive use by G. Stanley Hall who employed the questionnaire technique as a means of collecting various kinds of information, especially concerning adolescence. The questionnaire method of collecting information has been frequently abused and is therefore in disrepute as a technique of research. However, it must be admitted that there are certain types of information and factual data which may be collected economically by the questionnaire; the collection of such information by any other method such as interviews and personal observation might be so time-consuming and expensive as to be prohibitive. Trow[37] points out certain disadvantages in the use of the questionnaire method: a third to a half of the persons circularized do not answer; the report is biased, not only because the questioner is apt to select the reports that fit his theories, but also because there is a tendency on the part of the person filling out the questionnaire to give the questioner what he is looking for; and incidental memory is too fickle a thing to trust in scientific matters.

The fact that the questionnaire still has a legitimate place in educational investigation is attested by the following quotation which expresses the attitude of a well-known research worker and editor; these are the closing paragraphs of a lengthy editorial on the questionnaire.[38]

> We offer a word, therefore, in behalf of the questionnaire on these counts. First, it often affords the only means of securing information. Let the investigator take every reasonable precau-

[37] Wm. Clark Trow, *Scientific Method in Education*, pp. 100–103. Boston: Houghton Mifflin Co., 1925.

[38] "The Questionnaire," *Journal of Educational Research*, XIV (June, 1926), 54–58.

tion to assure himself that his problem falls under this head. Second, the topic must be worthy; it must not be trivial. Assured on these two points, the investigator should boldly decide to issue his blank. Third, the recipients of questionnaires owe something to the cause of education. Many who loudly condemn these instruments are glad enough to have the educational chariot move forward yet are unwilling to put their shoulders to the wheel.

Let the investigator look to his procedure. He must, of course, use a correct technique in writing the questionnaire. Others have said much on this point, and for that reason we leave the field to them. There are courtesies, however, to be observed not only because courtesy is a virtue but because it is effective. The investigator may well send out a preliminary inquiry and secure the assent of his prospective correspondents. He should discriminate in selecting even the preliminary group, and if he must send a second and more detailed questionnaire, he should obtain in the first one the names and addresses of the persons who are best informed about the details. From time to time the investigator should send progress reports to those who have cooperated with him, and at the close of the project, he should make a final report. He should at all times be quick to acknowledge the assistance he has received.

As we see it, therefore, the indiscriminate censure of the questionnaire is unjustified. Rightly used it is a proper and indeed an inevitable means of securing information. Moreover, a real obligation rests upon educational people to contribute something through this means to the general good.

Pointed criticisms of the questionnaire method have been voiced by a number of educational writers, and the student who contemplates the use of this technique of collecting data will do well to examine carefully all available criticisms and suggestions. Alexander discourages the use of the questionnaire in the field of school administration and urges the use of printed statistics and reports because of their greater accuracy.[39] The same writer[40] at another time calls attention to the

[39] Carter Alexander, *School Statistics and Publicity*, *op. cit.*, p. 59.

[40] Carter Alexander and Others, *Educational Research*, *op. cit.*, p. 15.

fact that students at Teachers College, Columbia University, may not send out questionnaires without the approval of the major professor and the Director of the School of Education. He also states that educators in the field will not answer unofficial questionnaires and that many school systems require the approval of questionnaires by the Secretary of the Department of Superintendence before answering them. Butterfield makes a caustic and withal humorous criticism of the questionnaire method in general and in particular of the technique as used in the Classical Investigation. Educational workers who contemplate the use of the questionnaire method in the collection of data should read Butterfield's article[41] and a critical editorial[42] in a similar vein in the *School Review.*

Probably the most common criticism of the questionnaire method is that only a fraction of the questionnaires distributed are returned, and therefore the sampling is inaccurate. Toops[43] describes a series of follow-up letters he used in such a way as to secure a return of 93 per cent of the questionnaires distributed. Wylie[44] presents some data which throw light on the reliability of the information secured by means of the questionnaire method. He concludes that one may rely upon the answers to school questionnaires with a reasonably high degree of assurance, provided certain simple working rules are observed in framing the questions.

[41] Ernest W. Butterfield, "The Plenary Inspiration of the Dotted Line," *Educational Review,* LXIX (January, 1925), 1–4.

[42] "Questionnaires," *School Review,* XXXIV (November, 1926), 649–50.

[43] Herbert A. Toops, "Validating the Questionnaire Method," *Journal of Personnel Research,* II (August-September, 1923), 153–69.

[44] Andrew Tennant Wylie, "To What Extent May We Rely upon the Answers to a School Questionnaire," *Journal of Educational Method,* VI (February, 1927), 252–57.

1. Ask only plainly worded questions concerning familiar facts and everyday experiences.

2. Ask a fairly large number of questions, if possible "interlocking" them in such a way that any vitally important point will be established by a sort of consensus of opinion among the answers and not rest merely upon one isolated statement.

3. Ask the questions of a sufficiently large number of individuals so that errors of judgment and of statement will have an opportunity to balance and correct one another and by so doing yield a net total which will be a reasonable approximation of the truth.

The National Committee on Research in Secondary Education voices certain cautions to the public-school investigator who would use the questionnaire method and lists certain rules which should be followed in the event this technique of collecting data must be used.[45]

In the first place let us remember that the questionnaire is often a lazy man's method of getting alleged information that could b much better obtained in some other way. It is easy to sit down in the quiet of one's study and make out questions for some one else to answer. But such a method is very wasteful of the time and energy of the one to whom it is sent and is frequently wasteful of the time of the maker, for these questionnaires not infrequently find their way into the waste-paper basket, and many of them should. One has no right to take the time of some one else in answering questions when he himself can find the answer elsewhere. Nor, on the whole, can he consistently ask some one to spend his valuable time in work that will not presumably prove of value to him or his school. After he has decided upon the data he wishes, he should search through all available material to see whether these data can be obtained through printed reports. If they can and he does not have the reports, he should send for them and get the data for himself. If the data given in the reports are not in the exact form in which he wishes them, he should change his own plan to fit the form used, where this is possible.

When he has exhausted all available material and feels that he must resort to the questionnaire method, let him observe the following directions and suggestions:

[45] *An Outline of Methods of Research with Suggestions for High School Principals and Teachers*, *op. cit.*, pp. 23–25.

1. Make the questionnaire as brief and concise as possible. One-page questionnaires are much more frequently answered than those of 2, 3, or 4 pages.

2. Organize it so that it can be answered by checks or by the insertion of a minimum number of words or figures.

3. Be careful of the spacing. Leave enough space for the answer.

4. Ask only for the information actually intended for use. The greater part of many questionnaires is never used and serves merely to clutter up the study.

5. Formulate each question so that it will have identically the same meaning to everybody who answers it; and, if necessary, give specific definition of terms.

6. Questionnaires should ordinarily call for facts, not opinions. Such questions are more frequently answered, take less time of the one who fills them out, and are more reliable.

7. When judgments or opinions are asked, the questions should be so framed as to exclude dogmatic answers based on enthusiasm and opinions, and to insure reflective thinking. So far as possible objective evidence for judgments should be called for . . .

. . . .

8. Before sending out any questionnaire it should go through the following stages:

(a) Very careful formulation by the author and arrangement in the form to be used.
(b) Submission to some expert for advice and correction.
(c) Try-out on teachers or others not primarily concerned—disinterested persons.
(d) A try-out of the revised questionnaire on a group as nearly like the ones to whom it is to be sent as possible. These try-outs will often show the inaccuracies of statement, the equivocal questions, and other undesirable features that can be corrected before the questionnaire is actually sent out for replies.

9. Be sure that each copy is clear and readable.

10. Always state clearly the purpose of the investigation.

11. Be sure that the investigator's name and address are clearly given on the questionnaire.

12. Provide a space for the signature of the one who fills out the questionnaire, together with his position and the date of filling it out.

13. Provide an extra copy so that the principal furnishing the data may have on file in his office a copy of the data collected.

14. A self-addressed envelope inclosed with the questionnaire will often bring good results.

15. Send a copy of the result of the investigation to each one who fills out the questionnaire.

Other suggestive lists of rules and principles to be observed in using the questionnaire method[46] are available, although the above list probably covers the essential points in a reasonably adequate manner.

The reader may with profit be referred to several recent investigations which have used the questionnaire technique in the collection of data. This method has been employed in investigations of children's interests in reading,[47] play behavior of children,[48] practices in handwriting instruction,[49] procedures in dealing with bright and dull children,[50] values derived from extensive reading of general-science material,[51] the training of

[46] Ward G. Reeder, *How to Write a Thesis*, pp. 35–38. Bloomington, Illinois: Public School Publishing Co., 1925.

W. C. Schluter, *How to Do Research Work, op. cit.*, pp. 84–87.

Harold O. Rugg, *Statistical Methods Applied to Education*, Chapter II. Boston: Houghton Mifflin Co., 1917.

[47] Carleton Washburne and Mabel Vogel, *Winnetka Graded Book List.* Chicago: American Library Association, 1926. Pp. 286.

[48] Harvey C. Lehman and Paul A. Witty, *The Psychology of Play Activities.* New York: A. S. Barnes and Co., 1927. Pp. xviii + 242.

[49] Paul V. West, *Changing Practice in Handwriting Instruction.* Educational Research Monographs, No. 9. Bloomington, Illinois: Public School Publishing Co., 1927. Pp. vi + 142.

[50] Harry J. Baker, *Characteristic Differences in Bright and Dull Pupils.* Bloomington, Illinois: Public School Publishing Co., 1927. Pp. viii + 118.

[51] Francis Day Curtis, *Some Values Derived from Extensive Reading of General Science.* Teachers College Contributions to Education, No. 163. New York: Teachers College, Columbia University, 1924. Pp. vi + 142.

modern foreign-language teachers,[52] and one-room and consolidated schools.[53] Examination of these selected studies should be more enlightening to the reader than further discussion of the questionnaire method. Attention may also be directed to two monographs which include data collected by questionnaire procedures; they deal with the length of elementary education[54] and the social composition of school boards.[55]

It is possible to check the accuracy of questionnaire data in some instances by the use of correspondence, oral questionnaires, interviews, and various means of direct observation; of course, these methods may also be used independent of any written questionnaire. Sturtevant and Hayes[56] present a helpful treatment of the interview in which they discuss the factors involved, preliminary steps, the interview in process, and suggestions as to technique; they include a bibliography. Schluter lists certain rules for con-

[52] Hugh Stuart, *The Training of Modern Foreign Language Teachers for the Secondary Schools in the United States.* Teachers College Contributions to Education, No. 256. New York: Teachers College, Columbia University, 1927. Pp. 112.

[53] Emil Leonard Larson, *One-Room and Consolidated Schools of Connecticut.* Teachers College Contributions to Education, No. 182. New York: Teachers College, Columbia University, 1925. Pp. xii + 68.

[54] *Report of the Commission on Length of Elementary Education.* Supplementary Educational Monographs, No. 34. Chicago: Department of Education, University of Chicago, 1927. Pp. xii + 168.

[55] George S. Counts, *The Social Composition of Boards of Education.* Supplementary Educational Monographs, No. 33. Chicago: Department of Education, University of Chicago, 1927. Pp. x + 100.

[56] Sarah M. Sturtevant and Harriet Hayes, "The Use of the Interview in Advisory Work," *Teachers College Record,* XXVIII (February, 1927), 551–62.

ducting correspondence, observations, and interviews.[57] Reference may be made to two studies which involve the interview[58] and to another which employs the method of observation.[59]

Statistical Methods of Investigation.—Most of the studies cited in preceding paragraphs of this chapter as examples of the various types of research discussed are also illustrations of some phase of statistical methods. In fact, Symonds presents a concise statement of the nature of statistical method in which he maintains that all research involves the use of statistical methods.[60]

> . . . ALL *research involves the use of statistical methods.* The vigorous opposition to this statement which has been expressed is due in part to a misunderstanding of the nature of statistical methods. To most people, statistical methods mean coefficients of correlation, biserial *r*, normal probability curve, correction for attenuation, probable error of the mean, etc. It means sheet after sheet packed closely with figures, complicated formulae, calculating machines, Greek letters. Not at all. Statistics *must* be used in research both in the solution of particular problems and in the solution of general problems. One cannot make an accurate observation without using numbers. "This boy is tall, is old, is honest," are observations, but they are inaccurate observations. One cannot answer how tall, how old, how honest, and give an answer without using numbers. (A comparison can be given,

[57] W. C. Schluter, *op. cit.*, pp. 79–84.

[58] John Rufi, *The Small High School.* Teachers College Contributions to Education, No. 236. New York: Teachers College, Columbia University, 1926. Pp. x + 146.

Donald Scott Snedden, *A Study of Disguised Intelligence Tests (Interview Form).* Teachers College Contributions to Education, No. 291. New York: Teachers College, Columbia University, 1928. Pp. 48.

[59] Inga Olla Helseth, *Children's Thinking.* Teachers College Contributions to Education, No. 209. New York: Teachers College, Columbia University, 1926. Pp. vi + 164.

[60] Percival M. Symonds, "A Course in the Technique of Educational Research," pp. 28–29, *Teachers College Record,* XXIX (October, 1927).

such as "is taller than," but this goes only part way in locating the answer to the question. An accurate answer can only be given when height is referred to some point on a scale.) And the treatment, handling, or combining of these numbers involves statistical methods. The simple average is a part of statistical methods. One does not need to do difficult or complicated things to be working in statistics. No generalization should be drawn on the basis of one case. Where two or more cases are involved and accurate observation (using observation in a broad sense) has been used, there is always the necessity of boiling down the figures to bring out certain characteristics of the data, and these are statistical methods. Even historical or legal research requires statistical methods. One would hardly dare to generalize on the nature of the eighteenth century academy on the basis of the description of a single instance. One would hardly dare generalize on the curriculum of a century ago from a single textbook or course of study. I venture the opinion that historians are not always as careful as they should be that their sampling is representative and adequate.

I have made it appear as though statistical methods could be made very simple. They can be. But statistics have often been used to prove both sides of an issue, as in the current prohibition controversy, and statistics have by a well known aphorism been made to seem the very antithesis of the truth. The pitfalls into which one may stumble both in using and in interpreting statistics are many. Consequently a smattering of statistical methods is not enough. One should proceed far enough with his statistical studies to be able not only to compute the common constants accurately, but to understand their accuracy or reliability and the factors influencing them. Only then is he competent to handle the very simplest research problem. As one student said after completing a research in a field where statistical methods had never before been used, "I have gained a great respect for numbers."

Reference may be made to two brief discussions of the nature of statistical method which supplement the preceding quotation.[61] An editorial writer points to

[61] Claude C. Crawford, *Methods of Study*, *op. cit.*, pp. 159–60. Wm. Clark Trow, *Scientific Method in Education*, *op. cit.*, pp. 103–109, 124–28.

the value of statistical methods to society and refutes the charge that statistical procedures have brought about an attempt to make all people alike.[62]

It has sometimes been asserted that the application of statistics has resulted in an attempt to make people all alike, to turn children out of the school like buttons out of a mill, each with the same handwriting, the same speed of reading, and the same accuracy in arithmetic. This is a charge which is entirely without foundation. The fact is that individual differences were never more clearly recognized than they have been since means of measurement and the statistical treatment of measurement have been employed. Never has personality been more easily distinguished nor more highly respected than in recent years. This is true in every walk of life. Even the physician recognizes that one may have a very common disease in a very personal way. We do not characterize men or children as brave, honest, generous, quick, accurate. We seek to express how much and how many, leaving to readers or hearers the task of deciding whether certain epithets apply. In accordance with the requirements of statistical thinking, we do not say that a man is tall, we say that his height is five feet eleven and three-fourths inches. Whether he is a tall man or not depends upon one's experience and use of language. Whether we say that a person who departs from the average by as much as three and three-fourths inches when the standard deviation is two inches, is in reality a tall man, is relatively unimportant. Knowing these numerical facts we have a much more valid basis for thought than any epithet can provide.

. . . .

The old dichotomous classifications no longer pass muster. It is not enough to divide creation into big and little, hot and cold, long and short; it is not enough to rate men as tall and short, fat and lean, rich and poor. Most things fall into statistical groupings. They exhibit a norm or type and are characterized by profoundly significant variations. Indeed, it is the variation which statistics is especially emphasizing. This corresponds to changing conceptions in social and economic matters. Variation and not type, diversity and not uniformity, development and growth rather

[62] "Thinking Statistically," *Educational Research Bulletin*, VI (March 30, 1927), 142–43. Columbus, Ohio: Bureau of Educational Research, Ohio State University.

than inertia, are at once the manifestations and the objectives of the social order . . .

. . . .

The objectives of modern life are also different now. How far has statistical method been instrumental in this? How far are both this and statistical method a common result of a more fundamental cause? We do not know, but it is well to remember in appraising the services of statistical science that it is peculiarly appropriate to modern thinking and to modern life. In particular, it exalts the individual; it distinguishes, discriminates, and evaluates, not on the basis of conformity but on the basis of personality, individual differences, and growth.

Presumably the same editorial writer, in a later issue of his bulletin, indicates that while statistics is a new and powerful instrument of thought, certain dangers are incident to the use of this procedure in the analysis of phenomena.[63] He emphasizes in particular the errors that may arise in the interpretation of coefficients of correlation.

The very attractiveness of statistical technique sometimes leads to our undoing. Under the influence of statistical method our thinking tends to lose flexibility, to harden, and to crystalize into set forms. When we decide to use measurement, and the analysis which measurement permits, we put our trust in precision, accuracy, and definition. This is desirable up to a certain point; but there are wide reaches of human thought where precision is not at present possible or where it can only be attained by non-statistical methods. To let our statistics dominate our thinking in these regions is to court disaster.

. . . .

The mechanical interpretation of the correlation coefficient is only one of a number of instances—the similar interpretation of the probable error of differences is another—in which users of statistics try to make their statistics cover too much territory. We shall never be relieved by statistics or by any other device from the necessity of original thinking.

[63] "Statistical Thinking Once More," *Educational Research Bulletin*, VI (May 25, 1927), 230–31. Columbus, Ohio: Bureau of Educational Research, Ohio State University.

Another editorial writer expresses a critical attitude toward mechanical procedures which have developed in the field of testing; he calls attention especially to a machine which tabulates and averages tests of mental abilities as an aid in vocational guidance.[64] A significant feature of a yearbook dealing with the problem of nature and nurture is that the statistical hazards involved in the investigations are pointed out in a separate chapter. Among the hazards mentioned are discussions of selection, inextricable causes, partial and multiple correlation, partial regression equations, coefficients of correlation, incommensurability of results from different tests, probable errors, etc.[65]

It is not within the province of this chapter to include a detailed treatment of statistical methods and procedures. This technique of educational research has received adequate treatment in a number of sources and the reader is referred to a number of standard treatments of the subject.[66]

[64] "After Testing—What?" *Peabody Journal of Education*, IV (November, 1926), 179–81.

[65] Barbara Stoddard Burks and Truman L. Kelley, "Statistical Hazards in Nature-Nurture Investigations," *Nature and Nurture: Their Influence upon Intelligence*, pp. 9–38. Twenty-Seventh Yearbook of the National Society for the Study of Education, Part I. Bloomington, Illinois: Public School Publishing Co., 1928.

[66] Henry E. Garrett, *Statistics in Psychology and Education.* New York: Longmans, Green and Co., 1926. Pp. xiv + 318.

Karl J. Holzinger, *Statistical Methods for Students in Education.* Boston: Ginn and Co., 1928. Pp. viii + 372.

Truman L. Kelley, *Interpretation of Educational Measurements.* Yonkers-on-Hudson, New York: World Book Co., 1927. Pp. xiv + 364.

William A. McCall, *How to Measure in Education.* New York: Macmillan Co., 1922. Pp. xiv + 416.

Walter S. Monroe, *The Theory of Educational Measurement.* Boston: Houghton Mifflin Co., 1923. Pp. xxiv + 364.

Although most of the investigations previously listed as examples of the survey and questionnaire techniques are at the same time good illustrations of statistical procedures, a few additional studies which employ statistical techniques may with profit be cited.[67]

C. W. Odell, *Educational Statistics.* New York: Century Co., 1925. Pp. xviii + 334.

Arthur S. Otis, *Statistical Method in Educational Measurement.* Yonkers-on-Hudson, New York: World Book Co., 1925. Pp. xii + 338.

G. M. Ruch and George D. Stoddard, *Tests and Measurements in High School Instruction.* Yonkers-on-Hudson, New York: World Book Co., 1927. Pp. xxii + 382.

Harold O. Rugg, *A Primer of Graphics and Statistics for Teachers.* Boston: Houghton Mifflin Co., 1925. Pp. vi + 142.

Harold O. Rugg, *Statistical Methods Applied to Education.* Boston: Houghton Mifflin Co., 1917. Pp. xviii + 410.

Percival M. Symonds, *Measurement in Secondary Education.* New York: Macmillan Co., 1927. Pp. xviii + 588.

L. L. Thurstone, *The Fundamentals of Statistics.* New York: Macmillan Co., 1925. Pp. xviii + 238.

Marion R. Trabue, *Measuring Results in Education.* New York: American Book Co., 1925. Pp. 492.

Frank N. Freeman, *Mental Tests.* Boston: Houghton Mifflin Co., 1926. Pp. xii + 504.

Truman L. Kelley, *Statistical Method.* New York: Macmillan Co., 1923. Pp. xii + 390.

[67] *Nature and Nurture: Their Influence upon Intelligence and Their Influence upon Achievement.* Twenty-Seventh Yearbook of the National Society for the Study of Education, Parts I and II. Bloomington, Illinois: Public School Publishing Co., 1928. Pp. x + 466, xiv + 398.

George E. Carrothers, *The Physical Efficiency of Teachers.* Teachers College Contributions to Education, No. 155. New York: Teachers College, Columbia University, 1924. Pp. x + 80.

Charles W. Odell, *Predicting the Scholastic Success of College Freshmen.* University of Illinois Bulletin, Vol. XXV, No. 2. Urbana, Illinois: University of Illinois, 1927. Pp. 54.

The Experimental Method.—It is to the experimental method that education must look for the solution of many of its most vexing problems. It is upon this basis that the ultimate establishment of education as a science must rest. Although the experimental problems yet unsolved in education are legion, a good beginning has been made; attention may be directed to the valuable contributions in reading, arithmetic, and foreign languages made possible by utilizing the technique of photographing eye movements at the University of Chicago. Trow describes the historical development of the experimental method including the early work of James, Woodworth, Thorndike, and Judd on transfer of training and the experiments by Ebbinghaus, Book, Bryan and Harter, Swift, and Starch dealing with the progress of learning.[68]

A bulletin intended particularly to serve public-school investigators describes the experimental method of securing data as follows:[69]

R. H. Ojemann, *The Constant and Variable Occupations of the United States in* 1920. University of Illinois Bulletin, Vol. XXIV, No. 39. Urbana, Illinois: University of Illinois, 1927. Pp. 48.

Clay Campbell Ross, *The Relation between Grade School Record and High School Achievement.* Teachers College Contributions to Education, No. 166. New York: Teachers College, Columbia University, 1925. Pp. viii + 70.

Ruth Strang, *Subject Matter in Health Education.* Teachers College Contributions to Education, No. 222. New York: Teachers College, Columbia University, 1926. Pp. vi + 108.

Frank Charles Touton, *Solving Geometric Originals.* Teachers College Contributions to Education, No. 146. New York: Teachers College, Columbia University, 1924. Pp. viii + 114.

Truman L. Kelley, *The Influence of Nurture upon Native Differences.* New York: Macmillan Co., 1926. Pp. viii + 50.

[68] Wm. Clark Trow, *Scientific Method in Education, op. cit.,* pp. 110–14.

[69] *An Outline of Methods of Research with Suggestions for High School Principals and Teachers, op. cit.,* pp. 13–16.

The experimental problem involves the discovery of the effect of a given element. Its method is direct manipulation, working with the given element, and observation. It is not historical, because it deals with a present situation; it actually introduces experimental elements or singles them out, and observes and evaluates outcomes. It is possibly the most difficult form of research to undertake outside a laboratory, but one that promises the best ultimate returns for the school in the improvement of practice. Its difficulty lies in the problem of isolation of elements, of control of conditions, and of actually determining whether the observed result is or is not the result of the element introduced.

The success of the experiment depends upon the following conditions:

1. Selection of a workable problem.
2. The ability of the experimenter to control conditions so as to keep all factors and elements the same throughout the experiment except the element or elements whose effect is to be studied.
3. Selection and introduction of elements that are not complex but comparatively simple.
4. The ability to measure the changes or results obtained.

Unless these conditions can be reasonably well assured, the time and energy spent on experimentation must largely be fruitless.

McCall describes three group methods of experimenting in education: the one-group method, the equivalent or parallel-group method, and the rotation-group method.[70] He states that a one-group experiment has been conducted when *one* thing, individual, or group has had *applied to* or *subtracted from* it some experimental factor or factors and the resulting change or changes have been estimated or measured. For example, a high-school group of pupils took five forms of a standard reading test, distributed over an equal number of weeks, in order to determine the effect on reading performance of varying mental attitudes which the experimenter sought to induce on the part of the pupils; these attitudes

[70] William A. McCall, *How to Experiment in Education*, Chapter II. New York: Macmillan Co., 1923.

were: normal, encouragement, skimming, discouragement, and reproduction.[71]

The fundamental assumption underlying a parallel-group method of procedure is that two or more groups are approximately equal in all respects. With carefully controlled conditions, only a single variable should be present and that is the given factor which the experimenter varies for the two groups and the effects of which he seeks to measure. For example, two high-school groups of pupils of equal mental ability and academic achievement were used to determine the effect of a single reading as compared with two readings of the same body of material.[72] One group read the material once, while the parallel group read the same subject matter twice; both groups took the same test as a measure of comprehension of the material read.

The rotation-group method may be a combination of two or more one-group methods or, if the various groups are equivalent, may be a combination of one-group and parallel-group methods. For instance, the latter procedure was employed in a study of the merits of textbook and supplementary reading.[73] The rotation-group method involves a reversal at intervals of the reading procedures followed by the parallel groups. After eight topics had been chosen for the purposes of the experiment mentioned, Group A was allowed to do only textbook reading on the first two topics selected, while

[71] Carter V. Good, "The Effect of Mental-Set or Attitude on the Reading Performance of High-School Pupils," *Journal of Educational Research*, XIV (October, 1926), 178–86.

[72] Carter V. Good, "The Effect of a Single Reading Versus Two Readings of a Given Body of Material," *Journal of Educational Method*, V (April, 1926), 325–29.

[73] Carter V. Good, "An Experimental Study of the Merits of Extensive and Intensive Reading in the Social Sciences," *School Review*, XXXIII (December, 1925), 755–70.

Group B did additional or supplementary reading on the same topics. The two groups exchanged reading procedures for the third and fourth topics so that Group A did supplementary reading, while Group B did only textbook reading. This procedure was continued in such a way that the parallel groups exchanged methods at the end of the second, fourth, and sixth topics; thus the groups were reversed three times in the course of the experiment. Each time parallel groups exchange reading procedures the results secured serve as a check on the data secured from preceding tests. The rotation method is desirable in investigating such a problem, even though the groups are equated on the basis of intelligence, due to the possibility that some uncontrollable factor such as industry or study habits may give one group a certain superiority in comprehending the reading material whether textbook or supplementary subject matter is used. However, if the group which does supplementary reading proves consistently superior, when the reading procedures are reversed at intervals, it seems reasonable to attribute this advantage to the material read or the method used.

Space does not permit a further description of more detailed experimental procedures employed in current investigations. However, attention may be directed to certain outstanding experimental investigations and the reader who would become proficient in such techniques must study carefully the procedures as described in the original sources. Special mention should be made of the considerable number of experiments dealing with the effect of nature and nurture upon intelligence and achievement as described in a yearbook of the National Society for the Study of Education; these studies are also excellent examples of statistical procedures.[74] A selected list of other investigations which employ experimental procedures may be examined with profit.[75]

[74] *Nature and Nurture: Their Influence upon Intelligence* and *Their Influence upon Achievement.* Twenty-Seventh Yearbook of the National Society for the Study of Education, Parts I and II. Bloomington, Illinois: Public School Publishing Co., 1928. Pp. x + 466, xiv + 398.

[75] G. T. Buswell and Lenore John, *Diagnostic Studies in Arithmetic.* Supplementary Educational Monographs, No. 30. Chicago: Department of Education, University of Chicago, 1926. Pp. xiv + 212.

G. T. Buswell, *An Experimental Study of the Eye-Voice Span in Reading.* Supplementary Educational Monographs, No. 17. Chicago: Department of Education, University of Chicago, 1920. Pp. xii + 106.

G. T. Buswell, *Fundamental Reading Habits: A Study of Their Development.* Supplementary Educational Monographs, No. 21. Chicago: Department of Education, University of Chicago, 1922. Pp. xiv + 150.

G. T. Buswell, *A Laboratory Study of the Reading of Modern Foreign Languages.* New York: Macmillan Co., 1927. Pp. xii + 100.

Joseph Seibert Butterweck, *The Problem of Teaching High School Pupils How to Study.* Teachers College Contributions to Education, No. 237. New York: Teachers College, Columbia University, 1926. Pp. vi + 116.

Stuart Appleton Courtis, *Why Children Succeed.* Detroit, Michigan: Courtis Standard Tests, 1925. Pp. 272.

Francis Day Curtis, *Some Values Derived from Extensive Reading of General Science.* Teachers College Contributions to Education, No. 163. New York: Teachers College, Columbia University, 1924. Pp. vi + 142.

Arthur I. Gates, *The Improvement of Reading.* New York: Macmillan Co., 1927. Pp. xii + 440.

Carter V. Good, *The Supplementary Reading Assignment: A Study of Extensive and Intensive Materials and Methods in Reading.* Baltimore: Warwick and York, 1927. Pp. xiv + 228.

Florence L. Goodenough, *Measurement of Intelligence by Drawings.* Yonkers-on-Hudson, New York: World Book Co., 1926. Pp. xiv + 178.

The Case-study Method.—The method of case analysis is proving exceedingly useful in the field of education. In the last few years this technique has been employed in studies of abnormality, brightness, dullness, pupil adjustment and guidance, adolescence, delinquency and problem children of various types, administration and supervision, special talents and defects, mental and physical growth, and school legislation. In making use of this valuable method of investigation, workers in education have followed the lead of investigators in the fields of law, medicine, social service, and the military sciences. Instead of dealing only with abstract theory in the form of lectures and textbook readings, the student may be presented with actual cases which illustrate the field of education under consideration, just as is done for the law student. Instead of dealing with all school pupils alike, the intelligent principal and teacher may collect all available information concerning the

---

Inga Olla Helseth, *Children's Thinking.* Teachers College Contributions to Education, No. 209. New York: Teachers College, Columbia University, 1926. Pp. vi + 164.

Charles Hubbard Judd, *Psychological Analysis of the Fundamentals of Arithmetic.* Supplementary Educational Monographs, No. 32. Chicago: Department of Education, University of Chicago, 1927. Pp. x + 122.

Charles Hubbard Judd and Guy Thomas Buswell, *Silent Reading: A Study of the Various Types.* Supplementary Educational Monographs, No. 23. Chicago: Department of Education, University of Chicago, 1922. Pp. xiv + 160.

Paul Washington Terry, *How Numerals Are Read: An Experimental Study of the Reading of Isolated Numerals and Numerals in Arithmetic Problems.* Supplementary Educational Monographs, No. 18. Chicago: Department of Education, University of Chicago, 1922. Pp. xiv + 110.

W. H. Winch, *Teaching Beginners to Read in England: Its Methods, Results, and Psychological Bases.* Journal of Educational Research Monographs, Number 8. Bloomington, Illinois: Public School Publishing Co., 1925. Pp. 186.

pupils under consideration and on the basis of such information diagnose difficulties and introduce remedial measures, just as the physician does for his patients.

A discussion of the case method, intended particularly to meet the needs of public-school workers, places special emphasis on the application of this technique to the study of problem children.[76]

> One of the methods of investigation that has come into general use within the past few years is the case method. This method has been developed mostly in certain phases of social work and has arisen because of the difficulty of securing reliable data regarding individuals and because of the complexity of the problem of diagnosis. It has come to occupy a very important place in education because every educational problem is a social problem and sooner or later must deal with individuals. At present it is used most frequently in so-called problem cases; that is, in the study of students who for various reasons are not properly adjusted and in consequence cause trouble or are likely to drop out of school. While these problem cases come up first for consideration, there is every reason to believe that the same methods may be used in studying other children and in diagnosing their problems.

The same bulletin presents an outline of the case method as adapted from Morrison's discussion[77] and includes the items of: symptoms, examination (psychophysical, health, educational, and mentality), health and physical history, school history, family history, social history and contacts, diagnosis, and treatment.

Burris[78] makes a strong plea for the introduction of the case method in the training of teachers rather than to depend solely on lectures and textbooks. He discusses at length the development and use of the case

[76] *An Outline of Methods of Research with Suggestions for High School Principals and Teachers*, *op. cit.*, pp. 21–23.

[77] Henry C. Morrison, *The Practice of Teaching in the Secondary School*, pp. 618–39. Chicago: University of Chicago Press, 1926.

[78] W. P. Burris, "The Case Method for the Study of Teaching," *School and Society*, XV (February 4, 1922), 121–30.

method in law and feels that teachers in training should come into contact with reported cases of teaching which illustrate the problems under consideration.

At present the most complete and adequate treatment of the case-study technique as applied to the counseling and guidance of pupils is Reavis' treatment of the subject; in the same connection Brewer's book should be mentioned.[79] Reavis discusses at length the historical development of the technique in other fields before it was adopted in education, describes the application of the technique to counseling and guidance, and presents in detail nine problem cases. Reavis mentions the following items in his outline of an individual case history: chronological data, intelligence, temperament, other mental conditions, physical condition, moral character, conduct, associates, amusements, education, vocational record, home conditions, and neighborhood conditions. A brief discussion of the case-study method of collecting data may be found in Trow's treatment of scientific method in education; his description of the procedure is concerned chiefly with its application to the study of problem children.[80]

The wide use of the case-study technique in education is made apparent by reference to the following investigations which involve applications of the procedure, that is, a study of cases, in one form or another: reading,[81]

[79] William Claude Reavis, *Pupil Adjustment in Junior and Senior High Schools*. Boston: D. C. Heath and Co., 1926. Pp. xviii + 348.

J. M. Brewer and Others, *Case Studies in Educational and Vocational Guidance*. Boston: Ginn and Co., 1926.

[80] Wm. Clark Trow, *Scientific Method in Education*, *op. cit.*, pp. 115–18.

[81] Arthur I. Gates, *The Improvement of Reading*, Part IV. New York: Macmillan Co., 1927.

William Scott Gray, *Remedial Cases in Reading: Their Diagnosis and Treatment*. Supplementary Educational Mono-

problem children,[82] superior children,[83] genius,[84] mental abnormality and deficiency,[85] adolescence,[86] mental hygiene,[87] personality,[88] special talents and defects,[89] supervision,[90] classroom method,[91] educational administration,[92] and the teaching of agriculture.[93]

---

graphs, No. 22. Chicago: Department of Education, University of Chicago, 1922. Pp. viii + 208.

[82] Mary B. Sayles, *The Problem Child in School.* New York: Joint Committee on Methods of Preventing Delinquency, 1925. Pp. 288.

[83] Lewis M. Terman and Others, *Genetic Studies of Genius*, Vol. I. Stanford University, California: Stanford University Press, 1925. Pp. xvi + 648.

[84] Catharine Morris Cox, *Genetic Studies of Genius*, Vol. II. Stanford University, California: Stanford University Press, 1926. Pp. xxiv + 842.

[85] Sidney L. Pressey and Luella Cole Pressey, *Mental Abnormality and Deficiency.* New York: Macmillan Co., 1926. Pp. xiv + 356.

[86] Winifred Richmond, *The Adolescent Girl.* New York; Macmillan Co., 1925. Pp. xvi + 212.

[87] Florence Mateer, *The Unstable Child.* New York: D. Appleton and Co., 1924. Pp. xii + 472.

William H. Burnham, *Great Teachers and Mental Health.* New York: D. Appleton and Co., 1926. Pp. xiv + 352.

[88] June E. Downey, *The Will-Temperament and Its Testing.* Yonkers-on-Hudson, New York: World Book Co., 1923. Pp. 340.

[89] Leta S. Hollingworth, *Special Talents and Defects.* New York: Macmillan Co., 1923. Pp. xx + 216.

[90] C. J. Anderson, A. S. Barr, and Maybell G. Bush, *Visiting the Teacher at Work.* New York: D. Appleton and Co., 1925. Pp. xviii + 382.

[91] Douglas Waples, *Problems in Classroom Method.* New York: Macmillan Co., 1927. Pp. xxii + 610.

[92] George D. Strayer, N. L. Engelhardt, and Others, *Problems in Educational Administration.* New York: Teachers College, Columbia University, 1925. Pp. xviii + 756.

[93] A. W. Nolan, *The Case Method in the Study of Teaching with Special Reference to Vocational Agriculture.* Educational Research Monographs, No. 10. Bloomington, Illinois: Public School Publishing Co., 1927. Pp. xii + 266.

Job Analysis, Activity Analysis, and Social-survey Methods.—The technique of activity analysis has been borrowed from the industrial world as an aid in determining what activities to emphasize in the school. It has been most frequently applied in the selection of curriculum content. Since it is no longer possible to include all knowledge in the school program of studies, activity analysts maintain that selection of subject matter should be determined on the basis of social need rather than on the basis of historical importance of the various school subjects, opinions of textbook writers and authorities, pronouncements of philosophers, consensus of current school practices, and committee recommendations. The applications of this method have been widespread, including analyses of the activities of pharmacists, librarians, and teachers, and surveys of social need or usage in spelling, arithmetic, grammar, etc.

Trow[94] and Crawford[95] present brief treatments of this technique of investigation. Phelps[96] discusses briefly the method of job analysis as applied to curriculum construction. Waples[97] describes this method in combination with the interview technique as a means of determining specific teaching difficulties; he discovered 424 typical difficulties which confront high-school teachers. Other investigators have applied the method of activity analysis to various fields: diversified curricu-

[94] Wm. Clark Trow, *Scientific Method in Education*, *op. cit.*, pp. 118–23.

[95] Claude C. Crawford, *Methods of Study*, *op. cit.*, p. 161.

[96] Shelton Phelps, "Curriculum Construction," *Peabody Journal of Education*, V (January, 1928), 223–29.

[97] Douglas Waples, "The Definition of Teaching Problems on the College Level," *Educational Administration and Supervision*, XIII (September, 1927), 391–98.

Douglas Waples, *Problems in Classroom Method.* New York: Macmillan Co., 1927. Pp. xxii + 610.

lum studies,[98] secretarial duties,[99] the pharmaceutical curriculum,[100] character development,[101] activities of teachers,[102] the high-school curriculum,[103] and difficulties in the teaching of reading.[104] The application of the technique under consideration may be made more concrete by reviewing briefly the studies reported in Bobbitt's monograph, *Curriculum Investigations.*[105] This summary is adapted from the writer's review of Bobbitt's work in the *School Review* for January, 1927.

Professor Bobbitt, with the cooperation of a number of graduate students, has prepared a monograph which describes the techniques of certain curriculum investigations and reports the results. In the first chapter

[98] W. W. Charters, *Curriculum Construction.* New York: Macmillan Co., 1923.

[99] W. W. Charters, *Analysis of Secretarial Duties and Traits.* Baltimore: Williams and Wilkins Co., 1924.

[100] W. W. Charters, A. B. Lemon, and Leon M. Monell, *Basic Material for a Pharmaceutical Curriculum.* New York: McGraw-Hill Book Co., 1927. Pp. 366.

[101] W. W. Charters, *The Teaching of Ideals.* New York: Macmillan Co., 1927. Pp. xiv + 372.

[102] W. W. Charters, *The Commonwealth-Fund Study of Teacher-Training Curricula: The Activities of Teachers.* Chicago: Tentative list of activities distributed by the author from the University of Chicago. Pp. 32.

[103] Franklin Bobbitt, *Curriculum-Making in Los Angeles.* Supplementary Educational Monographs, No. 20. Chicago: Department of Education, University of Chicago, 1922. Pp. vi + 106.

Franklin Bobbitt, *How to Make a Curriculum.* Boston: Houghton Mifflin Co., 1924. Pp. 292.

[104] Julia M. Harris, H. L. Donovan, and Thomas Alexander, *Supervision and Teaching of Reading.* Richmond, Virginia: Johnson Publishing Co., 1927. Pp. xxiv + 474.

[105] Franklin Bobbitt and Others, *Curriculum Investigations.* Supplementary Educational Monographs, No. 31. Chicago: Department of Education, University of Chicago, 1926. Pp. viii + 204.

the author sets forth his fundamental point of view and defends the technique of activity analysis as a method of curriculum investigation and as a guide in curriculum construction. The critics who maintain that the curriculum should be determined in terms of the philosophy and theory of education will find their objections to activity analysis carefully met in this first chapter and also in the interpretative discussions of succeeding chapters. Since relatively few individuals have achieved the highest and most desirable levels of human performance, a system of education may well seek ultimately to bring all individuals toward this high level, in so far as native capacity and environment will permit. Eventually the curriculum-maker may have to analyze the activities of different ability groups in order to determine what level of performance members of a given group should attain. The activities of childhood and of all growth levels need to be analyzed before one can be certain what activities are appropriate for a given age or growth level. However, the author considers it advisable, as a starting-point, to analyze human activities at the highest adult level, not by way of discovering what the child should do but for the assistance such an analysis gives in determining the activities normal at earlier stages.

An investigation of the major fields of human concern was made by an examination of the frequency of the topics listed in the *Reader's Guide to Periodical Literature* covering the years 1919–21 inclusive, a study of the column inches of space devoted to each topic in a newspaper over a period of time, an analysis of the number of columns devoted to each topic in *The Encyclopaedia Britannica*, a classification of the topics apparently referred to by the ten-thousand most frequently used English words, and a study of the topics treated in the

Literary Digest. An effort was made to determine the duties and traits of a good citizen by analyzing newspaper editorials, magazine articles on citizenship, and the opinions of leading citizens as expressed in interviews. Civic and social shortcomings were studied by an examination of the editorials of newspapers and magazines. The social problems of the labor group were determined by an analysis of ten widely used books and seven labor periodicals which deal with labor problems. A study of essays was made to discover the characteristics of human behavior that are approved and disapproved; a canvass of books, magazine articles, and books of etiquette was made to determine approved social behavior. Shortcomings in the written English of adults were discovered by an analysis of letters written for newspaper publication. The science articles in a random sampling of five general magazine and three books of popular science were studied to determine the mathematics used in popular science. The play activities of persons of different ages were discovered by having each individual check in a comprehensive list of play activities those in which he had engaged of his own volition and as play within the week preceding the investigation. The grade-placement of poems was investigated by analyzing courses of study, elementary-school readers, and books written by specialists in the teaching of English.

The author shows clearly that the frequency with which topics appear and the space devoted to them are not necessarily accurate indices of the relative importance of the topics. However, the fact that certain topics are frequently discussed shows them to be matters of major concern and therefore of significance to education; at least, frequency figures are one type of tangible evidence that can be used in evaluating the various fields of human concern. The monograph suggests the wide range of opportunity for investigation in the field of activity analysis as a guide in curriculum-making.[106]

Conclusion.—This chapter has described in some detail the various techniques of educational research available for the collection of data. These techniques are: philosophical and other subjective methods, historical and legal methods, comparative and survey methods, questionnaire-correspondence and interview methods, statistical methods, experimental methods, case-study methods, and activity-analysis and social-survey methods. It should be repeated that the educational worker or student who wishes to become proficient in the use of a given technique or techniques must study carefully appropriate original investigations such as have been cited rather freely in this chapter.

[106] Adapted from the writer's book review in the *School Review*, XXXV (January, 1927), 73–74.

Chapter VII

PROBLEMS INVOLVED IN THE ANALYSIS, ORGANIZATION, AND SUMMARIZATION OF DATA: TABULAR AND GRAPHIC PRESENTATION

The preceding chapter has indicated the various methods and techniques available for the collection of data. Logically, the next step is the organization and analysis of the information secured. It is not the purpose of this chapter to present a detailed or descriptive treatment of the analysis, organization, summarization, and tabular or graphic presentation of data. Such procedures have been adequately treated in available publications which will be cited at appropriate intervals. To attempt even a brief description of graphic and tabular methods in the presentation of data within the limits of a single chapter would be presumptuous in view of the fact that whole volumes have been devoted to these problems. While certain problems of mechanics and form arise in connection with a discussion of the analysis and organization of data, it seems advisable to defer a treatment of such matters until the problems of reporting educational research are taken up in Chapter IX.

In the light of the preceding comments, it seems appropriate to profit by the procedure followed by Monroe and Engelhart in their excellent bulletin,[1]

[1] Walter S. Monroe and Max D. Engelhart, *The Techniques of Educational Research.* University of Illinois Bulletin, Vol. XXV, No. 19. Urbana, Illinois: University of Illinois, 1928. Pp. 84.

namely, to suggest sources of information dealing with the problems treated in this chapter rather than to attempt detailed descriptions. Most of the readers of this volume will be sufficiently mature to profit by such a plan.

Problems Involved in the Analysis and Organization of Data.—Monroe and Engelhart[2] introduce their illustrative references dealing with the analysis, organization, and summarization of data as follows:

> The analysis and organization of data depend upon the form in which they were collected. For example, when data are taken from records or printed sources, their organization may be facilitated or made more difficult by the form in which they were copied. Hence this phase of educational research overlaps that described in the preceding chapter ["Collecting Data"].
>
> The phase of educational research described as "analyzing, organizing, and summarizing data" may make great demands upon the investigator's ingenuity. There are many decisions to be made, especially in summarizing data. Typical questions are: What form of table is to be made? How large intervals should be used? How may the data be summarized without obscuring significant details? Shall one large complex table be constructed, or a group of smaller tables?
>
> Much of the handling of quantitative data is accomplished by standard statistical methods . . . However, before an average or coefficient of correlation is calculated, the investigator must make decisions. In some instances these are very simple, but frequently an experienced investigator may need to experiment before he finally decides just what calculations to make.

The same authors[3] present illustrative references which throw light on a number of problems involved in the analysis and organization of data. Their outline, with the references omitted, is as follows:

A. Transference from original sources.
B. Interpretation by means of graphs
   1. Frequency polygon.

[2] *Ibid*, p. 42.
[3] *Ibid*, pp. 42–48.

2. Frequency curve.
3. Histogram.
4. Normal curve with experimental curve.
5. Bar graph.
6. Scatter diagram, or correlation chart.

C. Summarization by means of tables.
1. Simple table.
2. Open table.
3. Table doubled upon itself.
4. Table with subdivisions.
5. Table with varied divisions.

Transferring Data from Original Sources, Tabulating, Arranging, and Systematizing Data.—Space does not permit more than a listing of selected references which deal with the problems of tabulation and classification of data. Adequate treatments of the several problems involved in tabulation are available: the frequency table,[4] handling the results of testing and distribution of scores,[5] original and mechanical tabulation of educational data,[6] and types of tabulation and selection of tabulation forms and blanks.[7] Other discussions which include information on classification that is closely related to the problems listed in the preceding sentence may be mentioned.[8]

[4] L. L. Thurstone, *The Fundamentals of Statistics*, pp. 1–8. New York: Macmillan Co., 1925.

[5] Percival M. Symonds, *Measurement in Secondary Education*, Chapter XII. New York: Macmillan Co., 1927.

Frank N. Freeman, *Mental Tests*, Chapter XII. Boston: Houghton Mifflin Co., 1926.

[6] Harold O. Rugg, *Statistical Methods Applied to Education*, Chapter III. Boston: Houghton Mifflin Co., 1917.

[7] William A. McCall, *How to Measure in Education*, pp. 321–25. New York: Macmillan Co., 1922.

Carter Alexander, *School Statistics and Publicity*, pp. 71–89. New York: Silver, Burdett and Co., 1919.

[8] Karl J. Holzinger, *Statistical Methods for Students in Education*, Chapter II. Boston: Ginn and Co., 1928.

Harold O. Rugg, *op. cit.*, Chapter IV.

Interpretation of Data by Means of Graphs.—Graphic and pictorial representation of facts has come to be used not only in scientific treatises but even in popular magazine articles and newspaper discussions. School officers and educational investigators have made extensive use of the various types of charts and visual aids in presenting data. It must be recognized that scientific and correct procedure is fundamental to any investigation; yet the ability to supplement verbal description by the condensed and effective methods of graphic display is important. Especially do school surveys, testing programs, reports of school officers, professional books in education, and educational programs take on greater significance in the eyes of the reading public through correct charting of scientifically determined facts.

A brief statement may be made concerning the content of a valuable treatment of graphic methods in education.[9] This treatise includes discussions of the purpose and value of graphic methods and a list of the various materials and instruments which are used in the preparation of charts. Graphic representation is divided into 15 main types which are described in as many chapters. The methods of charting treated are: squares and simple areas, bar representations, circle representations, curves, frequency surfaces, individual frequency distributions, block diagrams, organization charts, maps, genealogical charts, architectural diagrams, picture graphs, verbal-

---

W. C. Schluter, *How to Do Research Work,* Chapter XII. New York: Prentice-Hall, 1926.

Henry E. Garrett, *Statistics in Psychology and Education,* Chapter I. New York: Longmans, Green and Co., 1926.

C. W. Odell, *Educational Statistics,* Chapter I. New York: Century Co., 1925.

[9] J. Harold Williams, *Graphic Methods in Education.* Boston: Houghton Mifflin Co., 1924. Pp. xviii + 320.

display charts, charts made with the aid of type, and special chart devices. A set of rules for judging graphic procedure and for checking up chart work and a five-division grading-scale for charts are suggested. The fifteen chapters which describe the various types of graphic representation include problems for charting. The book itself contains 148 figures which serve as good examples of the principles discussed. The author does not neglect to point out at appropriate intervals the misinterpretations which may accompany the use of graphic devices, although possibly he makes charting appear so easy as to result in misapplication and overworking, on the part of the novice and the publicity-seeker, of the excellent methods described.[10]

An elementary treatment of graphics and statistics,[11] prepared by a pioneer writer in the field of statistics, may also be summarized briefly. In this book directions are given for making a frequency table, plotting a frequency diagram, and graphing the grouped frequency distribution. Numerous illustrations are given to show how teachers of mathematics, science, and the social studies use graphic and pictorial devices in order to present their subjects more effectively. One chapter includes 17 suggestions which the Joint Committee on Standards for Graphic Presentation considered the more generally applicable principles of elementary graphic presentation. The author himself makes extensive use of tabular, graphic, and pictorial devices to illustrate the topics under discussion as evidenced by a total of 23 tables and 115 figures.

[10] Adapted from the writer's book review in the *School Review*, XXXIII (April, 1925), 314–15.

[11] Harold Rugg, *A Primer of Graphics and Statistics for Teachers*. Boston: Houghton Mifflin Co., 1925. Pp. vi + 142.

Standards for Graphic Presentation.—Seventeen suggestions concerning elementary graphic presentation are as follows:[12]

1. The general arrangement of a diagram should proceed from left to right.
2. Where possible, represent quantities by linear magnitude, as areas or volumes are more likely to be misinterpreted.
3. For a curve, the vertical scale, whenever practicable, should be so selected that the zero line will appear in the diagram.
4. If the zero line of the vertical scale will not normally appear in the curve diagram, the zero line should be shown by the use of a horizontal break in the diagram.
5. The zero lines of the scales for a curve should be sharply distinguished from the other coordinate lines.
6. For curves having a scale representing percentages, it is usually desirable to emphasize in some distinctive way the 100 per cent line used as a basis of comparison.
7. When the scale of the diagram refers to dates, and the period represented is not a complete unit, it is better not to emphasize the first and last ordinates, since such a diagram does not represent the beginning and end of time.
8. When curves are drawn on logarithmic coordinates, the limiting lines of the diagram should each be of some power of 10 on the logarithmic scale.
9. It is advisable not to show any more coordinate lines than necessary to guide the eye in reading the diagram.
10. The curve lines of a diagram should be sharply distinguished from the ruling.
11. In curves representing a series of observations, it is advisable whenever possible, to indicate clearly on the diagram all the points representing the separate observations.
12. The horizontal scale for curves should usually read from left to right and the vertical scale from bottom to top.
13. Figures for the scale of a diagram should be placed at the left and at the bottom or along the respective axes.
14. It is often desirable to include in the diagram the numerical data or formulae represented.

[12] *Report of the Joint Committee on Standards for Graphic Presentation.* New York: American Society of Mechanical Engineers, 1918. Pp. 50.

15. If numerical data are not included in the diagram it is desirable to give the data in tabular form accompanying the diagram.

16. All lettering and all figures in a diagram should be placed so as to be easily read from the base as the bottom, or from the right-hand edge of the diagram as the bottom.

17. The title of a diagram should be made as clear and complete as possible. Sub-titles or descriptions should be added if necessary to insure clearness.

Other Sources of Information on Graphic Methods.—Attention may be directed to two rather general and brief treatments of the preparation of illustrations[13] and to a number of rather specified discussions of graphs and charts which contain numerous illustrations of the topics treated.[14]

Summarization of Data by Means of Tables.—For references which illustrate the various types of tables the reader is referred to the helpful bulletin by Monroe and Engelhart.[15] For discussions of the construction of tables and additional examples of tabular methods a number of sources of information will be found helpful.[16]

[13] Ward G. Reeder, *How to Write a Thesis*, pp. 73–78, 119–29. Bloomington, Illinois: Public School Publishing Co., 1925.

W. C. Schluter, *op. cit.*, Chapter XIV.

[14] Carter Alexander, *op. cit.*, Chapters IV and XI.

Henry E. Garrett, *op. cit.*, Chapter II.

Karl J. Holzinger, *op. cit.*, Chapter III.

Truman L. Kelley, *Statistical Method*, Chapter II. New York: Macmillan Co., 1923.

William A. McCall, *op. cit.*, Chapter XIII.

C. W. Odell, *op. cit.*, Chapter II.

Harold O. Rugg, *Statistical Methods Applied to Education*, *op. cit.*, Chapter X.

Percival M. Symonds, *op. cit.*, Chapter XII.

L. L. Thurstone, *op. cit.*, Chapters II and III.

[15] Walter S. Monroe and Max D. Engelhart, *op. cit.*, pp. 46–48.

[16] Carter Alexander, *op. cit.*, pp. 204–33.

Karl J. Holzinger, *op. cit.*, Chapter III.

Translating Statistical Material for the Reading Public. Alexander calls attention to the uselessness of much of the tabular material in school reports due to lack of coordination and interpretation.[17] He makes some pertinent suggestions concerning the simplification of graphs and the translation of statistical ideas, relationships, and results into ordinary language for the benefit of the average reader who covers superintendents' reports and school survey reports.[18]

Truman L. Kelley, *op. cit.*, Chapter I.

William A. McCall, *op. cit.*, pp. 325–30.

Ward G. Reeder, *op. cit.*, pp. 65–72, 116–18.

Harold O. Rugg, *Statistical Methods Applied to Education*, *op. cit.*, Chapter X.

[17] Carter Alexander, *op. cit.*, pp. 200–203.

[18] *Ibid*, Chapter XII.

Chapter VIII

INTERPRETATION OF DATA AND FORMULATION OF CONCLUSIONS

Obviously, much that has been said in the preceding chapter is closely related to problems of interpretation and formulation of conclusions. The problems of organization and analysis of data, as well as tabular and graphic methods of presentation, in many instances cannot be definitely separated from the issues involved in the interpretation of data. Much of the information in Chapter IV, "Characteristics of Scientific Investigations," and Chapter VI, "Techniques of Educational Research Available for the Collection of Data," has a decided bearing on the problems of the present chapter. Special attention should be directed to the references listed under the various techniques of collecting data—philosophical, historical, survey, questionnaire, statistical, experimental, case-study, and activity analysis. These references contain usable suggestions applicable to the problems involved in the interpretation of data and the formulation of conclusions.

In discussing the problems of this chapter it seems advisable to use the plan followed in the preceding chapter, namely, to refer the reader to appropriate sources of information rather than to attempt a detailed descriptive treatment of determining conclusions. Such a plan should have a stimulating effect on the reader in that he chooses the particular references suited to his needs and is able critically to examine and evaluate the material in its original setting.

Monroe and Engelhart on Determining Conclusions.—The following quotation is appropriate in discussing the interpretation of data and the formulation of conclusions:[1]

Formulating Conclusions.—The conclusions are essentially the answers to the questions specified in the definition of the problem. Hence, in formulating the conclusions, an investigator is merely attempting to answer the questions that have guided him throughout the research. These answers should be formulated very carefully so that they will express precisely what the writer intended to say. It may be that the data justify only tentative or partial answers. If so, the statements should clearly indicate this fact.

Hypotheses and Verification.—Determining conclusions corresponds very closely to two steps of reflective thinking, formulation of hypotheses and verification. In determining the answers to the questions of the problem the investigator formulates tentative statements and then compares them with the data as a means of verification. Sometimes the meaning of the data is obscure and considerable ingenuity is required to formulate a hypothesis.

Being Scientific.—To be scientific is to know one's data and to use them with full recognition of the defects that they may possess. Hence in determining conclusions, especially in verifying tentative formulations, the investigator should have clearly in mind all the limitations of his data. It is obvious that he cannot do this unless he *knows* his data. One who has not made an extended and critical study of data is usually ignorant of their limitations. In educational research we seldom work with perfect data. Sometimes their imperfections are not significant but sometimes they are. The investigator is responsible for knowing his data. Failure to know them and use them intelligently means that he is not scientific.

Determining Conclusions versus Interpreting Data.—There appear to be two concepts of educational research. [One has been described in this book and in the present quotation.] According to the other, the problem and its definition are not made basic. The data collected are not necessarily restricted to those called for by the problem. In fact, investigators who have this concept of education frequently collect data without any clearly defined

[1] Walter S. Monroe and Max D. Engelhart, *op. cit.*, pp. 49–50.

problem in mind, or they may merely take data that have accumulated as a product of operating a school or engaging in some other activity. In such cases, the data are looked upon as material to be interpreted rather than used as a means of answering certain questions. As a result, we have reports of educational research that present a long list of "conclusions" which are demonstrated or suggested by the data, but which are not answers to questions raised at the beginning of the work. Although there are occasions when it is profitable to analyze, organize, and summarize accumulations, such activity is not educational research as conceived by the authors of this bulletin. Consequently, the references [a selected list] illustrate the determination of answers to questions rather than the interpretation of data.

The list of references referred to in the preceding sentence is organized according to the following outline:[2]

A. Statement of conclusions.
   1. Concise statements.
      a. Answers specifically connected with questions asked in statement of problem.
      b. Conclusions specifically connected to declarative statements of problems.
   2. General statements.

B. Statement of limitations in conclusions.
   1. Recognition of limitation due to faulty or incomplete data.
   2. Recognition of danger of generalization.

C. Application of conclusions.
   1. Suggestions for application to practice.
   2. Suggestion of problems for further investigation.

An Illustration of the Statement of Conclusions.—The reader will find the studies listed under the foregoing headings of real value as examples of the various ways in which conclusions may be stated. One concrete example will serve to illustrate the contribution made by Monroe and Engelhart. In a given experiment[3] this question is raised, "What effect has mental-set or attitude on reading

[2] *Ibid*, pp. 50–54.

[3] Carter V. Good, *The Supplementary Reading Assignment*, Chapter XV. Baltimore: Warwick and York, 1927.

performance?" After a summary of related investigations in this field and a description of the testing materials selected and the experimental procedures involved, the results are stated in a series of four paragraphs. Limitations of the experiment are mentioned:

It is realized that an attitude is a subjective quality and the experimenter cannot be certain whether the desired attitude has been induced. Possibly the stimulus employed causes a reaction on the part of one pupil, while another pupil is unaffected. However, in view of the fact that an effort was made to keep all factors constant, with the exception of the given attitude that the experimenter sought to convey to the pupils, the results secured should prove fairly tangible. When the average of the group on a form of the test is materially different from preceding or subsequent performances, it is reasonable to attribute at least a part of this difference to the mental-set or attitude with which the pupils approached the reading.

An extension of the investigation is suggested and application of the results is made to the guidance of children in their reading.

The attitude with which the pupil approaches his reading is significant; the attitude of parent and teacher toward the pupil's reading interests and assignments is also very important. The teacher and parent, by a sympathetic and encouraging attitude, may do much to promote desirable reading habits on the part of the pupil. Pupils profit from instructions in skimming and rapid reading methods. Encouragement induces an attitude more favorable to effective reading than does discouragement or indifference. Pupils are likely to read with a higher degree of comprehension if held responsible to a certain extent for the material covered.[4]

Other Sources of Information on Determining Conclusions.—Alexander mentions five points to be considered in arriving at conclusions:[5]

[4] *Ibid*, p. 217.

[5] Carter Alexander and Others, *Educational Research*, pp. 3–4. New York: Bureau of Publications, Teachers College, Columbia University, 1927.

1. Must be relevant to the problem.
2. Must be justified by the data studied.
3. May be positive or negative (but must be constructive).
4. Should be stated in terms which show bearing on present or future practice.
5. Must show that relevant conclusions from data presented have not been overlooked.

Trow discusses nine rules of scientific thinking which have a decided bearing on the interpretation of data and the formulation of conclusions:[6]

1. Give first place to facts.
2. Don't multiply theories unnecessarily.
3. Avoid reification of abstractions.
4. Regard analogy as a source of suggestion not as proof.
5. Apply the test of agreement.
6. Scrutinize all statements purporting to be true.
7. Avoid basing conclusions on too few cases.
8. Be consistent and coherent.
9. Use precise terms.

Other useful sources of information are available. A bulletin of the United States Bureau of Education sets up a hypothetical situation and suggests the tentative conclusions which may be inferred from the facts presented.[7] Dewey devotes a chapter to judgment or the interpretation of facts.[8] An article by a scientist

[6] Wm. Clark Trow, *Scientific Method in Education*, pp. 72–93. Boston: Houghton Mifflin Co., 1925.

[7] National Committee on Research in Secondary Education, *An Outline of Methods of Research with Suggestions for High School Principals and Teachers*, pp. 5–8. Bureau of Education Bulletin, No. 24, 1926. Washington: Bureau of Education.

[8] John Dewey, *How We Think*, Chapter VIII. Boston: D. C. Heath and Co., 1910.

emphasizes that judgment must be unprejudiced, must be impersonal, and must be suspended if the data are inadequate.[9] Sears discusses the interpretation of data secured in school surveys.[10] Schluter devotes a chapter to the analysis and interpretation of data.[11]

Interpretation of Educational Measurements and Statistics.—The references listed in Chapter VI which describe the experimental and statistical techniques of collecting data are useful in the interpretation of measurements and statistics. Special attention may be called to certain references, some of which were not mentioned in Chapter VI. These discussions are concerned with: interpretation of intelligence tests,[12] interpretation of educational measurements;[13] interpretation of the probable error and coefficient of correlation;[14] an understanding of the magnitude of errors;[15] statistical fallacies,

[9] Elliot R. Downing, "The Elements and Safeguards of Scientific Thinking," *Scientific Monthly*, XXVI (March, 1928), 231–43.

[10] Jesse B. Sears, *The School Survey*, pp. 16–17. Boston: Houghton Mifflin Co., 1925.

[11] W. C. Schluter, *How to Do Research Work*, Chapter XIII. New York: Prentice-Hall, 1926.

[12] Frank N. Freeman, *Mental Tests*, Chapter XVII. Boston: Houghton Mifflin Co., 1926.

[13] Truman Lee Kelley, *Interpretation of Educational Measurements*. Yonkers-on-Hudson, New York: World Book Co., 1927. Pp. xiv + 364.

"After Testing—What?" *Peabody Journal of Education*, IV (November, 1926), 179–81.

[14] Charles W. Odell, *The Interpretation of the Probable Error and the Coefficient of Correlation*. University of Illinois Bulletin, Vol. XXIII, No. 52. Urbana, Illinois: University of Illinois, 1925. Pp. 50.

[15] Walter S. Monroe, *The Constant and Variable Errors of Educational Measurements*. University of Illinois Bulletin, Vol. XXI, No. 10. Urbana, Illinois: University of Illinois, 1923. Pp. 30.

errors, and hazards;[16] and validation of statistical procedures.[17]

Honesty and Accuracy in Reporting Findings and Arriving at Conclusions.—An editorial writer emphasizes absolute honesty in reporting what is found without regard for whether such facts agree with tradition, the findings of colleagues, or with the investigator's individual theories and philosophy.[18] A quotation from this clear-cut editorial may be found in Chapter IV. Another quotation in Chapter IV points out the desirability of mathematical precision and accuracy, but suggests that under certain practical working conditions it is possible to carry precision to the point of absurdity.[19] Sometimes a well-meaning investigator deliberately

[16] Barbara Stoddard Burks and Truman L. Kelley, "Statistical Hazards in Nature-Nurture Investigations," *Nature and Nurture: Their Influence upon Intelligence*, pp. 9–38. Twenty-Seventh Yearbook of the National Society for the Study of Education, Part I. Bloomington, Illinois: Public School Publishing Co., 1928.

Karl J. Holzinger, *Statistical Methods for Students in Education*, Chapters V, XIII. Boston: Ginn and Co., 1928.

"Thinking Statistically," *Educational Research Bulletin*, VI (March 30, 1927), 142–43. Columbus, Ohio: Bureau of Educational Research, Ohio State University.

"Statistical Thinking Once More," *Educational Research Bulletin*, VI (May 25, 1927), 230–31. Columbus, Ohio: Bureau of Educational Research, Ohio State University.

Harvey C. Lehman and Paul A. Witty, "Statistics Show," *Journal of Educational Psychology*, XIX (March, 1928), 175–84.

Guy M. Whipple, "The Improvement of Educational Research," *School and Society*, XXVI (August 27, 1927), 249–59.

[17] S. A. Courtis, "The Validation of Statistical Procedure," *Journal of Educational Research*, XII (June, 1925), 31–40.

[18] "Research," *Educational Research Bulletin*, VI (April 13, 1927), 164–65. Columbus, Ohio: Bureau of Educational Research, Ohio State University.

[19] "Accuracy," *Journal of Educational Research*, VIII (June, 1923), 63–67.

distorts or colors facts in the interest of some piece of propaganda which may even aim toward a worthy objective. However, such a procedure is scored by an editorial writer.[20] The real scientist is distinguished by two characteristics, an insatiable desire to know the truth and an absolute honesty in reporting what is found.

[20] "Scientific Accuracy Versus Propaganda," *Elementary School Journal*, XXVI (January, 1926), 323–25.

CHAPTER IX

REPORTING EDUCATIONAL RESEARCH AND THE PREPARATION OF A MANUSCRIPT FOR PUBLICATION

Much of the value of an investigation or experiment depends on the effectiveness with which it is reported. This chapter will discuss briefly a number of problems involved in the reporting of educational research and in the preparation of manuscripts for publication. Numerous references which should prove of value to investigators and writers will be listed. Among the problems discussed are: criteria for planning a report of educational research, careless practices and common errors in educational writings, the guidance of graduate students in the preparation of theses, the necessity for absolute accuracy and intellectual honesty in research reports and other educational writings, hygienic requirements of printed materials and typographical considerations, placing material for publication with an appropriate journal or publisher, seeing articles or books safely through the press, and relations with other writers and publishers.

The Need for Careful Reporting of Educational Research. An editorial aptly emphasizes the desirability of improving the diction and style of educational writings.[1]

> . . . The experience of anyone who examines critically the form in which reports of educational investigations are written

[1] "Educational Writings," *Elementary School Journal*, XXVI (October, 1925), 91.

leads to the conviction that there is great need of more attention to diction and style of writing on the part of authors and publishers . . .

Until recently the energy of advocates of educational investigations has been devoted chiefly to the promotion of experiments and to the conversion of those who were doubtful about the possibility of measuring the results of educational endeavor. If anything whatever could be produced, it was thought of as indicating progress. It is still true that school people have to be urged vigorously to take time from their routine duties to make studies of the results which they secure.

The period in the evolution of educational science has come, however, when it is legitimate to urge that there be an improvement in the form of educational writing. It has been pointed out clearly . . . that there is a close relation between thinking and the style of expression. Where the latter is obscure and ill organized, there is ground for the suspicion that the former is inefficient and unsound. By all means, let us urge educators to write, but let us begin to demand that they write well.

Two Valuable Bulletins Dealing with the Reporting of Educational Research.—Special attention should be directed to two bulletins published by the Bureau of Educational Research of the University of Illinois. The earlier bulletin[2] is now out of print, but its contents are ably summarized in a chapter of a second bulletin[3] published three years later. Many of the problems involved in educational writing will not be treated in detail in the present chapter because of the excellent material made available by Professor Monroe and his associates. The contents of the last chapter of the second bulletin are indicated by the outline for planning a report of educational research, as given in a subsequent

[2] Walter S. Monroe and Nell Bomar Johnston, *Reporting Educational Research.* University of Illinois Bulletin, Vol. XXII, No. 38. Urbana, Illinois: University of Illinois, 1925. Pp. 64.

[3] Walter S. Monroe and Max D. Engelhart, *The Techniques of Educational Research,* Chapter VI. University of Illinois Bulletin, Vol. XXV, No. 19. Urbana, Illinois: University of Illinois, 1928.

portion of this chapter. A quotation makes clear the point of view from which both bulletins were written.[4]

Reporting an Important Phase of Educational Research.—The report of an investigation not only serves to record and communicate the procedure and the results but it also fulfills an important function in the process of research. In the act of writing, if it is well done, the research worker refines his thinking and the detailed record facilitates the critical testing of the work done. Thus an investigator should not consider that he has completed his task until a complete report has been prepared. If he is interested in communicating his work to others, the report must be well written in order to fulfill that purpose effectively.

The Communicatory Function of a Report of Educational Research. Usually, in preparing a report of a study, a research worker should not confine his purposes to "telling" the reader the answer that he has obtained to the problem studied. Instead, he should try to guide the reader to think about the problem in such a way that at the conclusion of his reading a dependable answer will have been attained. Thus a complete report of an investigation should guide the reader (1) to define the problem clearly so that he will understand just what questions are to be answered and in some cases their relation to other questions, (2) to understand the data introduced, especially to be aware of their limitations, and (3) to test critically the hypothesis which is to be accepted as the answer and as a result to qualify or limit it if the data indicate that this should be done. In case other hypotheses are likely to occur to the reader, the discussion should guide him to an understanding of the reasons for their rejection.

Criteria for Planning a Report of Educational Research. The outline given below indicates the points which should be considered by an investigator in making his report.[5] It may serve as a check list in determining whether important matters have been overlooked in the written account of an investigation. Monroe and Engelhart discuss each of these points and subpoints in some detail. The suggestion is made that such criteria

[4] *Ibid*, p. 57.

[5] Walter S. Monroe and Max D. Engelhart, *op. cit.*, pp. 58–61.

are of service in evaluating research reports as well as in planning or preparing written accounts of research.

Summary of Criteria

A. General structure of a report.
  1. Major divisions.
    a. Are the following divisions reasonably explicit: definition of problem, collection of data, treatment of data, discussion of each question to be answered, and the conclusion?
  2. Introduction.
    a. Is the problem introduced in such a way that a competent reader will understand and appreciate the purpose of the report?
    b. Has superfluous material been eliminated from the introduction?
  3. Definition of problem.
    a. Is the reader given a precise statement of the questions to be answered?
    b. In case the problem is related to other problems, are the relations made clear to the reader?
  4. Conclusion.
    a. Is the reader given in convenient form an explicit answer to each question included in the "definition of the problem?"

B. Development, evaluation, and organization of ideas.
  5. Trend of thought.
    a. As the reader "traces" the writer's thinking, will he be led from a clearly defined problem to a critical and scholarly answer by a route that is satisfying to him?
    b. Is an encyclopedic enumeration of ideas or facts avoided?
  6. Development of ideas.
    a. Has the writer avoided leaving "gaps" in his "trend of thought" for the reader to fill in?
    b. Have the important ideas been "developed" so that the average reader will fully comprehend them?
    c. Has the writer developed his ideas so completely that no points have been overlooked which might leave the reader with unanswered questions?

7. Evaluation of ideas.
   a. Have all irrelevant ideas been eliminated?
   b. Have the ideas been grouped properly with reference to their relative importance?
8. Accuracy of interpretation.
   a. Have the data been accurately interpreted?
   b. Do the statements agree with generally accepted opinion and "common sense?" If not, is attention called to such disagreements?
9. Precision of statement.
   a. Are the statements made so that they will convey to the reader exactly the meaning intended?
   b. Are all statements worded so that ambiguity or indefiniteness is avoided?

C. Details of structure and form.

10. Diction.
    a. Have appropriate words and phrases been used at all times?
    b. Have particular words and phrases been used with a consistent meaning?
    c. Have words and phrases to which common practice has assigned technical meanings been used correctly?
    d. Has attention been called explicitly to each word or phrase used with an unusual or restricted meaning?
    e. Has the "over-working" of certain words been avoided?
11. Clearness.
    a. Is the vocabulary suitable for the intended audience?
    b. Are the ideas expressed in simple yet definite language?
12. Rhetoric, grammar, spelling, and punctuation.
    a. Have the rhetorical rules relative to unity, coherence, and emphasis in sentence and paragraph construction been properly observed?
    b. Have rules of grammar been observed?
    c. Are all words correctly spelled?
    d. Has consistency in the plan of punctuation been observed?
13. Form of tables and graphs.
    a. Are the captions of tables at the top and those of graphs at the bottom?
    b. Are the captions, box headings, and other labels sufficiently complete so that a competent reader will be able to understand the table or graph without referring to the accompanying text?

14. Explanation and interpretation of tables and graphs.
    a. Has the enumeration of the facts summarized in a table or diagram been minimized in the accompanying text?
    b. Is the accompanying text sufficiently complete so that it is unnecessary for the reader to refer to the table or diagram in order to follow the trend of thought?
    c. Are references to tables and graphs sufficiently explicit so that the reader will have no difficulty in locating the correct table or graph?
    d. In interpreting a table or graph, is the introduction of irrelevant facts or comments avoided, so that the trend of thought is not broken?
15. References to sources of information.
    a. Are bibliographical references given for statements or facts taken from the works of other persons?
16. Bibliographical form.
    a. Are all references both in footnotes and in bibliographies given in an approved bibliographical form?
17. Chapter titles, table of contents, preface, title page, order of paging, spacing, kind of paper, and so forth.
    a. Have conventional rules with reference to chapter titles, table of contents, and so forth been observed?
18. Footnotes.
    a. Have footnotes been used to give needed explanations or other comments which will make more certain a correct and complete understanding by the reader?
    b. Has material which would tend to break the trend of thought but which is desirable to include been placed in a footnote or in an appendix?
19. Miscellaneous.
    a. Have conventional rules with reference to abbreviations, division of words, spelling out numbers, and so forth been complied with?

Careless Practices and Errors in Educational Writings.— Probably many of the points listed in the preceding outline will be made more concrete if examples are selected from current educational literature. It should be stated that the authors of the bulletin from which the outline was taken illustrate many of the criteria in an effective manner. The writer will use seventeen educational books published late in 1926 and during 1927 to illustrate certain careless practices and errors in educational writings. Twenty different authors and eleven publishing houses are represented. The fields of psychology, writing, arithmetic, elementary method, educational theory, method in history, how to study, rural education, extra-curricular activities, supervised study, reading, and secondary method are represented one or more times in the group of volumes under consideration. A part of the material on this topic is adapted from discussions which are already available.[6]

Difficulties in Handling Bibliographies and Citations.— One of the common sources of difficulty in educational writing seems to be the handling of bibliographies and references to other authors. It will not be disputed that bibliographies should be arranged alphabetically by authors and that references to other authors should be cited in footnotes. Yet one of the books under consideration neglects at times the alphabetical arrangement; at times the author's name is listed first, and on other occasions the title of the volume is mentioned first. Some writers who list author and title in correct order neglect to be consistent in citing the volume number and date of publication of a magazine article, that is, the order of giving this data is not always the same and at times part of the information is omitted entirely. Two books which include reasonably complete information in bibliographical references do not follow a consistent plan with regard to the order in which the data are listed.

Two books follow a plan midway between the practice of citing references to other authors in footnotes and of

[6] Carter V. Good, "Careless Practices in Educational Writings," *School and Society*, XXIII (May 29, 1926), 684–86.

Carter V. Good, "Educational Writings, Editing and Errors," *School and Society*, XXVII (February 4, 1928), 146–50.

mentioning the references in the body of the text, that is, about one-half the citations involve each plan. Certainly the finished writer follows without question the plan of using footnotes in citing related investigations or subject matter. If the use of footnotes is irksome to certain authors or an unusually large number of citations is involved, a plan employed in the writing of the late S. C. Parker is quite effective. This plan involves the insertion of a numeral or two numerals at the proper place in the body of the text referring to an item in the bibliography at the end of the chapter or volume; the second numeral gives the page reference. This scheme has been very advantageously used in such digests[7] as Gray's *Summary of Investigations Relating to Reading* and Buswell and Judd's *Summary of Educational Investigations Relating to Arithmetic;* the former includes 436 references and the latter 320 references. It is rather commonly agreed that information concerning a book should include the following items: author, title, place of publication, publisher, date of publication, and number of pages. References to monographs and bulletins should include the same data as given for a book, with the additon of a description of the publication (name of series, and volume and number of the series).

Inconsistency in Abbreviations of Journals.—A few writers today make use of abbreviations in listing the titles of magazines, which is hardly a finished procedure. Two of the seventeen books manage to include several

[7] William Scott Gray, *Summary of Investigations Relating to Reading*. Supplementary Educational Monographs, No. 28. Chicago: Department of Education, University of Chicago, 1925. Pp. viii + 276.

Guy Thomas Buswell and Charles Hubbard Judd, *Summary of Educational Investigations Relating to Arithmetic*. Supplementary Educational Monographs, No. 27. Chicago: Department of Education, University of Chicago, 1925. Pp. viii + 212.

forms of abbreviation for the same journal. One of the authors uses the following abbreviations, in addition to the full title of the journal in question: *Jour. Educ. Psychol.*, *Jour. Ed. Psychol.*, *Jour. of Educational Psychology*, and *Jour. of Educ. Psychol.* One author uses two spellings of another writer's name; a second author is about evenly divided between using the first name with the surname and the initials with the surname of a writer to whom reference is frequently made.

Desirability of Complete Information in Citing References.—Seven of the seventeen books under consideration fail to give complete information in citing references. The most common omissions are: place of publication of books, page references of magazine articles, volume number of magazine articles, title of magazine articles, and adequate description of monographs and bulletins. One rather well-known author does not list a single page reference in the footnotes cited, even in the case of books, and in many instances fails to give volume number and title of article in magazine citations.

It has been suggested that a uniform procedure is desirable in referring to the contributions of other writers in the field. Too many authors simply adopt the slipshod practice of stating that John Doe said so and so, without giving the reference where the indirect quotation may be found; other writers give the complete reference in the body of the text. Such practices may save the author the inconvenience of being exact in his quotation or facilitate printing; certainly the former practice does not promote a scientific or questioning attitude on the part of the reader who should be encouraged to read as many quotations as possible in the original setting and in relation to the context. Of course the commonly accepted plan is to give citations in footnotes. In a book not included in the seventeen books a rather unusual scheme of asterisks, daggers, and other symbols is used to refer the reader to footnotes; it seems that the conventional Arabic numerals would be less confusing.

Helpfulness of Lists of Tables and Figures and of an Index.—Nine of the volumes in question do not include lists of tables and figures. Included in this number is a monograph which contains 148 numbered tables and five unnumbered tabulations of data. In such a case, the reader finds it necessary to thumb through the volume until he locates the desired data, whereas if a list of tables is provided the search for a particular item of information is greatly facilitated. Certainly if statistical data are worth including in a book, it seems that the reader deserves the guidance of simple mechanical aids in locating desired information.

Two of the books have no index and this omission is so inexcusable as to require no comment. In three of the books errors were found in the indexes. In one of the books published by a reputable house, the names of four authors selected at random from the index were followed by incorrect page references. The present writer is at a loss to explain such wholesale errors, unless the author tried to prepare a page index from galley proof, or the publisher scrambled the page proof after it had been returned. Four volumes have errors in listing the names and initials of authors, or in titles, or in both.

Careless Practices in Handling Tabular Data.—Eight of the seventeen books under discussion, with regard to the handling of tabular material, are partially lacking in one or more of the following respects: table headings, numbering of tables, poor arrangement, and inadequate headings. When a table is lacking in either title or number, the writer is somewhat embarrassed in referring to the tabulation of data and the reader frequently finds difficulty in following the author's interpretation of the data. One author is especially inconsistent when he frequently uses the work, "table," in referring to tabulations of data, but has not dignified such data by a table heading or number. An especially bad practice found in one volume is that of splitting a table heading up into two or more clauses or phrases separated by periods. A table heading should be adequately expressed in a continuous title describing the nature of the data presented. A few tables which cover more than one page are divided in an unfortunate way; sometimes even monosyllabic words are split so as to appear on different pages. Certainly it is a difficult matter to locate information buried in a tabulation of data which has neither heading nor number, even though the book may contain a list of the numbered tables. In one book instances were found in which two tables bore the same number. This happens more frequently when the author has quoted a table from another source and has neglected to give the tabulation a new number in keeping with his own scheme.

Difficulty in Identifying Yearbook and Bulletin References.—Embryo authors and even writers of experience seem to have considerable difficulty in listing references to yearbooks. Very frequently the information given is so inadequate as to be almost useless in locating the yearbook in question, but the following examples taken from different books are worse than incomplete: (*National Yearbook for the Study of Education*, 1923, Part II) and (Baldwin, B. T. A Measuring Scale for Growth and Physiological Age. Fifteenth Yearbook, N. S. G. E., 1916). The writer's guess is that each reference is intended to designate a yearbook of the National Society for the Study of Education, but the reader is permitted to draw his own conclusion and to search for the remainder of the information which should have been included.

A book not included in the seventeen volumes gives this almost hopelessly incomplete reference, "*Educational Monograph*, University of Chicago, 1925." Since this rather vague reference is given at the close of a chapter on the subject of arithmetic, the well informed reader may deduce that the author had in mind Buswell and Judd's summary of educational investigations in arithmetic published in 1925. However, it should not be necessary for the reader to guess at the author, title, or publisher of a reference listed.

Lack of Organization.—Three of the books are so lacking in paragraph headings, sectional headings, summary statements, summary paragraphs, and transitional paragraphs and statements as to render it unnecessarily difficult to follow the author's basal outline, if he had any. It is true that a few educational writers and a few readers may consider it a reflection on the intelligence of the reader to label plainly with key sentences or phrases the paragraphs and sections of a chapter. However, most writers and readers recognize that the extensive, rapid-reading procedures made necessary by the large amount of subject matter to be covered require every legitimate mechanical aid the writer and publisher can devise for use in following intelligently the trend of the discussion presented.

Consistency in Giving the Locations of Publishers.—The accepted practice is to list the main office of a publishing house in a bibliographical reference. Two of the books under consideration do not follow this procedure. In fact, one of these volumes in successive references has Ginn and Co. located at both New York and Boston. It may be stated that one author located Houghton Mifflin, Ginn, and Heath at New York, whereas all three firms have their publication offices at Boston. Throughout one book the name of a well-known publishing house appears as MacMillan. In another volume the name of the same firm appears as: Macmillan and Co., Macmillan Co., and The Macmillan Co.

Miscellaneous Inaccuracies and Unfinished Practices. One volume refers a number of times to Part V, when in fact the treatment is divided into only four parts. Possibly in such a case the original plan was to include five parts and subsequent proofreading did not detect the misstatements. Another book has the body of the text divided into Part I and Part II, and the Table of Contents indicates the existence of Part I, but fails to show that there is a second part; in fact all the chapters appear under the caption, "Part I." Doubtless both the above cases are due to careless proofreading, as well as hurried editing.

Two books draw quite heavily on previously published magazine articles of the authors, but no allusion is made to this former appearance of the material. An author is entirely within his rights in omitting any reference to an earlier appearance of his material, but it seems that the reader would profit by having such information. One can interpret better the chapter of a book if information is available concerning the journal in which the material previously appeared or concerning the professional organization before which the paper was read.

Rather unfinished writers, in many instances, use so frequently the academic and professional titles of authors whose material is quoted directly or indirectly that the reiteration becomes monotonous to the reader. Occasionally a writer, in his anxiety to demonstrate his knowledge of the academic qualifications of other authors, wrongly bestows the Doctor's degree. For instance, one writer confers this title upon the late S. C. Parker, a mistake frequently made, when in fact Professor Parker never quite found time in his busy life of teaching, writing, professional service, and struggling with ill health to complete the formal requirements for the Ph. D. degree.

Questionable English Usage.—More frequently than should be the case writers are careless about the principles of English usage. Loose sentence and paragraph structure are common; the split infinitive turns up with amazing regularity and occasionally subject and verb fail to agree in number. A quotation from one of the books under consideration is an example of amazingly loose sentence structure.

"Is the irregularity of beginning and ending of lines an advantage to first grade children of normal age, i.e. should every line in a paragraph, excepting the first, which is customarily indented, and the last, which may fall short due to lack of material, begin and end so as to form a solid margin, i.e., one with no indentations, or should the right margin be solid and the left margin irregular, or should the left margin be solid and the right irregular, or should both margins be irregular?"

A revised edition of a book appeared some time ago that contained an inexcusable number of errors in grammatical structure, sentence structure, and common English usage. Split infinitives, plural subjects with singular verbs, and loose sentence structure were common. The fact that the volume is a revised edition makes such errors all the more inexcusable.

It is a matter of regret that the reader's attention is so frequently distracted from quite valuable and worth while information by lapses in the form, mechanics, English usage, and style employed by the author. The writer should never become so wrapped up in his subject or so careless as to neglect the points enumerated above; to some these points will seem minor, yet they play an important part in determining the sort of impression that is made on the reader.

Authors and Editors Must Share the Blame for Careless Practices and Errors.—Unquestionably the major portion of blame for the careless practices enumerated in the preceding paragraphs must be charged to the author who is either careless or ignorant concerning proper procedures. The rest of the blame can be charged to the editor and publishing house. However, in justice to editors and publishers, it should be stated that they make fairly decent articles and books out of manuscripts that look almost impossible on first examination. The editorial staff of two well-known journals and a monograph series is so careful in its work as to check even the data and citations of references in manuscripts which are submitted. Possibly two or three of the research journals in education are equally careful in the work of editing. Three or four of the publishers of educational textbooks can be relied upon to turn out almost mechanically perfect pieces of work. All too frequently the journal of limited resources and the small publishing house with an over-taxed editorial staff print material verbatim as it comes from the pen of the author with the result that errors and lapses are numerous. One publishing house has been especially lax in editorial matters in an effort to turn out a large number of educational textbooks in a short time.

Examples of Good Writing.—For excellent examples of book-making and editorial work the reader is referred to publications of the University of Chicago Press, including the *School Review*, the *Elementary School Journal*, and the *Supplementary Educational Monographs*, and to the *Journal of Educational Research*. The works[8] of the late S. C. Parker are excellent examples of the textbook writer's art. It is said of Professor Parker that he made a careful study of the good features of numerous books before he started his program of educational writing.

Guidance of Graduate Students Who Are Preparing Theses.—An examination of the various references cited in this chapter will indicate that most of the writing on reporting educational research has been done within the past three or four years. A few years ago the graduate student had available very little material for use as a guide in the preparation of his thesis. Today a survey of twenty of the larger graduate schools or departments of education indicates that most of them are making some systematic attempt to instruct students concerning the principles involved in educational research and particularly in the reporting of investigations. However, much is yet to be accomplished in this respect.

The writer was fortunate enough to receive from a number of these graduate schools copies of the materials placed in the hands of graduate students for their guidance. Some interesting information was received in response to the following request:

We are canvassing the practice in some twenty of the larger graduate schools and departments of education with regard to guidance of graduate students in the preparation of theses. Will you be good enough to forward any printed or mimeographed materials which you distribute to graduate students for their guidance and which throw light on any of the following items?

1. Lists of problems suitable for investigation as thesis projects.
2. Lists of graduate theses on file in the library which are recommended for examination to graduate students.
3. Suggestions regarding the mechanics of thesis-construction—title page, table of contents, lists of tables and figures, tables,

[8] Books on method and a history of education published by Ginn and Co.

diagrams, figures, graphs, sectional and paragraph headings, citations, bibliographies, typing or printing, English usage, etc.

4. A seminar or research course which may be conducted almost exclusively for the benefit of those preparing theses.

5. Any other available materials and suggestions placed in the hands of graduate students for their guidance.

The information received from the office of the Secretary of the Department of Education, University of Chicago, is so suggestive that it seems appropriate to reproduce the material at some length. Other schools were supplying similar information in some form or providing other types of guidance. It will be recognized that the information given below should be of value to all who are interested in reporting educational research in an effective manner.

The Thesis

The Master's Thesis a Minor Piece of Research.—The Master's thesis is intended to give the student training in methods of research. It is not to consist simply of compilations from the discussions of other writers.

Objective Methods.—Subjective opinions and *a priori* theorizing have no place in such investigations. Clearly formulated hypotheses are necessary, but objective verification of these constitutes the most essential step in all investigations. Impartial procedure, precise measurement, and a minute study of the technique to be employed are of the first importance.

Independence in Research.—The requirement of a thesis is one of the most characteristic respects in which a graduate curriculum differs from undergraduate study. In the thesis the candidate is required to exhibit a mastery of educational problems and a mastery of scientific methods of solving these problems which will make it clear that he has attained a degree of intellectual independence. The candidate should accordingly find a subject in which he can have genuine intellectual interest. Members of the Department are glad to suggest subjects and discuss possible lines of investigation but they will not prescribe subjects. The candidate must show initiative in the choice of a subject. In like fashion, the candidate must carry out his work with reasonable independence. Consultations are always proper, but not efforts to get the work of the thesis done or even corrected in detail by members of the Department. The judgment of the Department with regard to the propriety of conferring a Master's degree is very largely determined by the candidate's initiative and ability as exhibited in preparing a thesis rather than by his success in particular courses.

Suggestions for Procedure.—It is suggested that the following points be observed by the candidate as he proceeds with his investigation.

1. A problem should be selected that is sufficiently limited in scope to permit of detailed and thorough investigation.

2. The member of the Department of Education who is a specialist in the type of technique involved in the problem selected should be consulted. He should understand that the problem is for a thesis. Confusion sometimes arises when theses grow out of term papers.

3. What has already been done upon closely related problems should be ascertained by means of thorough bibliographical work.

4. A detailed plan of the investigation should be made and all aspects of the technique should be submitted to the most rigorous criticism.

5. The technique involved should be tried on a few cases and necessary revision should be made before the candidate attempts to secure a large amount of material.

6. When the candidate is convinced that the problem is suitable for a thesis, he should secure from the office of the Secretary of the Department of Education an approval sheet for the subject of the thesis. This approval sheet should be filled out by the candidate and then taken or mailed to the member of the Department who is a specialist in the field in which the subject falls. When the approval sheet has been signed by some member of the Department, it should then be returned to the Secretary of the Department, who will present it to the Faculty, together with the student's application for candidacy. When the subject has been approved, the member of the Department who signed the approval sheet will act as the student's adviser throughout the preparation of the thesis. His criticism should be secured at all stages of the investigation, and when the thesis is in complete form it should be submitted to him for approval. If he is not willing to approve it in such form he will return it for further revisions. If the Adviser is satisfied with the thesis, he will then transmit it to the Secretary

of the Department with his recommendations. Final acceptance will be acted upon by the Secretary of the Department.

Date of Presentation.—No thesis will be received for examination after a date four weeks (five weeks in the Summer Quarter) prior to the Convocation at which the candidate expects to receive the degree. In general, the candidate should plan to present his thesis earlier than this date. The greatest difficulty arises because some candidates feel it their privilege to be late. The above rule is therefore emphasized as final, and candidates are notified that excuses, explanations, pleas, and other efforts to secure exemption from its operation will be absolutely and rigidly refused.

Form.—The thesis is acceptable or not acceptable according to the scientific character of the material presented. But, since it is difficult for the person passing upon the thesis to give his undivided attention to content if the form of the thesis is poor, the candidate is required to meet certain stipulated requirements in relation to the form of the thesis. The candidate should clearly understand that form is not a consideration in the acceptance or rejection of a thesis but that Advisers have been instructed not to consider a thesis for final approval until the form meets the requirements to be described in the following pages.

The Department of Education has adopted the University Press style for the form of its theses. It should be understood that other forms may be equally correct but that for the sake of uniformity the style adopted by the University Press will be insisted upon. In the following pages detailed directions relating to the form of the thesis are given. The candidate will save himself a great deal of labor if he will study these pages carefully before beginning to write. Ultimate conformity to this style will be required before the thesis is accepted. Furthermore, the candidate will be held responsible for adherence to proper form on the part of the stenographer who copies the thesis.

Most of the inadequacies of English expression could be eliminated if the candidate would carefully revise his manuscript before submitting it. Since such careful revision will be insisted upon before the thesis is accepted, it will save time both on the part of the Adviser and the student if all editing is carefully done before the thesis is submitted. Difficulty is frequently experienced when the final copies of the thesis are prepared, due to the fact that the candidate expects the typist to edit the manuscript and correct errors in spelling, punctuation, and tabulations as well as to make the copy. Such editing is expert service and cannot be expected of a typist at the ordinary rates of typing. The obligation of the typist ceases when exact copies are made of the material which is presented. This means that the candidate is responsible for spelling, punctuation, and all matters of form.

The Acquisition Department of Harper Memorial Library requires that the following points be observed when the final copies of the thesis are made.

1. Embassy bond paper (sixteen-pound weight) should be used for all three copies of the thesis, including the original, the first, and the second copies.

2. Black ribbon and black carbons should be used.

3. The margin on the left-hand side of each page should be an inch and a half in width, and at least three quarters of an inch should be left on the other three sides. It is necessary that the same margins be left in case of charts, graphs, statistical tables, etc.

Specimen pages of various parts of the thesis are given on the following sheets. These specimen sheets will furnish general models of form for the various parts of the thesis, and they should be carefully observed. [It should be stated that in setting up in type the various specimen pages of the thesis it has not been possible in every instance to reproduce exactly the effect of a typewritten document.] A list of the items illustrated, together with explanatory notes calling attention to certain details which are frequently overlooked, follows.

1. Title-Page.
   (a) Spacing should be precisely the same as in the sample given.
   (b) All capital letters should be used.
   (c) The full name (including the middle name if there is one) should be used.
   (d) The month and year should be that of the Convocation at which the degree is expected.
2. Table of Contents.
   (a) Capital letters should be used as in sample.
   (b) Introductory material (including table of contents, list of tables, and list of figures) should be numbered in small Roman numerals at the bottom of the page, using "ii" for the first page of the table of contents and omitting "i" on the title-page. All other pages of the body of the thesis (including the bibliography) are numbered at the top of the page with the exception of the first page of each chapter, which has the number placed at the bottom.

(c) The title of each chapter and the subdivisions under each should correspond exactly with the headings as they appear in the body of the thesis.

3. List of Tables.
   (a) Tables should be numbered in Roman numerals.
   (b) Titles of tables in the list of tables should not be written in capitals.
   (c) The title of each table in the list of tables should correspond exactly with the title on the page where the table appears.
4. List of Figures.[9]
   (a) Figures should be numbered in Arabic numerals.
   (b) Titles of figures in the list of figures should not be written in capitals.
   (c) The title of each figure in the list of figures should correspond exactly with the title on the page where the figure appears.
5. Sample Tables.
   (a) The word "TABLE" (written in capitals), together with the number of the table in Roman numerals, should be centered above the table.
   (b) A double ruling should appear below the title of the table.
   (c) A single ruling should appear at the end of the table.
   (d) Vertical rulings should be inserted as needed, and care should be taken that the heading above each particular section applies only to that section.
   (e) Uncommon abbreviations should be explained in footnotes below the table.
   (f) Footnotes in connection with the table should be referred to by stars, asterisks, or letters rather than by figures.
6. Sample Figures.
   (a) Figures should be numbered in Arabic numerals, followed by a period and a dash.
   (b) The legend should be placed beneath the figure.
   (c) The scale for the figure should appear below for horizontal, at the left for vertical.
   (d) Sufficient explanation of symbols should be given below the figure. This applies to different cross rulings in a bar diagram, different kinds of lines or colors in a line diagram, etc.

[9] Suggestions for figures are also applicable to diagrams, charts, maps, etc., depending on the type of the thesis.

7. Body of Text.[10]
   (a) The word "CHAPTER" (written in capitals), together with the number of the chapter in Roman numerals, should be centered above each chapter.
   (b) The title of the chapter (written in capitals) should be centered two spaces below the number of the chapter.
   (c) Major subheadings of the chapter should be written in small letters, centered, and not underlined. Minor subheadings should be written in small letters, run into the regular paragraph, underlined and followed by a period and a dash.

[10] In case the candidate is unable to make the form of his thesis conform to that recommended for the body of the text, he should devise a plan which he can follow consistently throughout the investigation.

(Sample title-page for A.M. dissertation—The Graduate School of Arts and Literature. The candidate is requested to follow this form *exactly*.)

The University of Chicago

Salaries, Experience, and Training of Teachers in the Second-class Cities of Kansas, 1924–1925

A DISSERTATION SUBMITTED TO THE GRADUATE FACULTY IN CANDIDACY FOR THE DEGREE OF MASTER OF ARTS

DEPARTMENT OF EDUCATION

By
CLYDE ULYSSES PHILLIPS

CHICAGO, ILLINOIS
September, 1926

TABLE OF CONTENTS

LIST OF TABLES

LIST OF FIGURES*

* The list of figures in the thesis should be placed on a separate sheet from the list of tables.

(Sample Table)

TABLE I

ACTIVITIES OF RURAL SUPERVISORS AND THE NUMBER OF HOURS DEVOTED TO EACH

Activity	Number of Hours	Rank	Rank Value
1. Office activities:			
Preparing suggestions for teachers.	253.2	1	2
Records and reports............	241.3	2	15
Correspondence................	164.7	3	18
Conference with teachers........	130.9	4	1
Preparing for visits—collecting materials, reports, etc.........	94.7	5	5
2. Miscellaneous activities:			
County meetings...............	355.2	1	2
Sectional meetings..............	247.3	2	1
Fair-exhibit work...............	138.5	3	8
Recreational institutes, play days, community clubs, etc..........	28.3	4	10
Preparing for professional meetings........................	16.5	5	3

(Sample Table)

TABLE II

CHRONOLOGICAL AGES, MENTAL AGES, INTELLIGENCE QUOTIENTS, AND READING SCORES OF SIX PUPILS IN GRADE IV

Pupil	Chronological Age	Mental Age	I.Q.*	Monroe Silent Reading Test		T-Score—Thorndike-McCall Reading Scale
				Rate	Comprehension	
1..........	10–2	8– 8	85	131	7	35
2..........	10–1	8–10	87	106	4	35
3..........	11–3	10– 3	91	44	4	38
4..........	10–5	9– 4	89	81	7	36
5..........	10–4	9–11	95	72	5	45
6..........	10–2	10–11	107	128	8	43
September standard...	....	.....	...	122	7.7	39.6

* *Haggerty Intelligence Examination, Delta 2.*

(Sample Page of a Thesis)

CHAPTER IV

THE TESTS

Justification of the Use of Tests

Tests were used extensively throughout the experiment for the purpose of pre-testing, teaching, and checking results.

In order to have a definite and objective basis for comparing the results of the two methods of teaching, tests were constructed and given at the conclusion of each unit of the course. The results were then tabulated and analyzed. These comparisons form the chief basis for the conclusions of the thesis.

Criticisms of Tests.—There are many criticisms advanced regarding tests and their value for comparative purposes. However, specialists in the testing field seem to agree that such a use of tests is justifiable. Charles Russell, principal of the Massachusetts State Normal School at Westfield, Massachusetts, makes the following contention.

> One of the results of the testing which is now being done in the elementary schools is that a teacher may compare his class and the work of its individual members with like pupils in like classes in other places . . . Tests may furnish the only reliable means by which this can be done.[1]

The same author believes that the efficiency of a teacher may be measured by means of tests. If this is

[1] Charles Russell, *Classroom Tests*, pp. 7–8. Boston: Ginn & Co., 1926.

(Sample Figure)

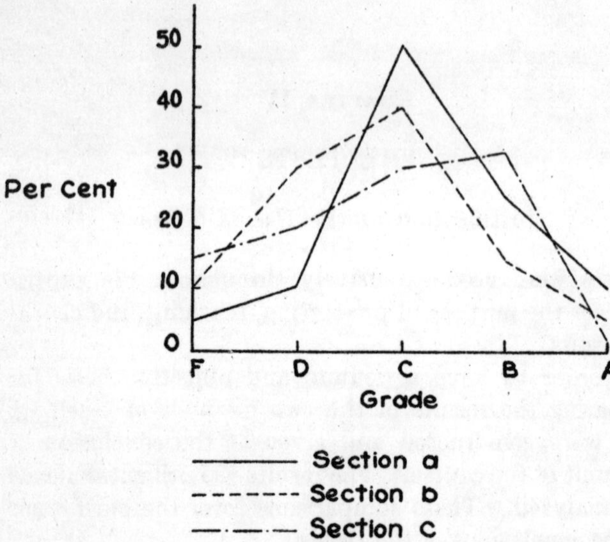

Fig. 21.—Distribution of grades for three sections of first-year algebra.

Bibliography

The bibliography conforms in style to that adopted by the *Elementary School Journal* and other publications of the Department of Education, University of Chicago, as illustrated by the following examples.

ARTICLES

Anderson, C. J. "The Use of the Woody Scale for Diagnostic Purposes," *Elementary School Journal*, XVIII (June, 1918), 770–81.

"Junior High Schools in Denver," *School Review*, XXXVI (February, 1928), 85–86.

BOOKS

Bode, Boyd H. *Modern Educational Theories.* New York: Macmillan Co., 1927. Pp. xiv + 352.

Guidance of Childhood and Youth: Readings in Child Study. Compiled by Child Study Association of America. Edited by Benjamin C. Gruenberg. New York: Macmillan Co., 1926. Pp. xii + 324.

Judd, Charles Hubbard. *Genetic Psychology for Teachers*, pp. 265–96. New York: D. Appleton & Co., 1903.

Matthews, Mary Lockwood. *Foods and Cookery.* Boston: Little, Brown & Co., 1926 (revised). Pp. xii + 298.

MISCELLANEOUS MATERIAL

Alter, Donald R., and Others. *Instructional Activities in the University High School.* Educational Research Circular No. 47. University of Illinois Bulletin, Vol. XXIV, No. 13. Urbana, Illinois: University of Illinois, 1926. Pp. 28.

Catalogue of Wesleyan University, 1927–1928. Wesleyan University Bulletin, Vol. XXI, No. 6. Middletown, Connecticut: Wesleyan University, 1927. Pp. 190.

The Courtis Standard Tests in Boston, 1912–1915: *An Appraisal.* School Document No. 15, 1916. Bulletin No. X of the Department of Educational Investigation and Measurement. Boston: Boston Printing Department, 1916. Pp. 48.

Elliott, Charles Herbert. *Variation in the Achievements of Pupils.* Teachers College Contributions to Education, No. 72. New

York: Teachers College, Columbia University, 1914. Pp. iv + 114.

Gray, William Scott. *Summary of Investigations Relating to Reading.* Supplementary Educational Monographs, No. 28. Chicago: Department of Education, University of Chicago, 1925. Pp. viii + 276.

High School Principals' Conference. Bulletin of the School of Education, Indiana University, Vol. III, No. 2. Bloomington, Indiana: University Bookstore, 1926. Pp. 28.

Report of a Survey of the State Institutions of Higher Learning in Indiana. Indianapolis, Indiana: Board of Public Printing, 1926. Pp. 206.

Studies in Education. Yearbook Number XV of the National Society of College Teachers of Education, 1926. Chicago: University of Chicago Press, 1927. Pp. viii + 206.

Wilson, G. M. "A Survey of the Social and Business Use of Arithmetic," *Second Report of the Committee on Minimal Essentials in Elementary-School Subjects,* pp. 128–42. Sixteenth Yearbook of the National Society for the Study of Education, Part I. Bloomington, Illinois: Public School Publishing Co., 1917.

The Winston Simplified Dictionary: Advanced Edition. Edited by William Dodge Lewis, Henry Seidel Canby, and Thomas Kite Brown, Jr. Philadelphia: John C. Winston Co., 1926. Pp. xx + 1260.

UNPUBLISHED MATERIAL

Osburn, W. J. "Improvement in the Fundamentals of Arithmetic." Madison, Wisconsin: State Department of Public Instruction, 1923 (mimeographed). Pp. 12.

Staker, Moses Roy. "A Study of the Mistakes in the Fundamental Operations in Arithmetic." Unpublished Master's thesis, Department of Education, University of Chicago, 1917. Pp. 71.

LEGAL MATERIAL

Atlantic Reporter, 1885–1927.

Legislative Acts of Ohio, 1850–1900.

Reports of the Supreme Court of Ohio, 1920–27.

Session Laws of Wisconsin, 1920–26.

FOOTNOTES

The form of a footnote reference is the same as that of a bibliographical reference except that the author's name is written as "C. J. Anderson" instead of "Anderson, C. J." and a comma instead of a period follows the name. For example, the footnote reference for the first item in the bibliography is written as follows:

[1] C. J. Anderson, "The Use of the Woody Scale for Diagnostic Purposes," *Elementary School Journal*, XVIII (June, 1918), 770–81.

Examples for footnotes in legal material follow.

[2] *Barry* v. *McCollom*, 81 Conn. 293, 129 Am. St. Rep. 215, 70 Atl. 1035.

[3] *Laws of Nebraska*, 1919, chap. 44, sec. 843.

[4] *Burn's Annotated Statutes of Indiana*, 1925, Vol. II, sec. 6448.

[5] *School Laws of Pennsylvania*, 1925, sec. 1432.

[6] *Compiled Statutes of Nebraska*, 1922, sec. 6509.

[7] *Revised Statutes of Kansas*, annotated, 1923, act. 48, sec. 28.

[8] *Smith* v. *Johnson*, 105 Neb. 61, 178 N. W. 835, 12 A. L. R. 231.

CHECK LIST FOR MASTERS' THESES

To the Candidate:

Before handing your thesis to your Adviser for his final approval, check each of the items listed below and secure Professor Breed's signature to the statement relating to the bibliography. Attach this sheet to the first page of your thesis. Advisers have been requested not to read a thesis until the items of form listed below have been checked by the student.

....1. Title-page according to mimeographed sample.

....2. Table of contents, list of tables, and list of figures according to mimeographed sample.

....3. Statistical tables checked for accuracy.

....4. Ruling and typing of tables according to sample.

....5. Title of each chapter identical in table of contents and body of thesis. Titles of tables and figures identical in lists of tables and figures and body of thesis.

....6. Tables and figures appear on page following their first mention.

....7. Pages properly numbered, including tables and figures.

....8. Carefully edited for punctuation, grammar, and sentence structure.

I have given careful attention to each of the items checked.

(Signed).....................................

(Candidate)

....

For Professor Breed:

I approve the present form of the footnotes and bibliography in the thesis of...

(Signed).....................................

(Mr. Breed)

Samples of Bibliographical Form.—In a previous discussion of this chapter it was stated that writers find difficulty in giving adequate information in a uniform manner concerning monographs, yearbooks, bulletins, and articles within yearbooks or monographs. A list of references has been compiled for the purpose of illustrating virtually every type of reference with which the student of education comes in contact in his work. The form is that used by the University of Chicago Press. It should be emphasized that the important thing is not so much to select the scheme used by a given institution or publishing house, but to follow consistently *some* good plan. Certainly the bibliographical form suggested below is one of the best. It will be recognized that educational workers who are preparing reports for a particular institution, journal, or publishing house will find it economical to use the plan followed by the institution or press in question.

The types and accompanying numbers of the references illustrated are as follows: book, 1; magazine article, 2; monographs, 3, 5, 6; article within a monograph, 4; bulletins, 8, 11, 12, 13, 14; school survey, 7; yearbook, 9; article within a yearbook, 10; thesis, 15; and term paper, 16.

Bibliographical references (books)
Author
Title
Place of publication
Publisher
Date
Pages

Bibliographical references (periodicals)
Author
Title
Name of periodical (in full)
Number of volume in Roman numerals
Month and year of publication in parentheses
Number of pages inclusive on which article appears

Bibliographical references (monographs and bulletins)
Author
Title
Description (name of series, volume and number of series)
Place
Publisher
Date
Pages

1. O'Brien, John A. *Silent Reading.* New York: Macmillan Co., 1921. Pp. xiv + 290.
2. Lyman, R. L. "How High-School Seniors Explain Common Errors in Reasoning," *English Journal,* XII (May, 1923), 293–305.
3. Buswell, Guy Thomas. *Fundamental Reading Habits: A Study of Their Development.* Supplementary Educational Monographs, No. 21. Chicago: Department of Education, University of Chicago, 1922. Pp. xiv + 150.
4. Beauchamp, Wilbur L. "A Preliminary Study of Technique in the Mastery of Subject-Matter in Elementary Physical Science," *Studies in Secondary Education,* I, pp. 47–87. Supplementary Educational Monographs, No. 24. Chicago: Department of Education, University of Chicago, 1923.
5. Curtis, Francis Day. *Some Values Derived from Extensive Reading of General Science.* Teachers College Contributions to Education, No. 163. New York: Teachers College, Columbia University, 1924. Pp. vi + 142.
6. *Improvement in the Teaching of Reading.* Supplement to the Course of Study in Reading, Elementary and Secondary

Grades. Bureau of Research Monographs, Number 1. Baltimore: Bureau of Research, City Department of Education, 1926. Pp. 130.

7. Ferriss, Emery N. *Rural School Survey of New York State: The Rural High School.* Ithaca, New York: Joint Committee on Rural Schools, 1922. Pp. 188.

8. Swift, Fletcher Harper. *The Public School System of Arkansas: Public School Finance.* Bureau of Education Bulletin No. 11, 1923. Washington: Bureau of Education. Pp. iv + 110.

9. *Educational Yearbook of the International Institute of Teachers College, Columbia University,* 1924. Edited by I. L. Kandel. New York: Macmillan Co., 1925. Pp. xiv + 650.

10. Gray, William S. "Individual Difficulties in Silent Reading in the Fourth, Fifth, and Sixth Grades," *Report of the Society's Committee on Silent Reading,* pp. 39–53. Twentieth Yearbook of the National Society for the Study of Education, Part II. Bloomington, Illinois: Public School Publishing Co., 1921.

11. *Health for School Children.* School Health Studies, No. 1. Washington: Bureau of Education, 1923. Pp. 76.

12. Monroe, Walter S. *A Critical Study of Certain Silent Reading Tests.* University of Illinois Bulletin, Vol. XIX, No. 22. Urbana, Illinois: University of Illinois, 1922. Pp. 52.

13. National Education Association (Research Division), "What National Defects Result from the Weak Spots in Our Public School System?" *Research Bulletin of the National Education Association, I* (September, 1923), 276–86.

14. Mooney, W. B. "Reading," *A Self-Survey of the Sterling Public Schools, District Number Twelve, Logan County, Colorado, Colorado State Teachers College Cooperating,* pp. 46–73. Colorado State Teachers College Bulletin, Series XVII, No. 5. Greeley, Colorado: Colorado State Teachers College, 1917.

15. Tingelstad, Oscar Adolf. "Religious Element in American School Readers." Unpublished Master's thesis, Department of Education, University of Chicago, 1913.

16. Clark, Sarah B. "The Amount of Reading in the First Three Grades of the Elementary School." Unpublished term paper on file in the office of the Department of Industrial Arts, Teachers College, Columbia University, 1917.

Other Sources of Information on Reporting Research.—A number of references are available to the educational worker who wishes assistance in the preparation of reports.[12] The various sources of information are listed without comment, since in most cases the title indicates the character of the contribution. An especially helpful section of a book in the curriculum field

[12] Carter Alexander, *School Statistics and Publicity*, Chapter XII. New York: Silver, Burdett and Co., 1919.

William F. Book, *Learning How to Study and Work Effectively*, Chapter XVIII. Boston: Ginn and Co., 1926.

Claude C. Crawford, *The Technique of Study*, Chapter XI. Boston: Houghton Mifflin Co., 1928.

Garland Greever and Easley S. Jones, *The Century Handbook of Writing*. New York: Century Co., 1918. Pp. xii + 228.

John Matthews Manly and John Arthur Powell, *A Manual for Writers*. Chicago: University of Chicago Press, 1913. Pp. viii + 226.

A Manual of Style. Chicago: University of Chicago Press, 1920. Pp. x + 300.

National Committee on Research in Secondary Education, *An Outline of Methods of Research with Suggestions for High School Principals and Teachers*, pp. 25–26. Bureau of Education Bulletin, No. 24, 1926. Washington: Bureau of Education.

Ward G. Reeder, *How to Write a Thesis*, pp. 49–132. Bloomington, Illinois: Public School Publishing Co., 1925.

Harold O. Rugg, *Statistical Methods Applied to Education*, Chapter X. Boston: Houghton Mifflin Co., 1917.

W. C. Schluter, *How to Do Research Work*, Chapters XIV–XVI. New York: Prentice-Hall, 1926.

Jesse B. Sears, *The School Survey*, pp. 17–18. Boston: Houghton Mifflin Co., 1925.

Standard Requirements for Written Work. Chicago: School of Education, University of Chicago, 1922. Pp. 8.

Style Manual of the Government Printing Office, ed., February, 1923. Washington: Government Printing Office, 1923. Pp. 224.

G. M. Wood, *Suggestions to Authors*. Washington: Government Printing Office, 1913. Pp. 64.

deals with editing the course of study.[13] The author was led to prepare this treatment as a result of finding many undesirable practices followed in the printed courses of study of public-school systems.

Accuracy and Intellectual Honesty in Educational Writings.—The need for accuracy in making statements and citing references has been emphasized a number of times in preceding discussions. The desirability of care in presenting any kind of information or data has been pointed out. This necessary qualification of the true scientist may be expressed once more in the form of a quotation from an excellent editorial.[14]

> The price of accuracy is quite evidently eternal vigilance. The degree to which it is feasible or desirable having been determined in the light of purposes and the nature of the data with which we deal, one must persistently strive for it by defining terms and simplifying procedure while gathering the information, by applying the known theorems concerning accuracy, by adopting an accuracy routine during the compiling, tabulating, and interpreting of the data, and finally by painstaking care during the period when the final report is passing through the hands of the printer.
>
> . . . .
>
> With particular reference to educational workers, we believe the ideals for insuring accuracy are not as high as they should be. Very likely this is likewise true of workers in other fields. Not only—as we have had repeated occasion to know in our editorial work—do figures in different tables of the same report often fail to "check up," but little effort appears to have been made to rid the data of such error as even an editor may detect. Some of the most competent workers are so much interested in devising tests and increasing the volume of material on which their conclusions rest that they have failed to devote the attention to accuracy which, in our judgment, it demands.

[13] Henry Harap, *The Technique of Curriculum Making*, pp. 229–34. New York: Macmillan Co., 1928.

[14] "Accuracy," *Journal of Educational Research*, VIII (June, 1923), 63–67.

Plagiarism and Intellectual Dishonesty.—When an author fails to give complete and exact information concerning the source of data or facts presented, it is ordinarily assumed that his training has been poor or that he has grown careless in his writing. When a writer takes data from the work of another and deliberately refrains from giving the source of the information, presenting the material as his own, the procedure is known as plagiarism. This is a form of intellectual dishonesty equivalent to theft of more tangible property and is likewise punishable under the law. Two examples will be used as illustrations of plagiarism.

Quite recently at a large graduate school of education a Doctor's thesis was accepted and published as a number of a well-known monograph series. The monograph was distributed to professional journals for review, advertised, and sold for a short time. Two or three experts in the field treated recognized fairly large portions of the thesis as ill-disguised paraphrasings of a previously published book on the same subject. When these facts were called to the attention of the graduate school in question appropriate regret was expressed and a request went out that all copies of the thesis be returned and that no reviews be published. Its number was struck from the list of the monograph series in question. It is said that the entire edition of the publication was burned, and the illegitimate Ph.D. was called back to his graduate school for severe criticism. The consequences of such intellectual dishonesty were far reaching in that discredit was reflected upon the graduate student involved, the faculty committee which accepted the thesis, the graduate school itself, and the cause of education.

An author of books on method in arithmetic found in a state teachers' journal an article which seemed strangely familiar. A little investigation proved that the article was made up almost entirely of material copied verbatim from one of his books on method; no recognition was given to the author of the book. The editor of the journal was contrite and demanded that the writer of the article, an obscure teacher in a small community, apologize to the author of the book which had been plagiarized. It is entirely possible that in this instance the offender may have been merely ignorant concerning professional ethics. Certainly in the case of the candidate for the Doctor's degree a similar explanation would not be acceptable.

Copyright Law and Professional Ethics.—The preceding discussion raises the question of copyright law and infringement of copyrighted material, which is punishable under the law. Copyright law cannot be stated in definite terms so as to cover all cases. In a given case decision as to what constitutes infringement is a problem for skilled lawyers and the courts. However, infringement or plagiarism may be described as copying in whole or in part the copyrighted work of another with intent to evade the law. According to the present writer's interpretation, slight alterations and paraphrasings made with a view to evading the law, would not avoid liability for infringement. Thus, dramatization of a copyrighted book would constitute infringement. It has not been definitely decided just what length a quotation or reproduction must be to constitute infringement. The safe rule is to secure permission to quote copyrighted materials, whatever the length, and certainly it is highly desirable to obtain such permission if the quotation is of any considerable length, such as a few sentences or a few lines. Publishers of copyrighted professional journals and monograph series as a rule are quite generous in granting permission to quote and ordinarily satisfactory arrangements for quoting can be made with commercial publishing houses. The young writer who observes the simple rules of accuracy and professional ethics should never find himself involved in tangles such as resulted in the cases of the graduate student and the contributor to the state teachers' journal. For an excellent brief statement of copyright law the reader is referred to a manual prepared by one of the high-grade publishing houses.[15]

Hygienic Requirements of Printed Materials and Typographical Information.—The reader who wishes information concerning certain mechanical problems involved in bookmaking will find several references on the subject available. Gray[16] has summarized the various experiments made to determine the hygienic requirements of printed materials, including style of type, legibility of different letters, length of line, regularity in length of line, distance between lines, size of type, thickness of vertical strokes, spacing, color of type, color and texture of paper, color of pictures, and size of book. Standards for size, spacing, and leading of type in school books have been prepared by a committee.[17] Specimens of types in use may be found in a manual published by the University of Chicago Press.[18]

[15] John Matthews Manly and John Arthur Powell, *A Manual for Writers*, pp. 205–10. Chicago: University of Chicago Press, 1913.

[16] William Scott Gray, *Summary of Investigations Relating to Reading*, Chapter XV. Supplementary Educational Monographs, No. 28. Chicago: Department of Education, University of Chicago, 1925.

[17] Committee on the Standardization of School Books of the American School Hygiene Association, *American Physical Education Review*, XVI (1911), 254–57.

[18] *A Manual of Style*, pp. 137–281. Chicago: University of Chicago Press, 1920.

Submitting a Manuscript to an Appropriate Journal or Publishing House.—The individual interested in publishing articles, monographs, or books should make a careful study of the professional periodicals, monograph series, and publishing houses in his field. Frequently a worth-while contribution is declined by a journal or publisher because the manuscript is unsuited to the established purposes of the periodical or the audience to which the publishing house caters. For instance, there is a professional journal which makes a specialty of publishing inaugural addresses of college administrative officers and papers delivered before learned societies; it would be out of place for authors to send such manuscripts to a technical research journal. The same periodical publishes a great deal of material dealing with problems of higher education; it would be inappropriate to send similar material to a journal of elementary or secondary education. It is almost a foregone conclusion that publishers of general educational textbooks will decline technical or highly specialized monographs, however meritorious they may be. However, there are a number of monograph series in which deserving contributions of this type may be made available. Two publishing houses in particular make available single contributions of the research type. The wise writer will study carefully the purposes and audiences of professional journals and publishing houses before submitting his manuscript for consideration. Such a procedure should prevent much embarrassment, disappointment, and discouragement.

Relations with Professional Journals.—In due time, after a manuscript has been accepted by the editor of a periodical, galley proof of the article is usually sent to the author. However, some editorial staffs publish articles without submitting proof to the author. Of course, in cases where proof is submitted the author is expected to make corrections and to return the corrected proof immediately. Certain subsequent remarks concerning proofreading and symbols used in proofreading apply alike to articles in periodicals and books. Preparation of reports of experimentation or investigation for publication in periodicals is considered a professional service for which there is usually no monetary reward; the writer knows of only two educational journals which buy articles and even in such cases the compensation is nominal. However, most educational periodicals recognize an author's efforts by supplying without cost to the author one or more of the following: copies of the issue in which the article appears, reprints (often involving a sum sufficient to cover the cost of printing), or subscription to the journal for a stated period of time.

Seeing a Book Safely through the Press.—The most common arrangement for publication with commercial houses is on the royalty basis, that is, the publisher assumes all responsibility relative to printing, advertisement, and sale of the book and pays the author a percentage of the sales, probably five to ten per cent.

It is assumed that the author has done his best to prepare a perfect copy before submitting the manuscript to the publisher, although in many cases this assumption is not valid. The various phases of preparing a report have been emphasized in preceding discussions. It should be added that it is highly desirable to number consecutively the pages of the copy; otherwise confusion may result in setting up the material, at considerable expense to publisher and author. Footnotes may well be numbered consecutively throughout a given chapter or section of the book. If the author has done a careful, conscientious piece of work, there should be a minimum of editorial work to be done on the manuscript by the publishing house. However, in any event, it is necessary to do a certain amount of editing in order to eliminate errors of various kinds which usually creep in; to apply the criterion of consistency in capitalization, punctuation, spelling, citations, bibliographies, etc.; to mark passages, chapter heads, etc. for the size and character of type to to be used; to prescribe rules for setting up tabular material; etc. Probably no better watchword than consistency could be suggested for the benefit of young writers.

In addition to the body of the manuscript the writer should submit, in the order given, the preliminary pages consisting of title page, preface, table of contents, list of tables, and list of figures or illustrations. If this material does not accompany the manuscript proper, it is likely to be overlooked. Of course the paging of the table of contents and list of tables or figures cannot be determined until page proof is available. It is likewise true that the index cannot be prepared until page proof is in the hands of the author. The importance of a good index cannot be overemphasized. In preparing an index it has proved helpful to copy the topics or names on cards which can be assembled and arranged in alphabetical order.

When the galley proof is received by the author he will find it helpful to have another person read aloud the copy or manuscript while he himself makes any necessary corrections on the proof. It must be kept in mind that to change even one punctuation mark or a single letter of matter set up on the linotype makes it necessary to reset the whole line. If insertions or deletions are made so as to involve a different length of line, it will probably be necessary to reset the material from that point to the end of the paragraph. When a word or phrase is changed it is desirable to use a new word or phrase of approximately the same length as the deleted material in order to avoid resetting the rest of the paragraph. Obviously, to make very many changes is expensive to publisher and author, though all essential corrections should be made. The economical plan is to have the copy in first-class condition when it is submitted to the publisher, then there will be only the usual typographical printer's errors to correct.

After the galley proof has been returned to the publisher, corrections are made and the type is broken up into pages. Page proof is then sent to the author who should read it carefully to see that paging and running heads (the lines at the top of pages) are correct, since these lines were not in the galley proof. The author should pay special attention to the lines at the top or bottom of pages, footnotes, letters and punctuation marks at the end of lines, tables and figures, and changes indicated in the galley proof. Page numbers may be inserted in the table of contents and lists of tables, figures, or illustrations. The index should be prepared. Attention should be given to any points in the body of the text where cross references have been made by page number. Changes in page proof are expensive, since the addition or deletion of a single line may mean that every following page to the end of the chapter must be made over in order to keep the pages of equal length.

The problems involved in seeing a book safely and accurately through the press or in seeing that an article appears in print in the most effective manner are important. More detailed information than that given above concerning these problems is available.[19]

[19] John Matthews Manly and John Arthur Powell, *op. cit.*, pp. 151–210.

Walter S. Monroe and Max D. Engelhart, *op. cit.*, pp. 78–84.

PROOFREADER'S MARKS

	Delete and close up
	Reverse
	Close up
#	Insert space
¶	Paragraph
□	Indent one em
[	Move to left
]	Move to right
	Lower
	Elevate
∧	Insert marginal addition
V∧	Even space
X	Broken letter
	Push down space
	Straighten line
‖	Align type
	Insert comma
	Insert apostrophe
	Insert quotes
=|	Hyphen
em|	Em dash
en|	En dash
;|	Insert semicolon
	Insert colon and en quad
	Insert period and en quad
?|	Insert interrogation point
	Query to author
	Use ligature
sp	Spell out
tr	Transpose
wf	Wrong font
bf	Set in **bold face** type
rom	Set in roman type
ital	Set in *italic* type
caps	Set in CAPITALS
sc	Set in SMALL CAPITALS
lc	Set in lower case
	Lower-case letter
stet	Let it stand
no ¶	Run in same paragraph
ld>	Insert lead between lines
hr #	Hair space between letters

Proofreader's marks in common use should be studied carefully and followed closely in making corrections on proof. The preceding list of symbols should prove generally satisfactory.[20]

Due Praise to the High-grade Editor and Publisher.—A discussion of reporting educational research would not be complete without a word of appreciation for the excellent work done by the editors of many professional journals and commercial publishing houses. These comments will be made with full recognition of the limitations of a regrettably large number of editors and publishers. The editor frequently makes a reasonably good book or article out of a manuscript which on first examination appears almost hopeless in form. It is to be regretted that the energies of editors so often must be consumed in such mechanical tasks. It is likewise a matter of concern that many writers are too careless, too unconcerned, or too ignorant to prepare first-class manuscripts. An editorial writer very appropriately has expressed a commendation of the work of editors in general.[21]

> A silent aid if not a "ghost writer" stands behind the finished work of many a successful author. He (or she) is the editor who labors for long hours over the manuscript, the galleys, and the page proof. In the finished production his name rarely appears; yet to him must go the credit for many a succinct phrase, for many an appropriate word, for a large part of the mechanical correctness, appropriateness, and beauty, and for the general form and style of the completed work. With him work the other less well known technicians who have to do with the making of books and magazines. To the editor and his helpers the author owes, but seldom gives, their due of praise and thanks.
>
> The making of a book or magazine is no simple task. Eternal vigilance is the price of perfection. In the securing of fine precision

[20] Forwarded with proof by the University of Chicago Press.

[21] "Praise to the Editor," *University of Pittsburgh School of Education Journal*, III (January–February, 1928), 58–59.

in diction, beauty of style, and mechanical beauty no person has quite so much influence as the careful editor. He catches the careless author at every turn. He has a fine ear attuned to dissonant words and phrases, a fine eye for the detection of misplaced marks of punctuation, a positive genius for the insertion of the illusive comma, the sturdy semi-colon, and the stalwart colon. To him the loose sentence is a simple thing, the split infinitive a matter of slight difficulty, and the misplaced phrase a problem of simple transposition. The printer's legend "one line short" is a trivial question of mere language ingenuity. With consummate care he puts in a shim here, tightens a bolt there, and adds the ever-needed lockwasher to keep the whole thing snug and workmanlike. Yet in all of this skilled and exacting work, the editor carries on in a modest manner; he is courteous and kindly. He constantly says to the struggling author, "Would you prefer this, or shall we let the original stand?" Truly in the making of books and magazines he has a grand and noble part.

In the making of educational books, the editor has a very large share. Such work is exacting and technical. Facts are facts, principles are principles, and must be accurately stated. And it may be said, without casting reflections upon any one, that writing is an art which many educational workers do not possess. The fine appearance, the mechanical correctness, and the smooth and effective style of many of our educational books and magazines, therefore, owe a great deal to the ever present, but generally silent, editor. Praise to him, and to her—for in an astonishingly large number of cases it is "her." Women seem to have a special aptitude for the making of magazines and books.

Chapter X

EVALUATING EDUCATIONAL WRITINGS AND PROFESSIONAL BOOKS

The Need for Critical Evaluation.—Nearly 450 publications[1] dealing with teaching and school administration were issued in 1927. Probably 1,500 to 2,000 articles appeared in educational periodicals during the same year. Since it is humanly impossible for a single individual to read this entire mass of material, methods of evaluating articles and books must be developed as an aid in selecting significant contributions for reading, study, textbook use, and supplementary assignments. Even the comparatively small portion of the total output of educational writings which is perused by a given individual should be subjected to a process of critical evaluation. Undergraduate and graduate students, public-school workers, and investigators are frequently confronted with the necessity of determining the significance of a new book or article. This judgment involves an evaluation of both content and form.

Criteria to be considered in planning a report were outlined at some length in Chapter IX. The same criteria are equally applicable in judging the worth and effectiveness of a completed work prepared by one's self or by another writer. Chapter IV, which deals with the characteristics of scientific investigations, should prove of service in evaluating a report of educational research.

[1] "Sixty Educational Books of 1927," *Journal of the National Education Association*, XVII (March, 1928), 95–98.

In fact, most of the information included in Chapters III-IX should be useful in determining whether appropriate standards of technique, content, and form have been maintained in reports of investigations and experiments, educational writings, and professional books. This evaluation may be merely an oral estimate presented informally before a group of students or colleagues or in conversation with a person of similar interests. It may appear in the form of a published book review or a critical comment in an article or book. There may be only the unexpressed and inarticulate evaluation of the publication in the mind of the reader.

Other Criteria for Use in Evaluating Educational Research.—In addition to the comprehensive list of criteria outlined in Chapter IX, two other discussions of standards may be mentioned. Brooks[2] states that the most important standards in evaluating a given piece of educational research are: (1) the exact delimitation of the problem; (2) its thoroughgoing analysis into constituent elements or subordinate problems; (3) its historical background, especially those researches which contribute toward its solution; (4) the selection and use of the method or methods best suited to its investigation; (5) the careful collection and critical evaluation of data bearing upon it; (6) the sound interpretation of data in relation to it; and (7) reaching the solution or conclusion to which the data most reasonably lead. He mentions a number of the more common deficiencies found in educational studies.

Alexander[3] lists the standards by which a dissertation in educational administration at Teachers College,

[2] Fowler D. Brooks, "Criteria of Educational Research," *School and Society*, XVIII (December 22, 1923), 724–29.

[3] Carter Alexander and Others, *Educational Research*, pp. 2–4. New York: Bureau of Publications, Teachers College, Columbia University, 1927.

Columbia University, is judged. These criteria are grouped under six headings: the problem, data, method, presentation, conclusions, and mechanics.

Characteristics of Good Textbooks.—Today a great deal of careful research goes into the writing of a good educational textbook. Consequently the evaluation of textbooks may very appropriately be discussed in this chapter. Certainly, educational workers are quite frequently confronted with the necessity of selecting appropriate textbooks for personal use, professional libraries, or for students. Worcester[4] discusses certain problems which should be kept in mind by those who write and select college textbooks: general comprehensibility and vocabulary difficulties, burden of detail, titles of tables and graphs, appropriateness for a given group of students, accuracy in mechanics and statements, modern point of view, agreement on minimum essentials especially for beginners, and outstanding problems yet unsolved in the field studied.

Hall-Quest[5] devotes a chapter to the selection and judging of textbooks and presents lists of standards for evaluating texts in a number of the school subjects. Another chapter is concerned with certain mechanical aids such as summaries, illustrations, questions and problems, references for supplementary reading, cross references, etc.

Rating Courses of Study.—Attention should be directed to an attempt which has been made to work out a technique for rating elementary courses of study. This experiment involves 107 judges and 191 courses of study,

[4] D. A. Worcester, "Some Characteristics of a Good College Textbook," *School and Society*, XXVII (February 18, 1928), 193–96.

[5] Alfred Lawrence Hall-Quest, *The Textbook: How to Use and Judge It*, Chapters IV and V. New York: Macmillan Co., 1918.

distributed among twelve fields such as art, civics, and geography.[6]

A Score Card for Rating Terms Papers.—An interesting attempt has been made to work out an objective method of evaluating term papers and written projects. The use of such a scheme should make more objective and uniform an instructor's methods in rating the work of his students. The score card[7] is reproduced in full.

[6] Florence B. Stratemeyer and Herbert B. Bruner, *Rating Elementary School Courses of Study*. Studies of the Bureau of Curriculum Research, Bulletin No. 1. New York: Teachers College, Columbia University, 1926. Pp. xiv + 194.

[7] Devised by Dr. W. A. Brownell of the School of Education, University of Michigan, and Dr. H. P. Rainey of Franklin College, (tentative form).

Score card for rating term papers	Possible score	Actual score
1. Introduction........ (Must include statement of problem, together with careful location of problem in field of education)	5	
2. Selection of material........ (Note amount, quality, and relevancy of material)	20	
3. Organization of material........ (Presentation should be clear, logical, coherent, sequential, progressive)	15	
4. Conclusions........ (Must be warranted by the material canvassed and by its treatment; neither over- nor under-stated)	10	
5. Bibliography........ (Credit only for annotated bibliography. Range and quality of reading partly covered under 2 above. See note below for form of bibliography)	10	
6. General appearance........ (Consider (a) neatness and legibility; (b) evidence of structure, explained in note below)	10	
7. Expression, i.e., English........ (Papers below a certain level of quality of English should be refused credit; in the scale here used 0 represents grade just acceptable; limit, 10 points)	10	
8. Proportionate allotment of space........	10	
9. Allowance for special merit........ (Intended to introduce a certain amount of flexibility. Special credit is thus available for high quality of research, originality, etc. Where not present, should not be allowed)	10	
Possible points	100	

Notes.—

1. Bibliography should contain, in addition to factual statements of contents of reference, these items—(a) for periodical: author's full name, title of article, name of periodical, volume, issue, pages inclusive; for book reference: author's full name, title of book, publisher, place of publication, year, edition, if more than one is extant.

2. Evidence of structure.—The form of the paper, by means of a table of contents, outline, or well-placed phrases inserted in the body of the material, *should show* the structure as a whole.

3. When certain items in the above scale, as the bibliography, are *justifiably* omitted, proceed with the scale as usual, adding to the total points earned an amount equal to total—times—per cent—represented—by—omitted—point. Thus, 10 per cent for the bibliography.

Evaluations of Educational Writings Frequently Appear in the Form of Book Reviews.—Obviously the worker in education must depend to a considerable extent on published book reviews as an aid in deciding whether new publications are to be added to his professional library or selected for classroom use. Certainly the practice of scanning the review departments of six or eight good professional periodicals is an important means of keeping pace with current educational literature.

Varying Characteristics of Reviews in Educational Journals.—Many of the professional journals devote considerable space to the review of new books and current literature in their respective fields. The style and content of the reviews published vary widely when a comparison is made between individual reviewers and between individual periodicals. This wide divergence of practice has led the writer to set forth in this discussion his impressions gained over a period of years from the reading and writing of book reviews.[8]

[8] Carter V. Good, "The Art of Book Reviewing," *School and Society*, XXIV (July 31, 1926), 142–43.

The professional journals in the field of education may be roughly classified into three groups with regard to the type of book review published. Probably six or eight of these journals provide bona fide, critical estimates, prepared by recognized authorities, of new books. Certain other periodicals conduct rather uncritical, informal, occasionally "gushing," and almost always complimentary "book chats" concerning current literature in the field. A third group of journals publishes little more than brief book notices that have in many instances been culled from the preface of the new book or from the publisher's advertisement.

The author of these remarks is a firm believer in the critical point of view, thoroughness, and professional tone embodied in the book reviews of the first class of journals mentioned above. It is with such evaluations of new literature that these remarks are in large part concerned. It must be admitted that even in this class of reviews, written in a serious-minded and professional manner, certain practices call for critical comment.

Elements of a Carefully Written Review.—It seems that a carefully written book review should include three fairly distinct parts. An introductory statement or paragraph may give the setting of the "stage" upon which the new book appears or a brief comment on the need for the new publication. Frequently it is the skill with which this introductory paragraph is written that lends tone to the rest of the review and attracts the attention of the reader.

In the second place, it is the duty of the reviewer to give a brief summary of the contents of the book under review, together with such critical comment as he deems necessary. Too frequently reviewers lack the skill necessary to condense a large amount of material into a small space, and either extend this summary to unusual length or neglect to give a statement of the contents of the volume. In the latter instance the reader secures from the review little more than the personal impressions and generalizations of the reviewer. However, it must be recognized that in some cases the general statement of a recognized authority regarding a new book is worth a great deal, even though he has neglected to present concrete evidence as a basis for his expressed opinion; undoubtedly this type of review would take on added meaning if adequately provided with factual evidence taken from the book under review.

In the third place, a review should present a critical evaluation and summary statement of the place the book seems destined to fill in its given field. This third part of the review may not in every instance be definitely separated from the second phase, although such a brief statement at the close of the review serves to summarize in a definite way the reviewer's conclusion. The three phases of the review may well be treated in the book review itself in the same order as listed above.

Attention to Matters of Form and Mechanics.—The critical reviewer gives attention to the form and mechanics of the volume under consideration, as well as to the content. Probably reviewers are universally lenient with regard to departures and lapses in the so-called mechanical features of a new book; they are reluctant to call attention to such matters for fear that their comments may distract the attention of the reader from quite worth while content material. However, lapses in form, mechanics, English usage, and sentence structure frequently detract greatly from a valuable message that an author has to convey; the critical comment of reviewers concerning such matters should do much to eliminate careless practices.

The writer[9] has elsewhere called attention to a number of careless practices in the more mechanical phases of educational writings, and in this discussion will do no more than enumerate certain of these lapses. The reviewer may well consider the following: care in giving citations and footnotes; uniformity in listing references; completeness of information given in bibliographies; English usage, including sentence and paragraph structure; care in presenting tabular, graphical, and statistical material; whether lists of tables, figures, plates, and illustrations are provided; whether an index is included; use of introductory, transitional, and summary statements or paragraphs; use of stimulating or thought-provoking exercises and problems; etc.

Cautions to the Reviewer.—Too frequently, certain excellent practices in themselves are overdone in book reviewing. A well chosen quotation often sets forth an author's point of view to advantage. However, the review which is largely a mass of quotations soon becomes tiresome to the reader, and causes one to wonder whether the reviewer did not resort to "padding" in turning out a hurried piece of work. Quite often there are valid occasions for quoting the exact title of a given chapter or section of the book under review; on the other hand it seems almost puerilely descriptive to reproduce verbatim a list of twenty or more chapter titles as given in a table of contents. Probably the tendency in book reviewing is to be over-complimentary rather than the reverse. The reviewer needs to deal out his praises critically and impartially. If his strongest superlatives are used

[9] Carter V. Good, "Careless Practices in Educational Writings," *School and Society*, XXIII (May 29, 1926), 684–6.

Carter V. Good, "Educational Writings, Editing and Errors," *School and Society*, XXVII (February 4, 1928), 146-50.

Also see Chapter IX for a discussion of common errors in matters of mechanics and form.

without discrimination, one is led to wonder what remains to be said for the publications of the future or whether further investigation and writing on the subject are even necessary.

No Attempt Made to Prescribe a Formula for Reviewing.—The author of these remarks does not presume, in any sense of the word, to prescribe a formula for reviewing books. A writer's or reviewer's style is his individual possession just as much as is his name or facial contour. However, an examination of the reviews printed in the various professional journals will show that the above comments are not wholly unwarranted.

Even Careful, Scholarly Reviews Vary in Type.—In the half-dozen journals which publish at regular intervals reviews of special interest to educational workers may be found three fairly distinct types of reviews, as well as combinations of two or more of these types. The first type of review involves, in part, some creative writing or a brief essay suggested by the book under consideration. In fact, the reviewer uses the book as a starting point or "spring board" from which to launch forth into his discussion. This method often gives a desirable setting, orients the reader in the given field, and raises pertinent problems; however, it may easily be overdone in that the content of the volume and critical evaluation receive little attention. The second type is concerned chiefly with a summary of the content of the book, which ordinarily subordinates the impressions or personality of the reviewer to a descriptive account of the author's work. The third type of review lays special stress on careful, academic analysis and critical evaluation of both the content and form of the work under consideration. Combinations of two or more of these three types of reviews probably appear more frequently than does a review which follows wholly a single line of emphasis.

Of course the type of treatment varies considerably with the personality and background of the individual reviewer.

Illustrations of Reviews of Educational Books.—The types of reviews described in the preceding paragraph may be labeled by certain key words: (1) essay, (2) summary, (3) analytical, and (4) combination. The four reviews which are reproduced on subsequent pages illustrate fairly well these four types of treatment; the reviews are in the same order as the types of treatment are listed in the preceding sentence. It should be pointed out that in very few instances does all the material of a given review belong exclusively to one type of treatment. However, in the four examples given the lines of emphasis are reasonably clear.

ESSAY TYPE OF REVIEW[10]

The Legal Basis of Public-school Administration.—A knowledge of the principles of law applicable to practical problems of school administration is highly beneficial to those who are charged with the duty of directing the work of the public schools. The expenditure of large sums of money, the employment of teachers, the issuance of bonds and the building of schoolhouses, the enforcement of rules and regulations—these and many other matters give rise to a great number of legal problems. For example, such questions as the following may arise at almost any time: May a board of education permit the use of school property for other than school purposes? What discretion does a board of education have in the selection of school sites? In the construction of its buildings, must the school board conform to the building regulations of the city council? What disposition is to be made of the demand of a parent that his child be excused from taking a particular subject? Is a board of education liable to teachers and pupils for injuries resulting from defective buildings and equipment? What con-

[10] By I. N. Edwards, *Elementary School Journal*, XXVIII (March, 1928), 547–48.

Harry Raymond Trusler, *Essentials of School Law.* Milwaukee, Wisconsin: Bruce Publishing Co., 1927. Pp. xlvi + 478

stitutes legal cause for the dismissal of teachers? What authority has the board of education to make rules and regulations for the government of the schools? In order to deal intelligently with many aspects of school administration, boards of education, superintendents, and principals should be familiar with those principles of law which in many cases must govern their action.

A knowledge of school law, however, does more than enable local administrative officers and teachers to avoid litigation and to form sound judgments with regard to specific administrative problems. It enables those who undertake to shape the educational policies of the state to do so with greater intelligence and understanding. Since the policy of the state finds expression through law, those who would understand that policy or undertake to shape it should know the law both in its present form and in its historical development.

A recent book undertakes to reduce to systematic organization the principles of case or common law applicable to many practical problems of school administration. The author has not made an exhaustive study of the decisions of the courts of final jurisdiction relating to education but has limited his attention to those problems that are likely to be the most perplexing. On the whole, the book is good and should prove exceedingly helpful to the legal profession and to school officers and teachers. One is inclined, however, to criticize the general organization of the subject matter. The book reads like a series of isolated chapters. In a number of instances, moreover, the conclusions of the author may well be challenged. It should be kept in mind that the common law represents an attempt to apply to social situations the principles of justice and fair dealing. Principles of law tend to become crystallized, while social institutions are constantly changing. A rule, therefore, which was reasonable and necessary yesterday may be unreasonable and arbitrary today. This is to say that the courts and all who undertake to formulate principles of law applicable to public education need to be informed with respect to the purposes of the modern school. At times the author seems to be more conversant with legal formulas than with present-day educational purposes. For example, in the case of the use of school property for other than school purposes, the author agrees with the older decisions which hold that such use should not be permitted in the absence of specific statutory authority. Taxation, it is said, may not be exercised for a private purpose. This point of view loses sight of the functions of the modern school, which seeks to serve the community in more ways than by giving classroom instruction. There is both reason and judicial authority for permitting school boards to allow the use of school buildings for various kinds of political and social meetings. In fact, if one considers the more recent cases, the weight of authority permits a wide use of school property for other than strictly school purposes. Other instances might be cited where the author is inclined to follow the more conservative cases.

SUMMARY TYPE OF REVIEW[11]

An Appraisal of Preschool Education.—An increasing interest in preschool education has been developing with the increasing recognition of the importance of the preschool years in the formation of character and personality. A critical survey of the present situation and a historical account of the various theories and forms of preschool education are contained in a book which should prove interesting to those whose special interest is the preschool child and to those who wish a general survey of the field.

The book is historical for the most part. The child-study movement is traced, and an account is given of the various forms in which schools for very young children have been organized—kindergarten, day nursery, and nursery school. An interesting section of the book shows how the forms and objectives of preschool education have been molded by the social and moral ideas current in different periods. The historical section describes the contributions of Froebel, Pestalozzi, Rousseau, Montessori, and others. In showing the effects of the writings and teachings of these leaders, the author pays particular attention to the practical implications of their several philosophies. An excellent account is given of the earliest nurseries and nursery schools in Europe and of their subsequent development.

The relation of the nursery school to the home is made the subject of a critical discussion. It is pointed out that, when nurseries do more than look after the physical well-being of the child, they provide advantages which no home, not even the wealthiest, can provide. Consequently, nursery schools should be available for

[11] By R. C. Scarf, *Elementary School Journal*, XXVIII (January, 1928), 393.

Ilse Forest, *Preschool Education:* A Historical and Critical Study. New York: Macmillan Co., 1927. Pp. xiv + 414.

all children, not merely for the children of the poor, as has usually been the case. The role of the nursery school in giving training to parents is emphasized.

The book ends with a note of commendable caution. The author does not favor a sudden expansion of nursery schools. Such schools are expensive; trained personnel is not available; and it is not yet certain what results may be obtained. Much more study of the child and his experiences is needed before a widespread program of nursery schools can be undertaken.

ANALYTICAL TYPE OF REVIEW[12]

Discussions and studies of the adolescent period may be roughly classified according to type as follows: general methods at the secondary level; special high-school methods; psychology of the high-school subjects; selection, organization, and administration of subject-matter and the program of studies; organization, administration, and supervision of the secondary-school period of training, including extra-class activities; general psychology of adolescent traits and characteristics; and specialized investigations of adolescence, including analyses of physical growth, health, mental development, emotions, delinquency, moral and religious attitudes, pubescence, abnormality, sex hygiene, etc. According to style of writing and scheme of organization, treatments of the adolescent period may be grouped in a three-fold classification: popular, entertaining discussions of adolescence; rigid, scientific studies of a rather specialized nature which often fail to make a direct application to school procedure; and textbooks which attempt to show the relation between the psychology of adolescence and the principles of organization, administration, supervision, method, and curriculum-construction involved in conducting a secondary school. Books of the latter type have not been very successful in making this application of psychology definite and concrete.

A new book dealing with the adolescent period is concerned primarily with problems of special method, and is a companion volume to *Adolescence and High-school Problems* in which an attempt was made to solve problems of social administration and

[12] By Carter V. Good, *Educational Administration and Supervision*, XIII (December, 1927), 639–42.

Ralph W. Pringle, *Methods with Adolescents*. Boston: D. C. Heath and Co., 1927. Pp. xviii + 438.

the high-school program of studies. The general problems of method in education, the adolescent intellect, general classroom procedure, mathematics, foreign languages, and science are treated in separate chapters. Chapters dealing with algebra, geometry, biological sciences, physical sciences, history, social sciences (civics, economics, and sociology), English composition, literature, Latin, and modern languages are included in the volume. The title of Chapter II, "The Adolescent Intellect," is not sufficiently inclusive, since virtually all the important characteristics of adolescence are summarized briefly. General, unified, or correlated mathematics is passed over with little more than the statement that such types of organization of materials and method do exist. The differences between algebra and geometry are emphasized to the virtually complete neglect of any similarities that may exist. Bare mention only is made of current developments in general science and unified social science, while general language courses are not referred to at all in the discussion. The author presents a vigorous defense of Latin, placing almost exclusive emphasis on the translation method. In the modern languages the acquisition of reading ability is advocated as the only immediate objective of instruction; the direct method receives little attention. More space might well have been given to methods of correlation between English and the other school subjects.

The influence of Stanley Hall is at all times evident in the discussion. The writings of Judd, Thorndike, Dewey, Bagley and others are drawn upon freely, although page references are never given and many times the volume or article is not cited. The author is not at all consistent in referring to other writers; the practices of mentioning the reference in the body of the text and in footnotes are employed with approximately equal frequency. The use of topical and paragraph headings would have improved the organization of the book and aided materially the reader. The book is written in a rather popular style which at times approaches the sentimental, as evidenced by snatches of poetry quoted at intervals, rather than in the academic, scientific manner which is becoming increasingly prominent in educational circles. The author does not draw freely in any direct manner upon the large body of experimental data available. Specific mention may be made of Gray's summary of reading investigations, Curtis' summary of science investigations, Buswell and Judd's studies of reading and foreign languages, Washburne and Vogel's canvass of children's reading interests, Huber, Bruner and Curry's study of preferences in poetry, Marshall and Judd's work in social science, Rugg's method of unification of the social sciences and the important contributions of Breslich and Schorling in mathematics.

It may be said, and the Foreword of the book makes this statement, that critical observation, increased knowledge of the psychological traits of the adolescent, definite techniques of measurement, and sociological factors have in turn influenced our conceptions of adolescent education. The writer of the volume under review apparently has been influenced most by the first two lines of development in the study of adolescence. If it is granted that books on method, general or special, fall roughly into a three-fold classification—discussions of the theories, principles, and philosophies of method, treatments rich in materials drawn from the classroom and experimental investigations, and studies employing the problem method and case analysis—Professor Pringle's book is of the first type. As such, the treatment is one or two steps removed from the latest developments in the field of method.

Statements made in a preceding paragraph indicate that a careful editing of the mechanical features of the book would have been desirable; it may be added that the title of Morrison's *The Practice of Teaching in the Secondary School* is misquoted on page 199. A yearbook reference on page 284 (*National Year Book for the Study of Education*, 1923, Part II) is a glaring misquotation and no doubt refers to a publication of the National Society for the Study of Education. The initials of Arthur G. Bovée (p. 414) and H. C. Hines (p. 428) are misquoted; the name of C. H. Handschin (p. 428) is misspelled. Only the surname of Naomi Norsworthy (p. 430) is correct, the name being given as Robert M. Norsworthy. The index could have been made more valuable by including the names of the numerous authors referred to in the discussion. The volume includes a selected bibliography.

The favorable reception with which the author's *Adolescence and High-school Problems* met a few years ago causes the reviewer to venture the prediction that the present volume will be widely adopted and used. However, in no sense of the word may it be ranked with such books as Parker's *Methods of Teaching in High Schools*, Morrison's *The Practice of Teaching in the Secondary School*, and Judd's *Psychology of High-school Subjects*, now revised under the title, *The Psychology of Secondary Education*.

COMBINATION TYPE OF REVIEW[13]

A Comprehensive Treatment of the High-school Program of Studies. Since the appearance in 1918 of Bobbitt's pioneer book, *The Curriculum,* probably no subdivision of the field of education has received so much attention as has the program of studies. For the past four years the yearbooks of the Department of Superintendence have dealt with the curriculum; the 1928 yearbook of this organization is devoted to the senior high school curriculum and the 1929 yearbook will discuss the articulation of the units of the American school system. Both parts of the 1927 yearbook of the National Society for the Study of Education were concerned wholly with the curriculum field. The books, monographs, yearbooks, and articles dealing with this topic may be classified roughly under the following headings: treatments of the historical development of curriculum philosophies, materials, and methods; statements of theories, principles, and objectives formulated by individual workers; recommendations of committees; surveys of current practices in curriculum-making; compilations of present-day courses of study and curriculums; detailed discussions of the separate school subjects; and reports of investigations made to determine desirable materials and methods of instruction.

Probably the most comprehensive and satisfactory curriculum treatise for textbook purposes available at present is the book by Professor Uhl. It is divided into six parts, made up of a total of seventeen chapters, which include discussions of the following topics: historical development of the high-school curriculum, criticism of secondary-school curriculums, educational objectives, pupils and curriculums, local conditions and curriculums, and the reconstruction and administration of present-day curriculums. The author's conception of the five problems most important in present-day curriculum-making includes consideration of: (1) educational objectives and curriculums; (2) pupils' equipment, interests, and needs in relation to curriculums; (3) local conditions and curriculums; (4) the reconstruction of curriculums to provide for the best possible pupil activities in the mastery of subject matter; and (5) a study of present-day practices as a final guide in formulating standards for constructing and administering curricu-

[13] By Carter V. Good, *School Review,* XXXVI (March, 1928), 227–28.

Willis L. Uhl, *Secondary School Curricula.* New York: Macmillan Co., 1927. Pp. xx + 582.

lums. However, for some reason a treatment of typical current courses of study and specific curriculums in actual use was not included in the book.

At various points in the discussion there is evidence to indicate that the author has been materially influenced by the work of Bobbitt and is in general sympathy with it. Since approximately one-half the book is devoted to a consideration of the historical development of curriculum theories, philosophies, objectives, materials, and methods, many readers will think that the historical phases of the problem have been overemphasized, valuable as such information is in providing perspective and a general background for the student in the curriculum field. Certainly a part of this space might well have been devoted to a survey of typical current courses of study and curriculums. With the qualifications mentioned in the two preceding sentences, it may well be said that the book presents a comprehensive and well-rounded treatment of curriculum problems which writers have tended to analyze separately or in various combinations rather than to discuss in full within the limits of a single volume. The book includes twenty-five tables, five charts, well-selected references, and profuse footnotes, which substantiate the conclusions reached by the author.

Additional Sources of Information on Book Reviews.—Averill and Mueller[14] report an analysis of the book reviews which appeared in 1926 in seven educational journals. The study was concerned with the length of the review, practice with regard to signing reviews, and the reviewer's attitude (favorable, unfavorable, doubtful, or impersonal). The report closes with a recommendation relative to the preparation of evaluations of books in education.

It would seem to the present writers that the only proper function of reviewers should be to present the aims and general scope of the books which they review in a wholly impersonal and unbiased way. It should reasonably be left to the intelligence of the reader to form his own judgment concerning a book's merits or demerits, and the likelihood of its being a desirable volume

[14] Lawrence A. Averill and Alfred D. Mueller, "An Analysis of Book Reviews," *School and Society*, XXVI (December 31, 1927), 848–49.

for him to add to his list. As it is, too often a reviewer is inclined either, on the one hand, to cater to the good will of publishing houses or, on the other, to express freely the favor or disfavor with which he personally—and often narrowly—reacts to a new volume according as it is or is not in line with his own individual philosophy or viewpoint.

The present writer is not able wholly to agree with this conception of the purpose of reviewing, as is evident on comparing the above quotation with the writer's discussion of the elements of a careful review.

Gard[15] has prepared a helpful treatment of the literary review which is applicable in many instances to the preparation of evaluations of educational books. His discussions of the reviewer's aims and methods, editors' opinions on reviews, and types of reviews are especially significant.

Keeping Pace with Educational Literature through Reviews.—Among the general educational journals most valuable for their careful, analytical evaluations of recent professional and research works are: *Educational Administration and Supervision*, *Elementary School Journal*, *Journal of Educational Psychology*, *Journal of Educational Research*, and the *School Review*.

The *Book Review Digest* indexes important books and gives abstracts of reviews published in about fifty of the most important English and American periodicals. It extends from 1906 to date and appears monthly, cumulating quarterly and annually.

[15] Wayne Gard, *Book Reviewing*. New York: Alfred A. Knopf, 1927. Pp. xii + 160.

CHAPTER XI

TRAINING RESEARCH WORKERS AND GUIDANCE OF GRADUATE STUDENTS

The reader may wonder why a separate chapter is devoted to the training and guidance of the research worker and graduate student when the whole book is concerned with various phases of the same general problem. However, there are certain specific suggestions gathered from the literature on educational research and from the large graduate schools of education which very appropriately may be brought together in this chapter. The literature includes concrete illustrations of the efforts made by graduate schools to inform workers concerning the techniques of educational research. Correspondence with departments and schools of education indicates a real interest in this problem, although in few instances is there a carefully outlined program involving adequate materials which can be placed in the hands of the graduate student. In many quarters there is still a tendency to allow the educational worker to proceed by the trial and error method in securing information concerning the techniques of educational research. Granted that even the writer of a Master's thesis should exhibit independence in research, it does seem that before undertaking a thesis problem the student should have the benefit of systematic instruction in methods of research.

Pleas for Productive Scholarship and Conservation of Research Ability.—One group of thinkers insists on greater productivity on the part of college and university teachers, although certain difficulties which confront teachers interested in research are recognized. The American Historical Association conducted a questionnaire survey in order to determine the status of research in colleges.[1] The returns from the questionnaire indicate that colleges are placing more emphasis on research due to the method of training Doctors of Philosophy, the emphasis placed on the dissertation, the place of research in the sciences and in modern industrial life, and the belief that it is a desirable method of education. Certain reasons for the lack of productivity are mentioned: the ability of the candidates for the Ph.D. and the fact that the degree has become a commercialized teaching degree, the low social value placed on productive scholarship in the United States as compared with European countries, and a widespread belief that the research worker is not adequately rewarded materially for his efforts. The report suggests the desirability of conferring two different degrees, one indicating research ability and the other fitness for teaching. Remedies for the comparatively low level of productive scholarship are: the development of a greater interest in research, greater encouragement to Doctors of Philosophy who are capable of advanced work, more "weeding out" of candidates for the degree, more money for travel and publication, and greater recognition of scholarship in the professional world. While these comments are intended to apply particularly to the field of history, they have a very pertinent bearing on the field of education.

Buckingham deplores the fact that many recipients of graduate degrees have become well informed along cer-

[1] "Productive Scholarship," *School and Society,* XXVI (October 22, 1927), 528.

tain lines, usually in connection with the thesis investigation, and later fail to pursue further research in the same fields.[2]

> . . . A certain limited number of high-grade students obtain Ph.D. degrees every year. At the moment of receiving the degree it is not unlikely that each of them is better posted concerning some aspect of his major field than any other man in the country. Yet, after taking their degrees, only a few Ph.D. students—and these are the wisest of them—pursue the topic which of all others they may pursue with the greatest likelihood of success. Much the same may be said of those who secure their master's degree. They have majored in a certain field and very likely have written a thesis in that field. No other area is for them so important as the one to which they have just given major attention. This particular topic offers them a greater chance than any other of securing recognition among their contemporaries. Differing in degree but not in kind is the major subject of the undergraduate student. Recent studies concerning the training of teachers have shown that too many of those who have fitted themselves abundantly to teach a certain subject enter some other line of service, thus dissipating their energies and incurring both for themselves and for society an unremunerative expense.

Is the College or University Teacher Only Incidentally a Research Worker?—Another point of view is expressed by educational workers who believe that the business of the college teacher is almost entirely that of teaching. The narrowing influence of graduate specialization and the dissertation are deplored, while the importance of human interest and social contacts as essential elements of the successful college teacher's makeup are emphasized. McMurry[3] emphasizes friendship and close personal relations with students as the most important thing in

[2] B. R. Buckingham, "The Greatest Waste in Education," *School and Society*, XXIV (November 27, 1926), 653–58.

"The Greatest Waste in Education," *Journal of Educational Research*, XII (November, 1925), 311–14.

[3] Frank M. McMurry, "The Biggest Thing in Teaching," *Teachers College Record*, XXVIII (November, 1926), 215–19.

teaching. Another writer[4] advocates a greater interest in the world of human affairs on the part of graduate students and teachers. Especially in the field of English has there been heated debate concerning the requirements for the Ph.D. degree. Wykoff[5] refers to ten of these published discussions and urges that both teaching and research degrees be offered in English. He suggests the requirements for the teaching Ph.D. degree in English: (1) three years of satisfactory graduate study, (2) no thesis, (3) intensive survey courses of the whole field of English and American literature, (4) broad but thorough survey courses of other literatures by means of English translations, (5) broad survey courses of fields allied to literature, (6) a reading knowledge of two modern languages, (7) a group of courses in education, (8) a year of actual experience or teaching interneship, and (9) a high standard of scholarship in all courses pursued.

Pressey[6] studied current opinions relative to the requirements for the Doctor's degree by circularizing 214 recipients of Ph.D. degrees who belonged either to the American Psychological Association or the Educational Research Association. The returns indicated that a majority of time went to teaching; that many made no use whatever of foreign languages in their work; and that changes were desirable in present requirements for the Ph.D. degree. The changes suggested included modification of the foreign-language requirement, adaptation of training to future needs, and greater freedom from

[4] Nathan G. Goodman, "More about Ph.D.'s," *School and Society*, XXIV (October 2, 1926), 429–30.

[5] George S. Wykoff, "On the Revision of Ph.D. Requirements in English," *English Journal*, College Edition, XVII (March, 1928), 213–20.

[6] S. L. Pressey, L. C. Pressey, and Others, *Research Adventures in University Teaching*, pp. 140–47. Bloomington, Illinois: Public School Publishing Co., 1927.

detailed requirements. It was pointed out that the program for the degree had remained essentially the same over a period of seventy-five years during which extraordinary educational and cultural changes had taken place.

Buswell reports a personnel study of 242 graduate students who received the Master's degree in education at the University of Chicago from 1924–1927. The facts disclosed caused Professor Buswell to raise the question of whether the Master's degree is for training in research or teaching.[7]

Numerous problems are suggested by the facts which have been presented. However, in the writer's judgment, the major problem revealed is that of the selection of graduate students. A redefinition of graduate work is being forced. The efforts of the graduate school must be focused either upon the task of stimulating fundamental research on educational problems or upon the task of providing an additional period of training beyond the bachelor's degree, but with emphasis upon practice rather than research. If the former purpose is adopted, the selection of students will need to be much more rigid than if the latter purpose is accepted. Both purposes are worthy; but the mixing of the two in the same department and the granting of the same degree for each will become increasingly difficult as the demand for the master's degree continues to increase. The master's degree needs definition. Either it stands for preliminary training in research or it does not. Perhaps it may be desirable to consider it a teaching degree. The writer does not so believe. The same type of outside pressure which now makes the master's degree in great demand will in another generation or sooner be applied to the doctor's degree. The problem is fundamental. Education must have men for scientific research; it must also have men skilled in teaching and administration. But the degrees which have formerly represented scientific achievement are more and more being desired by a selection of students whose chief interest is practice rather than

[7] G. T. Buswell, "A Personnel Study of Students Who Have Received the Master's Degree from the University of Chicago," *School and Society*, XXV (June 18, 1927), 730–36.

research. The writer believes that a clear-cut differentiation between students interested in research and students interested in practice is essential in a subject as new as education. Whatever may be the decision of the graduate school regarding its obligation to give training in practice and regarding its recognition of such training by a degree, its principal obligation will be the selection of a competent group of students and the giving to this group a rigid scientific training which will cumulate in critical, productive scholarship. This type of interest is utterly foreign to many first-year graduate students as now selected.

Possibly the solution of the problem is separate graduate degrees for teaching and for research. Probably adequate training and an appropriate balance between teaching and research activities, with conditions in the college or school system improved so as to facilitate research, is the desired solution when the recipient of a graduate degree takes up his own teaching work. Certainly the teacher who periodically conducts some investigation in the field of his interest will bring to the classroom or laboratory an inquiring attitude which should prove stimulating to students.

Qualifications of a Research Worker.—It has been suggested that in order to do successful research work the individual should have the following qualifications:[8]

1. Emotional factors—drive.

One can not do successful research work unless (a) he has the urge that comes from curiosity, (b) he takes pleasure in self-expression, in creation, (c) he feels that such work will be of real value either to himself or to others.

[8] National Committee on Research in Secondary Education, *An Outline of Methods of Research with Suggestions for High School Principals and Teachers*, p. 11. Bureau of Education Bulletin, No. 24, 1926. Washington: Bureau of Education.

S. A. Courtis, "The Development of Ability in Research," *Studies in Education*, pp. 85–93. Yearbook Number XV of the National Society of College Teachers of Education. Chicago: University of Chicago Press, 1926.

2. Knowledge—efficiency.

No one is ready to do effective research until he has developed the following:

(a) Ability to find quickly, to select, and to utilize the results of previous research.
(b) Knowledge of and facility in using approved experimental procedures, inductive and deductive processes, logic and experimentation.
(c) Skill in using approved educational measuring instruments.
(d) Skill in analytical methods, statistical and graphic.
(e) Ability to generalize, to know when and how to make safe generalizations.
(f) Skill in verification involving criticism and prediction.
(g) Ability to select and organize the materials used in the investigation and to report the methods and results.

3. Volition—control.

The volitional factors necessary may be outlined as follows:

(a) Visible evidence.
  (1) Courage.
  (2) Persistence.
  (3) Open-mindedness.
  (4) Humility.
  (5) Faith.
(*b*) General powers.
  (1) Self-direction—independence in thought.
  (2) Self-appraisal—power to know one's strength and limitations.
  (3) Self-control—power of self-control.
(*c*) Convictions.
  (1) About nature—unity of law, evolution, cause and effect.
  (2) About self—potentialities, social consciousness, control of self.
  (3) About opportunity—reality and possibility of discovery of truth, possibilities of growth in self and progress of society.

Buckingham presents an effective statement of the characteristics of a leader in educational research:[9]

[9] B. R. Buckingham, "Leadership in Educational Research," *Journal of Educational Research*, XV (April, 1927), 239–45.

In this plea for leadership in research I have asserted that due to the educational conditions of today, there is need of quantity production in research. In order to produce the verified and scientifically defensible body of knowledge which is thus demanded, there must be leaders and followers. I have tried to give some of of the qualities of leadership which seem to me to be desirable. The leader should have practical school experience. He should be able to enlist the support and win the confidence of teachers. He must be able to train workers. He must have the ability to analyze larger problems into their simpler elements and to combine selected parts of complex problems for the purpose of cooperative research. He must be a scholar in his chosen field and must be able to state problems with authority. If he is a real leader he will have what I have called "extractive power." He will be able to put his program over and to secure from people who would otherwise be indifferent the information he needs. He will be well informed as to the nature of scientific method and will know how to apply such a method to educational data. On the other hand, he will know the limitations of strictly objective treatment. He will be expert in thinking as well as in figuring. He will follow the figures where they lead, impartially and without bias or prejudice, but he will know how to interpret them and to supplement them. Finally, he will study a question long enough and hard enough to bring out something more substantial than tentative conclusions or a timid turning over of his chosen question to the educational public for further study.

Discussions of Factors Involved in the Training of the Research Worker and Graduate Student.—Attention may be directed to a number of helpful treatments of graduate work and the improvement of educational research. Bay[10] recommends as a part of the training of a research worker in education a year of philosophy, a year of mathematical analysis at the college level, and a year of statistics with emphasis on statistical analysis. Hunt[11] discusses several problems of the graduate

[10] James C. Bay, "The Training of a Research Worker in Education," *School and Society*, XXV (March 5, 1927), 274–78.

[11] Rockwell D. Hunt, "The Doctor of Philosophy Degree," *School and Society*, XXIII (January 9, 1926), 31–37.

school: residence requirements, the preliminary examination, the dissertation, language examinations, and the final oral examination. Phelps[12] stresses independence on the part of the graduate student in conducting his piece of research by setting up three requirements: the student must choose his own problem, must assume full responsibility for the research, and must verify his own solution. Newlon[13] urges that effective educational research depends upon the maintenance of intimate contacts with actual classroom and administrative procedures and with the public. Some excellent suggestions for beginners in research may be found in a number of the *Phi Delta Kappan*.[14] A Research Committee[15] discusses briefly five stages of activity which should be clearly understood by research workers: (1) recognition of the needs or problems for study and investigation; (2) securing acquaintance with and skill in use of the techniques and materials involved in such researches; (3) publication and dissemination of material secured by study, investigation, and research; (4) interpretation of published results and their application to existing conditions; and (5) checking and verifying the utility of applications. Whipple[16] treats the improvement of research from several angles: cardinal features of scientific work, ignorance of the work of predecessors, futile problems, hasty formulation of problems, neglect of

[12] Shelton Phelps, "Independence in Research," *Phi Delta Kappan*, X (December, 1927), 123–25.

[13] Jesse H. Newlon, "A Background for Practical Research," *Phi Delta Kappan*, VIII (April, 1926), 1–6.

[14] "Research," *Phi Delta Kappan*, IX (February, 1927), 97–99.

[15] A. R. Mead, W. C. Bagley, E. I. F. Williams, and K. Anthony, "Research in Supervised Student-Teaching and Allied Problems: Report of Research Committee, 1926," *Educational Administration and Supervision*, XII (May, 1926), 346–51.

[16] Guy M. Whipple, "The Improvement of Educational Research," *School and Society*, XXVI (August 27, 1927), 249–59.

direct observation, use of the experimental technique, value of preliminary trial, use of the questionary, use of measurement, typical statistical errors, and intelligible presentation of results.

Tools of Research Used in the Preparation of the Doctor's Dissertation.—Some interesting figures concerning the use of foreign languages and statistics in the preparation of dissertations in education are available. Bay[17] analyzed 204 theses in the series, *Teachers College Contributions to Education,* Columbia University. He raises a question concerning the desirability of the foreign-language requirement for the Doctor's degree in education. The results of his analysis stated in per cents are as follows: 1905–1915, employing foreign languages 38, employing statistics 41, employing neither foreign languages nor statistics 30; 1916–1926, employing foreign languages 16, employing statistics 78, employing neither foreign languages nor statistics 18.

A Suggested Program for Training Research Workers.—Crawford[18] calls attention to the fact that the individual method of training graduate students has certain limitations in that the expert research man may not be skilled in training apprentices in methods of investigation. The apprentice method is time-consuming, since the professor must repeat work with each student, while the student is apt to spend unnecessary hours by the trial and error method in discovering things which could be taught permanently and effectively in a regular course in methods of research. However, Professor Crawford is far from suggesting that a program of direct

[17] James C. Bay, "Tools of Research Needed in the Preparation of Dissertations for the Doctorate in Education," *School and Society,* XXV (January 8, 1927), 53–54.

[18] C. C. Crawford, "Training Research Workers," *Journal of Educational Research,* XIII (May, 1926), 366–70.

and formal training is to replace individual work; it is rather to serve as a foundation for individual work and to make possible the continuance of such work on a a higher level. The suggested program for training research workers follows:

I. *The Collection of Suitable Material Bearing on the Methods of Research.*—The three principal sources of such material are:

1. *Available Reports of Scientific Investigations.*—The summarization of these data would involve the sifting out of the best contributions to be found in books on historical and statistical methods, as well as a substantial body of periodical literature. Much useful material has not been reduced to printed form and would have to be collected from other sources.
2. *Professors and Deans of Graduate Schools.*—Much wisdom concerning methods of research has been gathered from experience and is stored in the memory of the professors who have been directing students in their theses. By interviewing these men and recording their suggestions concerning the methods of planning and carrying out investigations in their respective fields, we could secure a wealth of material that would be invaluable for the guidance of others.
3. *Graduate Students.*—From interviews with graduate students much might be learned regarding the difficulties met in the process of making investigations and in formulating the reports. These difficulties may have been overlooked by the deans and professors directing graduate work.

II. *Teaching This Material in a Regular Course.*—The course in research methods should resemble other courses in form and should include the use of textbooks, lectures, quizzes, and laboratory exercises. Such a course should be given equal status with any other scientific or professional course. Instruction should be given in class groups rather than individually; and all prospective graduate students should be allowed the opportunity of taking it, regardless of the subject or field in which they expect to do their graduate work.

This course should be offered during the first semester of the senior year to all students who give promise of research ability and followed in the second semester by courses in methods of research in the various fields such as natural science, historical research, statistical methods, etc. Various reasons for placing it in the senior year may be given. Such a course would reach more students in the senior year than later, it would be instrumental in inspiring Seniors to remain for graduate study and research. Also much of the ordinary feeling of dread that attaches to the idea of preparing a thesis would thus be overcome. After such a course the student would enter the graduate school ready to begin work, and even if he did not return for graduate study such training would be valuable as a preparation for practical research work in his chosen field of activity.

III. *Giving Assistance to Individual Students.*—Each graduate student should receive all the individual direction and training possible in connection with his actual research work.

Outline of a Course in Educational Research.—Symonds[19] describes a course in educational research which is based on an analysis of twenty-one studies in the series, *Teachers College Contributions to Education.* He listed all the different operations that were performed in the theses and in a check list noted the frequency of occurrence. In all, 201 items were listed and the fifty having the greatest frequency were selected and organized as the outline of a course in educational research. The outline follows:

- I. Choice of problem.
  1. Statement.
  2. Purpose.
  3. Importance.
- II. Bibliography.
  1. History of topic.
- III. Analysis of problem.
  1. Definitions of terms.
  2. Determination of units of measurement.
  3. Sampling—selection of material, subject, place.
     a. Representativeness.
     b. Adequacy.

[19] Percival M. Symonds, "A Course in the Technique of Educational Research," *Teachers College Record*, XXIX (October, 1927) 24–30.

IV. Collection of data.
  1. Observation.
  2. Rating.
  3. Questionnaire.
  4. Testing.
  5. Secondary statistical sources.
V. Treatment of data.
  1. Scoring.
  2. Tabulation.
    a. Tabulation of questionnaires.
      (1) Interpretation of tables.
    b. The frequency distribution.
      (1) Smoothing.
  3. Statistical methods.
    a. Measures of central tendency.
      (1) The arithmetic mean.
      (2) The median.
    b. Measures of variability.
      (1) The standard deviation.
      (2) The quartile deviation.
      (3) Percentiles.
    c. Measures of relationship.
      (1) Pearson coefficient of correlation.
      (2) Mean square contingency coefficient.
      (3) Per cent of overlapping.
    d. Measures of reliability.
      (1) P.E. of mean.
        (a) P.E. of difference.
      (2) P.E. of *r*.
    e. Miscellaneous.
      (1) Transmutation of scores.
      (2) Spearman-Brown formula.
      (3) Weighting.
    f. Important statistical concepts.
      (1) Criteria.
      (2) Validity.
      (3) Reliability.
    g. Partial correlation.
  4. Graphical methods.
VI. Construction of administrative formulae.
VII. Legal aspect of problem.
  1. Analysis of regulations.

VIII. Recommendations.
IX. Summary—conclusions.
X. Organization.
  1. Chapters.
  2. Lists of:
    a. Content.
    b. Tables.
    c. Charts.
  3. Title.
  4. Acknowledgments.
XI. Publication.

The Typical Bureau of Research and the Training of the Director.—Chapman[20] presents descriptions of the typical bureau of research, its functions, and the training of the director.

City Bureau.—The typical bureau of research in city-school systems was established in 1920; it has a staff of four persons, a director, an assistant, a general clerical helper, and a psychologist, if the director is not a psychologist himself. The director received a Bachelor's degree thirteen years ago, and since that time he has procured the Master's degree. He receives a salary of $4,150. For 1925–26 he had a salary budget of $7,800 and an operating budget of $1,500. In the list of functions the director of the median city bureau checked the following items: achievement testing; school finance other than budgeting; curriculum revision; experimental study of curricular and instructional problems; educational guidance; mental testing; psychological clinic; supervision of special classes; training teachers for special testing work; surveys and special investigations; classification of pupils; devising record and report forms; experimental study of special problems relating to administration.

During the year ended June 30, 1925, this bureau engaged in the study of seven distinct projects, four of which were special problems of research, and three were routine studies or services. The bureau is responsible to the superintendent of schools. It is expected to recommend policies, and it has a limited amount of responsibility for the execution of approved policies.

[20] Harold B. Chapman, *Organized Research in Education*, pp. 210–12. Bureau of Educational Research Monographs, Number 7. Columbus, Ohio: Ohio State University Press, 1927.

University Bureau.—The typical university bureau was established in 1922. It has a staff of five persons, a director on part time, a full-time assistant director, a general assistant, a statistical assistant, and a general clerk-stenographer. The director received his Bachelor's degree eighteen years ago and since then, his doctorate. His salary is $4,750. During 1925–26 his bureau had an operating budget of $1,083 and a salary appropriation of $4,833.

Eleven general functions were checked by the median university bureau. These were as follows: giving mental and achievement tests; studying curricular and instructional problems; making surveys and special investigations; classifying pupils; devising record and report forms; studying problems related to administration; guiding the research studies of students; constructing tests; giving educational information; caring for problems of student personnel; and providing teaching service.

During the year ended June 30, 1925, this bureau worked upon six different projects of which four might be called research problems and two routine problems. This bureau is responsible to the dean of the college of education.

Teacher-training Bureau.—The typical bureau in a teacher-training institution was established in 1920. It has the benefit of the services of three persons, each of whom devotes a small portion of his time to the bureau as its needs demand. One of the three acts as a general secretary.

The director received his Bachelor's degree fifteen years ago and since then, his doctorate. His median salary is $4,062; his 1925–26 salary budget was $6,050 and his operating budget, $850. The functions performed by this bureau were the same as those performed by the median university bureau. It is responsible to the president of the institution.

State Bureau.—There is no typical state bureau. It has already been pointed out that only three of the five cooperating bureaus were highly developed. These three resemble the typical university bureau and perform practically the same functions. The typical salary is $4,100; the director has a doctorate, and it has been fifteen years since he received his Bachelor's degree.

Training the Investigator Who Works in Public-school Systems.—Alexander[21] describes three possible methods

[21] Carter Alexander, "How to Equip the School Administrator with Methods of Locating Data Which Will Carry Over When He Is on the Job," *Teachers College Record*, XXVIII (May, 1927), 890–99.

of training superintendents: work in ordinary courses, interneship, and school surveys. The same authority discusses the special equipment necessary for the man who would do successful research in educational finance.[22]

> Valuable researches in this field are unlikely to be made by men who are merely hunting thesis or dissertation problems and want to work here because it has more than ordinary interest just now. They may be only babies reaching for the moon. But if a man has some special equipment for the work and will choose some phase of the educational finance field in accordance with that equipment, the chances for worth while research that will be duly noticed, are promising. This special equipment may be any one of a large number of lines—statistical method, economics, history, history of education, accounting, law, advertising, journalism, salesmanship, psychology, or a knowledge of practical politics. This last may provoke a smile at first thought. But as a matter of fact, for achieving reforms in educational finance through public support, substantial help will come from adequate studies of how practical politicians of the best type achieve their ends, especially in securing good legislation. A man who likes to study this greatest of all games, practical politics, preferably one who has had enough experience in playing it and still has not let it master him, may contribute much of value. For such work, too, popular political articles like those of the *Saturday Evening Post* or of *Colliers* may be worth several times the pronouncements of closet psychologists and sociologists.

Sears devotes a chapter to research bureaus, the school survey, and research problems in the public-school system.[23]

Guidance and Training of Graduate Students.—Inquiry among colleges and schools of education[24] indicates a

[22] Carter Alexander, "Opportunities for Research in Educational Finance," *Educational Administration and Supervision*, IX (April, 1923), 209–22.

[23] Jesse B. Sears, *The School Survey*, Chapter XVII. Boston: Houghton Mifflin Co., 1925.

[24] These schools have been good enough to answer the writer's inquiry and in many instances have forwarded mimeographed or printed materials and detailed personal letters: California,

real interest in more effective guidance of graduate students. A composite list of the methods used to promote better graduate work and more satisfactory theses includes: seminar or research courses in which techniques of research, sources of information, bibliographical procedures, and other matters of content and form are treated; lists of suggested problems; lists of accepted theses recommended for examination; individual conferences and individual guidance; advice on selection of courses of special value to the student conducting an investigation; field work such as surveys, testing programs, and interneship; scholarships and fellowships involving work as reader, assistant in instruction, and service to educational periodicals; and advice concerning publication of the thesis. A frequently expressed comment is concerning the lack of comprehensive and organized materials on research to which the student can be referred. This comment is not a surprising one. In fact, it is only within the past few years that educational workers have begun to write extensively on the subject of research. Even a casual inspection of the numerous references cited in this book shows how widely scattered the information is. It is the hope of the present writer that this book will be of some service to the graduate student, research worker, and seminar group in education in its attempt to bring together and organize the relatively large body of information on research now available.

Stanford, Yale, Chicago, Northwestern, Illinois, Indiana, Iowa, Michigan, Minnesota, Columbia, New York, Ohio State, Pennsylvania, Pittsburgh, Texas, and Wisconsin.

Chapter XII

PROGRESS IN EDUCATIONAL RESEARCH

This Book Made Possible through Recent Progress in Educational Research.—In this last chapter it seems appropriate to raise a question concerning the progress which has taken place to date in educational research. Of course, the discerning reader will answer at once that such a treatment of research as that set forth in this book would not be possible except for the labor and thought of a large number of conscientious research workers, experimenters, and investigators. So it may be said without exaggeration that the comparatively large body of material brought together in the preceding pages of this volume is evidence of real progress in the field of educational research, especially within the past few years. The very valuable research periodical, the *Journal of Educational Research,* was established as recently as 1920.

Development of Different Techniques of Research.—It is a matter of interest to note the limited scope of the types of educational research advocated from fifteen to twenty years ago. In a discussion[1] of research in education Cubberley mentioned the fields of finance, county reorganization, and units of cost as major fields in need of investigation; Dearborn and Thorndike urged experi-

[1] E. P. Cubberley, W. F. Dearborn, Paul Monroe, and E. L. Thorndike, "Research within the Field of Education, Its Organization and Encouragement," pp. 1–54. *The School Review Monograph,* Vol. I. Chicago: Department of Education, University of Chicago, 1911.

mentation and quantitative measurement; and Monroe emphasized cooperation in research. It was at this time when education was known in many quarters as pedagogy which was probably a transitional stage between the parent philosophy and present-day education. One writer of that day bore the title, Dean of the School of Pedagogy of New York University.[2] The historical method of research was also receiving relatively more attention than at present.[3]

The philosophical and historical methods of investigation were early in favor in education, but are not employed extensively at present. The questionnaire and survey methods of collecting data were widely adopted a little later and still serve a purpose when properly used. Today the statistical[4] and experimental methods appear to be in favor, including certain specialized forms of statistical procedure such as case study and activity analysis. Terman[5] expresses his confidence in the future of the testing movement which is probably the most widely used form of the statistical method.

> A hundred years from now the educational historian will probably characterize the present era as the one which saw the birth and development of the testing movement. From a half-dozen points of view the introduction of standard tests of intelligence and of school achievement must be regarded as of capital importance, for these devices are already leaving their mark upon school organization and administration, instructional methods, curricular content, textbooks, and even educational ideals.

[2] Thomas M. Balliet, "Undergraduate Instruction in Pedagogy," *Pedagogical Seminary*, XVII (March, 1910), 63–69.

[3] Paul Monroe, "Opportunity and Need for Research Work in the History of Education," *Pedagogical Seminary*, XVII (March, 1910), 54–62.

[4] James C. Bay, "Tools of Research Needed in the Preparation of Dissertations for the Doctorate in Education," *School and Society*, XXV (January 8, 1927), 53–54.

[5] L. M. Terman, "The Ultimate Influence of Standard Tests," *Journal of Educational Research*, XVII (January, 1928), 57–59.

Buckingham[6] speaks of America as possessing a government originally established on the experimental basis and a people convinced of the value of the experimental method. He describes the public-school system extending from the kindergarten through the university and professional school as America's great experiment. His view of the experimental method is of interest:

It is the favorite observation of certain writers and speakers that the future historians of our contemporary education will characterize the present period as an era of experimentation. Very likely those who thus wax prophetic are themselves interested in experimental education and attribute to it a significance beyond its just deserts. Whether the long backward look, with its inexorable application of the laws of perspective, will in fact see the resort to objective data as more than an episode, it is certain that the movement toward experiment in education is both suggestive and promising.

Has Education Become a Science?—Naturally educational workers frequently raise among themselves a question with regard to the status of their chosen field as a science. Courtis[7] discusses this matter in a characteristically vigorous fashion:

It is about fifty years since man established the first laboratories for the scientific study of human nature, about forty years since the beginning of intelligence testing, about twenty years since the mental-age concept was clearly formulated and about fifteen years since the publication of the first standardized measure of educational products. Unnumbered millions of mental and educational tests have been given, whole libraries of books on tests and statistics have been written, endless meetings and conferences have been held, and thousands of experiments have been conducted. What is the net outcome? To what stage of development have we attained?

[6] B. R. Buckingham, "The Great Experiment," *Journal of Educational Research,* XVI (December, 1927), 375–78.

[7] S. A. Courtis, "Education—A Pseudo-Science," *Journal of Educational Research,* XVII (February, 1928), 130–32.

If we study the transition from an art to a science in any field of human endeavor, in astrology or alchemy, for instance, we can distinguish four general levels or stages. The first is action and explanation based on crude, natural, common-sense observations. During this stage the major elements in the field become isolated in consciousness, and folklore explanations gradually accumulate to satisfy the natural demand for understanding.

Eventually, however, the folk tales stimulate in exceptional individuals a higher form of curiosity. Systematic observation begins. It is biased observation, however. The investigators select data in terms of their preconceived notions and rationalize in terms of their selected data. They even invent what are apparently measuring instruments and experimental techniques. Observations multiply and theories, also. Controversies arise; investigation and publication are carried forward at a feverish pace. The beneficial consequences are that the minds of many are trained to a new point of view, and many data are accumulated which later prove of real value. But, judged as impersonal verifiable enduring truth, the net gain during this stage is small.

Finally, a time comes when the mass of data and conflicting views and theories serve as a stimulus to still higher types of curiosity and discontent. Investigators rise above their preconceptions, and careful analytical search of pertinent experience soon reveals truly elemental factors. New terms, new methods, new measuring instruments make their appearance, and ultimately, demonstrable truth prevails. Thus development enters its third stage and becomes a crude but true science yielding enduring knowledge, basic laws, and certain control.

The fourth stage is the golden age of science. Measurement is refined to the *n*th degree; techniques are perfected and standardized. The entire field is mapped out, knowledge is systematized, potentialities are developed, and control is based on exact knowledge applied in service to the common good. The science achieves a position of prominence and respect. Its yield of new truth is continuous and certain; its benefits, wide spread.

If now one asks, "In what stage is the science of education?" the answer must be "the second," or the stage of biased observation and uncritical acceptance of assumptions. We have measuring instruments of a sort, but no means of interpreting the results of our measurements except in terms of assumptions which have not been proved to fit the conditions. We speak of ability, capacity, nature, nurture, although none of these concepts is more than vague suggestion of obscure trends . . .

. . . .

The stage through which we are passing has served a good purpose. Today, thousands of workers are trained to a scientific point of view and are ready to use the new methods of control as soon as they are discovered. What Copernicus did for astronomy, what the skeptical chemist did for alchemy, that some modern leader will yet do for education. Our critical standards have been too low. We have deceived ourselves into considering our progress to be on a higher level than it really is. The challenge of the opportunity before us is as vast as it is unperceived by the rank and file of those in education whose intent is to be scientific.

Evidences of Progress in Educational Research.—The justice of the point of view expressed by Courtis in the foregoing quotation must be admitted. However, rapid gains are being made and even where progress is slow, there is no reason for pessimism or discouragement on the part of workers in education. Buckingham[8] has expressed in a stimulating way the progress which may result from the accumulation of even small gains in educational knowledge and slight improvements in procedure. It seems appropriate to list the visible evidences of progress in educational research. A logical starting point is to note the increase in numbers of those who, by virtue of their training, must be the leaders in research. In 1890 the number of Ph.D. degrees[9] granted was only 126, while in 1924 the number was 1,064; in 1926 the total for the United States was 1,302. The following types of evidence, which are discussed in some detail in Chapter II, indicate real progress in educational research:

[8] B. R. Buckingham, "The Accumulation of Minute Advantages," *Journal of Educational Research*, XVI (September, 1927), 136–38.

[9] B. R. Buckingham, "The Great Experiment," *Journal of Educational Research*, XVI (December, 1927), 375–78.

Graduate theses.
Professional and learned societies and organizations.
Bibliographies and abstracts.
Research periodicals.
Bulletins, monographs, and studies published by teacher-training institutions.
Bulletins and reports published by state and city school systems.
School survey reports.
Yearbooks, proceedings, reports, journals, and bulletins of educational organizations.
National foundations and boards for the advancement of education.
United States Bureau of Education.
Certain offerings of commercial publishing houses.
Summaries of investigations in given fields.
Research bureaus.

Certain bibliographies are of special significance in indicating recent experimentation and investigation.[10] The presidential addresses delivered at the annual meetings of the Educational Research Association direct attention to significant research.[11] Summaries of the literature in certain subdivisions of the field of education indicate a state of vigorous activity.[12] An

[10] *Bibliography of Secondary Education Research*, 1920–1925. Bureau of Education Bulletin, No. 2, 1926. Washington: Bureau of Education. Pp. viii + 96.

Walter S. Monroe and Ollie Asher, *A Bibliography of Bibliographies.* University of Illinois Bulletin, Vol. XXIV, No. 36. Urbana, Illinois: University of Illinois, 1927. Pp. 60.

[11] W. W. Theisen, "Recent Progress in Educational Research," *Journal of Educational Research*, VIII (November, 1923), 301–14.

Clifford Woody, "A Survey of Educational Research in 1923," *Journal of Educational Research*, IX (May, 1924), 357–81.

E. J. Ashbaugh, "A Bibliography of Research Articles Published in 1924," *Journal of Educational Research*, XI (May, 1925), 368–79.

M. R. Trabue, "Educational Research in 1925," *Journal of Educational Research*, XIII (May, 1926), 336–44.

[12] Guy Thomas Buswell and Charles Hubbard Judd, *Summary of Educational Investigations Relating to Arithmetic.* Supple-

interesting report of a survey conducted for the American Council of Learned Societies covers the research work done by learned societies, colleges, universities, bureaus, foundations, business houses, and individuals.[13]

Research Has Extended to Fields until Recently Neglected. It has been rather common to center investigation in education at the elementary and secondary level. Probably this has been a desirable procedure in the beginnings of educational research, although many workers will not grant the problems at such levels to be any less complex than at the college or university level. Be that as it may, within the past few years considerable activity in research has been manifest at the college level.[14] Even in the field of religious and character

---

mentary Educational Monographs, No. 27. Chicago: Department of Education, University of Chicago, 1925. Pp. viii + 212.

William Scott Gray, *Summary of Investigations Relating to Reading*. Supplementary Educational Monographs, No. 28. Chicago: Department of Education, University of Chicago, 1925. Pp. viii + 276.

F. D. Curtis, *A Digest of Investigations in the Teaching of Science in the Elementary and Secondary Schools*. Philadelphia: P. Blakiston's Son and Co., 1926. Pp. x + 342.

E. A. Lincoln, *Sex Differences in the Growth of American School Children*. Baltimore: Warwick and York, 1927. Pp. xii + 190.

Earle Rugg, *Studies in Curriculum Construction in the Social Sciences*. Forthcoming publication of Colorado State Teachers College, Greeley, 1928.

R. L. Lyman, summary of investigations in English composition to be published at the University of Chicago.

Yearbooks of the Department of Superintendence for 1925, 1926, 1927, and 1928 for summaries of curriculum studies in various fields.

[13] F. A. Ogg, *Research in the Humanistic and Social Sciences*. New York: Century Co., 1928. Pp. 454.

[14] Carter V. Good, "Bibliography on College Teaching with Special Emphasis on Methods of Teaching," *Studies in Education*, pp. 66–95. Yearbook XVI of the National Society of College

education, which has depended largely on subjective procedures, there is a marked attitude in favor of scientific investigation.[15] An examination of two numbers of *Religious Education* gives evidence of this recent tendency.[16]

Investigation of Problems of College Teaching.—The investigation of problems at the level of higher education may be illustrated by mentioning specific studies. This topic should be of especial interest to the reader of this book who will be in many instances either a graduate student or college professor. This fact is sufficient justification for the discussion, if justification is necessary. It has been only eight years since the appearance

---

Teachers of Education. Chicago: University of Chicago Press, 1928.

Carter V. Good, "The Literature on College Teaching," *School and Society*, XXVII (April 21, 1928), 481–87. A part of the subsequent discussion of college teaching is adapted from this article.

George Willard Frasier and Frederick Lamson Whitney, "Experiments in Teachers College Administration: I—Educational Research," *Educational Administration and Supervision*, XIV (January, 1928), 1–8.

[15] For example, the work of Hartshorne and May at Teachers College, Columbia University.

[16] "Research Projects in Religious Education," *Religious Education*, XXIII (April, 1928), 376–87. A list of current research problems.

Galen M. Fisher, "Standards of Research in Morals and Religion," *Religious Education*, XXIII (March, 1928), 186–90.

George H. Betts, Norris L. Tibbetts, Blanche Carrier, and Jessie Allen Charters, "Four Areas of Experimentation," *Religious Education*, XXIII (March, 1928), 229–39.

Martin H. Bickham, "Technique for Studying College Students," *Religious Education*, XXIII (March, 1928), 220–27.

A. E. Holt, "Case Method and Teaching at Chicago Theological Seminary," *Religious Education*, XXIII (March, 1928), 207–12.

of Klapper's pioneer book, *College Teaching*,[17] which was prepared by an impressive array of subject-matter specialists in science, social science, language and literature, arts, and vocational subjects. However, there is hardly a reference in the whole book to a factual or experimental investigation of methods of teaching, even in discussing the teaching of psychology and education. No doubt two reasons, the interests of the various subject-matter specialists and the limited number of investigations available at that time, are responsible for the subjective character of the twenty-eight chapters of the book. Certainly, a survey of the literature of the past eight or ten years indicates real progress in the improvement of college teaching and active investigation of teaching problems at the college level.

Kelly[18] has said:

> . . . It seems sure that a brighter day is coming in the training of college teachers. The first and foremost need in ushering in that brigher day is a clear recognition by the graduate schools that one of their principal functions, if not the principal function, is to train college teachers. This will involve a fundamentally different sort of curriculum than now prevails in the requirements for a degree of Doctor of Philosophy. The second essential of this movement is the development of a spirit of experimentation and investigation on the part of college faculties themselves, in order that there shall grow up a body of definitely proved material in the fields of college organization and teaching. In the third place, it is necessary that, in the professional aspects of teacher training, the education courses should develop out of the new experimental material which is developing and should not be "warmed-over" courses from the field of elementary and secondary education. Apprenticeship teaching should take place under the supervision of only thoroughly trained and recognized college teachers.

[17] Paul Klapper, *College Teaching.* Yonkers-on-Hudson, New York: World Book Co., 1920. Pp. xvi + 584.

[18] F. J. Kelly, "The Training of College Teachers," *Journal of Educational Research,* XVI (December, 1927), 332–41.

An examination of the educational literature which has appeared since Kelly made the foregoing statement indicates that his prophecy is coming true. There are other and later studies, which indicate an interest in and improvement of college teaching, than those mentioned in December, 1927, by Haggerty before Section Q of the American Association for the Advancement of Science.[19]

The foregoing statements concerning the progress made in the improvement of college instruction should be substantiated by reference to specific contributions to recent educational literature. A few contributions are mentioned which to the casual observer appear to apply primarily to teaching at the secondary level, for instance, Waples' *Problems in Classroom Method*[20] and Morrison's *The Practice of Teaching in the Secondary School.*[21] However, a more careful examination of such contributions and the opinions of specialists consulted indicate that distinct applications to college teaching may be inferred.

Attention may be directed to the following contributions: research in college teaching, a monograph by the Presseys and their students;[22] teachers' colleges and teacher training, studies by Armentrout[23] and McMul-

[19] M. E. Haggerty, "The Improvement of College Instruction," *School and Society*, XXVII (January 14, 1928), 25–37.

[20] Douglas Waples, *Problems in Classroom Method.* New York: Macmillan Co., 1927. Pp. xxii + 610.

[21] H. C. Morrison, *The Practice of Teaching in the Secondary School.* Chicago: University of Chicago Press, 1926. Pp. viii + 662.

[22] S. L. Pressey, L. C. Pressey, and Others, *Research Adventures in University Teaching: Eighteen Investigations Regarding College and University Problems.* Bloomington, Illinois: Public School Publishing Co., 1927. Pp. vi + 152.

[23] W. D. Armentrout, *The Conduct of Student Teaching in State Teachers Colleges.* Colorado Teachers College Education Series, No. 2. Greeley, Colorado: State Teachers College 1927. Pp. viii + 198.

len,[24] and Robertson's attempt[25] to promote a standard terminology in education; problems of liberal-arts colleges and junior colleges, the notable investigations of Kelly,[26] Koos,[27] and Proctor;[28] problems of general method, the previously mentioned work of Morrison[29] and Waples,[30] the Rollins College experiment,[31] and Good's study of supplementary and textbook reading procedures.[32] In the field of special method are: Buswell's utilization of the technique of photographing eye movements in studying the reading of modern foreign languages,[33] Stuart's investigation of the training of modern foreign language teachers for secondary schools,[34]

[24] L. B. McMullen, *The Service Load in Teacher-Training Institutions of the United States.* Teachers College Contributions to Education, No. 244. New York: Teachers College, Columbia University, 1927. Pp. viii + 98.

[25] D. A. Robertson, "Standard Terminology in Education," *Educational Record* (January, 1927). Washington, D. C.: American Council on Education. Pp. 32.

[26] F. J. Kelly, *The American Arts College.* New York: Macmillan Co., 1925. Pp. xiv + 198.

[27] L. V. Koos, *The Junior College Movement.* Boston: Ginn and Co., 1925. Pp. 436.

[28] W. M. Proctor and Others, *The Junior College: Its Organization and Administration.* Stanford University, California: Stanford University Press, 1927. Pp. x + 226.

[29] H. C. Morrison, *op. cit.*

[30] Douglas Waples, *op. cit.*

[31] G. E. Carrothers, "An Experiment at Rollins College," *School Review*, XXXV (March, 1927), 184–87.

G. E. Carrothers, *Rollins Plan of College Instruction.* Winter Park, Florida: Rollins College, 1927. Pp. 24.

[32] Carter V. Good, *The Supplementary Reading Assignment.* Baltimore: Warwick and York, 1927. Pp. xiv + 228.

[33] G. T. Buswell, *A Laboratory Study of the Reading of Modern Foreign Languages.* New York: Macmillan Co., 1927. Pp. xii + 100.

[34] H. Stuart, *The Training of Modern Foreign Language Teachers for the Secondary Schools in the United States.* Teachers College Contributions to Education, No. 256. New York: Teachers College, Columbia University, 1927. Pp. x + 112.

and Wood's experiments with new-type modern language tests;[35] Carpenter's study of chemistry,[36] Curtis' summary of investigations in the teaching of science,[37] and Nolan's treatment of the case method in teaching agriculture;[38] the discussion of the teaching of the social studies by Dawson and others;[39] Gray's summary of investigations in reading and the annual supplements published in the *Elementary School Journal;*[40] Blackstone's compilation of research studies in commercial education[41] and Lyon's investigations in the field of business education;[42] and Ready's canvass of the status of physical education in American colleges and universities.[43]

[35] B. D. Wood, *New York Experiments with New-Type Modern Language Tests.* New York: Macmillan Co., 1927. Pp. xxii + 340.

[36] W. W. Carpenter, *Certain Phases of the Administration of High School Chemistry.* Teachers College Contributions to Education, No. 191. New York: Teachers College, Columbia University, 1925. Pp. viii + 74.

[37] F. D. Curtis, *A Digest of Investigations in the Teaching of Science in Elementary and Secondary Schools.* Philadelphia: P. Blakiston's Son and Co., 1926. Pp. x + 342.

[38] A. W. Nolan, *The Case Method in the Study of Teaching with Special Reference to Vocational Agriculture.* Educational Research Monographs, No. 10. Bloomington, Illinois: Public School Publishing Co., 1927. Pp. xii + 266.

[39] E. Dawson, *Teaching the Social Studies.* New York: Macmillan Co., 1927. Pp. 406.

[40] W. S. Gray, *Summary of Investigations Relating to Reading.* Supplementary Educational Monographs, No. 28. Chicago: Department of Education, University of Chicago, 1925. Pp. viii + 276.

[41] E. G. Blackstone, *Research Studies in Commercial Education.* University of Iowa Monographs in Education, First Series, No. 7. Iowa City, Iowa: University of Iowa, 1926. Pp. 160.

[42] L. S. Lyon, *Education for Business.* Chicago: University of Chicago Press, 1922. Pp. xiv + 618.

[43] Marie M. Ready, *Physical Education in American Colleges and Universities.* Bureau of Education Bulletin, No. 14, 1927. Washington: Bureau of Education. Pp. vi + 52.

Reference may also be made to the following publications which have a bearing on college teaching: Book's[44] and Crawford's[45] investigations of methods of study and problems of orientation; Spence's[46] and Wood's[47] treatments of problems involved in the measurement of instruction and college entrance; and Seashore's studies of problems of college entrance, guidance, and the adjustment of work to the individual student.[48]

Cooperative Research.—One of the important current movements in education is to coordinate the research activities of various organizations and individuals. An editorial writer deplores the fact that duplication of effort has often taken place because of the lack of some central coordinating agency which would make known the various researches completed and the problems under way in the field.[49] Another writer lists three requirements for cooperative investigation: a well-selected committee to define major issues in the field of investigation, to suggest methods of investigation, and to review findings previous to publication; a personnel to conduct the investigation sponsored by the committee,

[44] W. F. Book, *Learning How to Study and Work Effectively.* Boston: Ginn and Co., 1926. Pp. xviii + 476.

W. F. Book, *How to Succeed in College.* Baltimore: Warwick and York, 1927. Pp. 192.

[45] C. C. Crawford, *Methods of Study.* Published by the author, University of Idaho, Moscow, Idaho, 1926. Pp. 164.

[46] R. B. Spence, *The Improvement of College Marking Systems.* Teachers College Contributions to Education, No. 252. New York: Teachers College, Columbia University, 1927. Pp. viii+90.

[47] B. D. Wood, *Measurement in Higher Education.* Yonkers-on-Hudson, New York: World Book Co., 1923. Pp. xii + 338.

[48] C. E. Seashore, *Learning and Living in College.* University of Iowa Studies, Volume II, Number 1. Iowa City, Iowa: University of Iowa, 1927. Pp. 124.

[49] "Competitive Research," *Journal of Educational Research,* XV (January, 1927), 52–53.

that is, to do the work; and some provision for travel expense. With these conditions met, he finds the possibilities for group research good.[50]

> Provided with these essentials, group research bears fruit. It avoids some of the weaknesses which frequently characterize individual effort. The topics of investigation are likely to be well chosen, and bias in the interpretation of results is reduced. The best methods of investigation are likely to be employed. Most important of all, a group of people with prestige are familiar with the findings of the study which, therefore, is far more likely to get over into practice. It is at this point that many individual investigations fail. Every time one prepares a comprehensive bibliography he is struck by the number of significant researches already in existence which have received little or no attention as far as modified school practice is concerned.

Chapman[51] discusses the promotion of group research by educational foundations and professional societies and the coordination of research agencies. His summary statement concerning the coordination of research agencies is as follows:[52]

> Integration of the efforts of research bureaus and of other research workers has been brought through the establishment of a central agency which would serve as a clearing-house. Both the National Education Association and the United States Bureau of Education have undertaken the task of coordination with some degree of success. The recent plan of cooperation between these organizations through committees of workers in special fields and the National Education Association's research service holds promise of bringing the problem more nearly to a solution. Experiments are already under way for a similar improvement of international relations in education.

[50] John K. Norton, "Cooperative and Individual Research," *Journal of Educational Research*, XVII (March, 1928), 216–18.

[51] Harold B. Chapman, *Organized Research in Education*, Chapters XII, XIII. Bureau of Educational Research Monographs, Number 7. Columbus, Ohio: Ohio State University Press, 1927.

[52] *Ibid.*, p. 141.

A Bulletin Showing a Decade of Progress in Educational Research.—The Bureau of Educational Research of the University of Illinois at this writing is engaged on an important bulletin which will appear in the fall of 1928 under the tentative title, "Ten Years of Educational Research, 1918–1927." The contents will probably include chapters showing progress in curriculum construction and educational measurement. A feature of the bulletin will be a bibliography of educational research reported outside of educational periodicals. This bibliography will include a complete list of the titles of all Doctors' theses in education.

The Accumulation of Small Gains in Education.—The writer has attempted to collect, organize, and interpret in an impartial manner the literature of educational research. The mature reader may select that which meets his needs and read and evaluate such material in its original setting. In paging through the rather formidable array of information on research which has been assembled, the writer has found his confidence in the efforts of experimenters and investigators strengthened; it is expected that the reader will have a similar experience.

In the present chapter some of the achievements of educational research have been cited. In Chapter V information was given concerning completed studies or partially solved problems in education and concerning problems in need of investigation. The beginner in research may select some one of these unsolved problems, small though it may be, and work toward its solution with this assurance of an able research worker and editor in mind:[53]

[53] B. R. Buckingham, "The Accumulation of Minute Advantages," *Journal of Educational Research*, XVI (September, 1927), 136–38.

We are familiar in mathematics with the doctrine of the summation of infinitesimals. The result is a finite magnitude whose size may indeed be very great. Each method, which through patient investigation is proved to be a little superior to the methods hitherto in operation, is one of the small quantities entering into this summation. Let us not suppose that any one of these procedures must produce a large effect in the complex learning process. Let us be prepared to accept small gains and to combine them for the purpose of producing large gains. Let us work bit by bit toward the master method. Let us play the educational game as the chess masters are now playing their game. Let us be content with an accumulation of small advantages.

APPENDIX

SELECTED BIBLIOGRAPHY OF BOOKS, MONOGRAPHS, AND BULLETINS ON CONDUCTING AND REPORTING EDUCATIONAL RESEARCH

Alexander, Carter, and Others. *Educational Research.* New York: Bureau of Publications, Teachers College, Columbia University, 1927. Pp. vi + 42.

Alexander, Carter. *School Statistics and Publicity.* New York: Silver, Burdett and Co., 1919. Pp. xx + 332.

Baldwin, Bird T. *Educational Research.* Bureau of Education Bulletin, No. 42, 1923. Washington: Bureau of Education. Pp. 76.

Book, William F. *Learning How to Study and Work Effectively.* Boston: Ginn and Co., 1926. Pp. xviii + 476.

Buckingham, B. R. *Research for Teachers.* New York: Silver, Burdett and Co., 1926. Pp. viii + 386.

Chapman, Harold B. *Organized Research in Education with Special Reference to the Bureau of Educational Research.* Bureau of Educational Research Monographs, Number 7. Columbus, Ohio: Ohio State University Press, 1927. Pp. x + 222.

Crawford, Claude C. *Methods of Study.* Published by the author, University of Idaho, Moscow, Idaho, 1926. Pp. 164.

Crawford, Claude C. *The Technique of Research.* Los Angeles: University of Southern California, 1928.

Dewey, John. *How We Think.* Boston: D. C. Heath and Co. 1910. Pp. vi + 224.

Educational Research Bulletin, Ohio State University, (fortnightly).

Freeman, Frank N. *Mental Tests.* Boston: Houghton Mifflin Co., 1926. Pp. xii + 504.

Gard, Wayne. *Book Reviewing.* New York: Alfred A. Knopf, 1927. Pp. xii + 160.

Garrett, Henry E. *Statistics in Psychology and Education.* New York: Longmans, Green and Co., 1926. Pp. xiv + 318.

Good, Carter V. *The Supplementary Reading Assignment.* Baltimore: Warwick and York, 1927. Pp. xiv + 228.

Greever, Garland, and Jones, Easley S. *The Century Handbook of Writing.* New York: Century Co., 1918. Pp. xii + 228.

Hall-Quest, Alfred Lawrence. *The Textbook: How to Use and Judge It.* New York: Macmillan Co., 1918. Pp. xvi + 266.

Harap, Henry. *The Technique of Curriculum Making.* New York: Macmillan Co., 1928. Pp. xii + 316.

Ho, Ching-Ju. *Personnel Studies of Scientists in the United States.* Teachers College Contributions to Education, No. 298. New York: Teachers College, Columbia University, 1928. Pp. 60.

Holzinger, Karl J. *Statistical Methods for Students in Education.* Boston: Ginn and Co., 1928. Pp. viii + 372.

Johnston, Charles Hughes, Newlon, Jesse H., and Pickell, Frank G. *Junior-Senior High School Administration,* pp. 65–88. New York: Charles Scribner's Sons, 1922.

Journal of Educational Research, (monthly).

Kelley, Truman L. *Interpretation of Educational Measurements.* Yonkers-on-Hudson, New York: World Book Co., 1927. Pp. xiv + 364.

Kelley, Truman L. *Statistical Method.* New York: Macmillan Co., 1923. Pp. xii + 390.

McCall, William A. *How to Experiment in Education.* New York: Macmillan Co., 1923. Pp. xvi + 282.

McCall, William A. *How to Measure in Education.* New York: Macmillan Co., 1922. Pp. xiv + 416.

Manly, John Matthews, and Powell, John Arthur. *A Manual for Writers.* Chicago: University of Chicago Press, 1913. Pp. viii + 226.

A Manual of Style. Chicago: University of Chicago Press, 1920. Pp. x + 300.

Monroe, Walter S., and Asher, Ollie. *A Bibliography of Bibliographies.* University of Illinois Bulletin, Vol. XXIV, No. 36. Urbana, Illinois: University of Illinois, 1927. Pp. 60.

Monroe, Walter S. *The Constant and Variable Errors of Educational Measurements.* University of Illinois Bulletin, Vol. XXI, No. 10. Urbana, Illinois: University of Illinois, 1923. Pp. 30. (Out of print.)

Monroe, Walter S. *Definitions of the Terminology of Educational Measurements.* University of Illinois Bulletin, Vol. XX, No.

6. Urbana, Illinois: University of Illinois, 1922. Pp. 18. (Out of print.)

Monroe, Walter S., and Johnston, Nell Bomar. *Reporting Educational Research.* University of Illinois Bulletin, Vol. XXII, No. 38. Urbana, Illinois: University of Illinois, 1925. Pp. 64. (Out of print.)

Monroe, Walter S., and Engelhart, Max D. *The Techniques of Educational Research.* University of Illinois Bulletin, Vol. XXV, No. 19. Urbana, Illinois: University of Illinois, 1928. Pp. 84.

Monroe, Walter S. *The Theory of Educational Measurement.* Boston: Houghton Mifflin Co., 1923. Pp. xxiv + 364.

National Committee on Research in Secondary Education. *An Outline of Methods of Research with Suggestions for High School Principals and Teachers.* Bureau of Education Bulletin, No. 24, 1926. Washington: Bureau of Education. Pp. vi + 32.

Nature and Nurture: Their Influence upon Intelligence and *Their Influence upon Achievement.* Twenty-Seventh Yearbook of the National Society for The Study of Education, Parts I and II. Bloomington, Illinois: Public School Publishing Co., 1928. Pp. x + 466, xiv + 398.

Odell, Charles W. *Educational Statistics.* New York: Century Co., 1925. Pp. xviii + 334.

Odell, Charles W. *A Glossary of Three Hundred Terms Used in Educational Measurement and Research.* University of Illinois Bulletin, Vol. XXV, No. 28. Urbana, Illinois: University of Illinois, 1928. Pp. 68.

Odell, Charles W. *The Interpretation of the Probable Error and the Coefficient of Correlation.* University of Illinois Bulletin, Vol. XXIII, No. 52. Urbana, Illinois: University of Illinois, 1925. Pp. 50.

Ogg, F. A. *Research in the Humanistic and Social Sciences.* New York: Century Co., 1928. Pp. 454.

Otis, Arthur S. *Statistical Method in Educational Measurement.* Yonkers-on-Hudson, New York: World Book Co., 1925. Pp. xii + 338.

Phi Delta Kappan, (bimonthly).

Pressey, S. L., Pressey, L. C., and Others. *Research Adventures in University Teaching.* Bloomington, Illinois: Public School Publishing Co., 1927. Pp. vi + 152.

Reavis, William Claude. *Pupil Adjustment in Junior and Senior High Schools.* Boston: D. C. Heath and Co., 1926. Pp. xviii + 348.

Reeder, Ward G. *How to Write a Thesis.* Bloomington, Illinois: Public School Publishing Co., 1925. Pp. 136.

Robertson, David A. *Standard Terminology in Education.* Educational Record Supplement (January, 1927). Washington, D. C.: American Council on Education. Pp. 32.

Ruch, G. M., and Stoddard, George D. *Tests and Measurements in High School Instruction.* Yonkers-on-Hudson, New York: World Book Co., 1927. Pp. xxii + 382.

Rugg, Harold O. *A Primer of Graphics and Statistics for Teachers.* Boston: Houghton Mifflin Co., 1925. Pp. vi + 142.

Rugg, Harold O. *Statistical Methods Applied to Education.* Boston: Houghton Mifflin Co., 1917. Pp. xviii + 410.

Sears, Jesse B. *The School Survey.* Boston: Houghton Mifflin Co., 1925. Pp. xxx + 440.

Schluter, W. C. *How to Do Research Work.* New York: Prentice-Hall, 1926. Pp. viii + 138.

Standard Requirements for Written Work. Chicago: School of Education, University of Chicago, 1922. Pp. 8.

Style Manual of the Government Printing Office, ed., February, 1923. Washington: Government Printing Office, 1923. Pp. 224.

Symonds, Percival M. *Measurement in Secondary Education.* New York: Macmillan Co., 1927. Pp. xviii + 588.

Thurstone, L. L. *The Fundamentals of Statistics.* New York: Macmillan Co., 1925. Pp. xviii + 238.

Trabue, Marion R. *Measuring Results in Education.* New York: American Book Co., 1925. Pp. 492.

Trow, Wm. Clark. *Scientific Method in Education.* Boston: Houghton Mifflin Co., 1925. Pp. xii + 160.

Voegelein, L. Belle. *List of Educational Subject Headings.* Columbus, Ohio: Ohio State University, 1928. Pp. xiv + 338.

Williams, J. Harold. *Graphic Methods in Education.* Boston: Houghton Mifflin Co., 1924. Pp. xviii + 320.

Windes, E. E., and Greenleaf, W. J. *Bibliography of Secondary Education Research,* 1920–1925. Bureau of Education Bulletin, No. 2, 1926. Washington: Bureau of Education. Pp. viii + 96.

Wood, G. M. *Suggestions to Authors.* Washington: Government Printing Office, 1913. Pp. 64.

INDEX